CHRISTIE'S

Review of the Season 1992

CHRISTIE'S
Review of the Season 1992

Edited by
FRANCIS RUSSELL

Assisted by
PETER FERGRIEVE BROWN

CHRISTIE'S

Copyright © Christie, Manson & Woods Ltd., 1992

All rights reserved. No part of this publication may be reproduced, stored in a retrieval system or transmitted, in any form or by any means, electronic, mechanical or otherwise, without the prior permission of the publisher.

A CIP catalogue record for this book is available from the British Library

ISBN 0–903432–42–0

Printed and bound by Watmoughs, Bradford and London

Cover illustration:
GIOVANNI ANTONIO CANAL, IL CANALETTO
(1697–1768)
The Old Horse Guards, London (detail)
46 × 93 in. (117 × 236 cm.)
London, 15 April 1992, £10,120,000 ($17,770,000)

Frontispiece:
HANS HOLBEIN II (German, 1497/8–1543)
Portrait of a Lady with a Squirrel
oil on panel
22¾ × 16 in. (57.8 × 40.8 cm.)
Sold by private treaty to the National Gallery, London

All prices include the buyer's premium where applicable. The currency equivalents given throughout the book are based on the rate of exchange ruling at the time of sale.

CONTENTS

FOREWORD

by Lord Carrington

Life at Christie's can never be static. Each year has its own pattern, as anyone who looks at previous *Reviews of the Season* can see. This volume once again documents the many developments of the last year, not only in our major salerooms in London and New York, but also in the other centres in which we hold auctions.

Every country in the world takes a just pride in its artistic inheritance. This year Christie's has had the privilege to sell, in circumstances described in greater detail by Charles Allsopp elsewhere in this volume, a masterpiece of Holbein's brief first period in England. This has now found an appropriate home in the National Gallery. More recently a major work by Antonello da Messina, who is particularly well represented at Trafalgar Square, was sold by private treaty to the Louvre, but Major Old Master pictures continue to appeal to the private collector, as the sale of Canaletto's *Old Horse Guards* demonstrated so dramatically.

The year has seen notable successes in other areas, including Old Master prints and books. The Messer collection of English furniture sold in London, the Tremaine and McCarty-Cooper collections of modern pictures and the McCarty-Cooper collection of tribal art are considered in articles in this volume. Equally remarkable was the sale of the Vung Tau cargo in Amsterdam, to whose markets so many such shipments were originally directed. The auction, which drew on the worldwide experience of the firm, offered yet another instance of the international nature of our business.

HOLBEIN, CHRISTIE'S AND CHRISTOPHER PONTER

by Charles Allsopp

On 31 March 1992 the National Gallery announced that, through the good offices of Christie's, it had acquired Hans Holbein the Younger's *Portrait of a Lady with a Squirrel* (frontispiece) from the Marquess of Cholmondeley for a net figure, after tax, of £10,000,000. This was the highest price ever paid by the Nation for any work of art. The picture ranks among the most beautiful to appear on the market for many years and is certainly the most important painting by an old master to have been sold since Velazquez's portrait of Juan de Pareja was auctioned by Christie's in November 1970. The acquisition is a major success for the Gallery's director, Neil Macgregor, and his negotiator, Jack Baer.

Lord Cholmondeley and his advisors had set themselves the task of raising from the sale of the Holbein and various other chattels the sum of £20,000,000 after tax, which was necessary to ensure the maintenance of his two estates, Cholmondeley in Cheshire and Houghton in Norfolk, and for his own and family's needs. Like others who have succeeded to landed fortunes, rich in buildings and works of art, he found himself with heavy potential liabilities and almost no money to meet these.

The easy solution for Lord Cholmondeley and his advisors would have been the sale at auction of the Holbein. The picture was not part of the historic collection housed at Houghton, the house designed by Colen Campbell and William Kent for Sir Robert Walpole, the first Prime Minister, which contains the unique and almost entirely untouched corps of early eighteenth-century furniture and works of art commissioned for the house. *The Lady with a Squirrel* by contrast had been bought, shortly after its arrival from Holland, by a Cholmondeley ancestor, the third Earl, in 1761, and had been at Cholmondeley where it was found on a back staircase in 1925 by Lord Cholmondeley's grandmother, Sybil. While any owner would regret the sale of a painting as beautiful as *The Lady with a Squirrel*, money had to be raised, and something had to be sold. The Holbein was the obvious choice.

Lord Cholmondeley chose to accept the offer from the National Gallery despite the advantages inherent in a sale at auction and without any parallel agreement about the sale *in situ* at Houghton of furniture designed for the house. This demonstrates his confidence that the Nation will honour its moral commitment to help to secure the future of Houghton. Proposals are being put to the National Heritage Memorial Fund, which, if accepted, will result in the achievement of Lord Cholmondeley's aims, albeit over a longer period than he would ideally have liked. These negotiations will be carefully watched by other owners of historic houses whose contribution to the preservation of this country's heritage is so often taken for granted.

No one can deny that the arts, particularly the visual arts represented by Britain's great museums, have been under-funded for too long. It is ironic that this has not always been the case. How much posterity owes to Disraeli's decision as Prime Minister to advance special funding at the time of the sale of the Barker Collection at Christie's in 1874 and thus to secure Botticelli's *Mars and Venus* for the National Gallery. His successors have not always shown such vision. In recent decades funding in real terms – that is when money available is compared with the cost of works of art – has inexorably decreased, the worst blow coming when the Minister for the Arts in Mrs. Thatcher's second administration froze museum grants.

Nonetheless the record of the National Gallery in acquiring works by old masters is second to none and compares favourably with that of such splendidly well-endowed bodies as the John Paul Getty Museum at Malibu and the Kimbell Art Museum in Fort Worth. Much of this success is due to the 1956 Finance Act and subsequent amendments to this which provided for surrender *in lieu* of tax of pre-eminent works of art.

Christie's led the way in advising our clients to take advantage of these new provisions and in 1957/8 acted for the Chatsworth Trustees in the surrender of a group of masterpieces to national museums. Subsequently notable pictures from other collections found their way to the National Gallery, including in 1964 Lord Derby's magnificent *Belshazzar's Feast* by Rembrandt. By 1965 the benefits of the *in lieu* provisions had become sufficiently well-known to persuade the executors of the late Captain E. G. Spencer Churchill to set aside the provisions of his will, which stipulated that the entire collection should be sold at public auction. In order to maximise financial benefits for the beneficiaries, the executors directed Christie's to surrender *in lieu* or sell by private treaty works of art which passed to no fewer than seven museums.

Acting on behalf of the Executors Christie's then Chairman, I. O. Chance, negotiated with an official at the Revenue who seemed to take a particularly sympathetic view of such sales, while properly protecting the Nation's interest. In the light of the understanding attitude adopted by that official, Christopher Ponter, he was subsequently invited to join Christie's, becoming in 1970 the Director of a new department dealing with taxation and private sales. The catalogue of his successes is long and includes the sale to the National Gallery of such notable pictures as the Luton Hoo Altdorfer, the gross price of which in 1980 exceeded by far that of any picture then sold at public auction. In a number of instances, negotiations with which Mr. Ponter has been concerned have set new precedents. The sale of the Blenheim archive to the British Library required a change of the law in 1973. With the transfer in 1980 of five important portraits at Arundel Castle which is vested in a private charitable trust, Christie's was associated with establishing a key precedent that would be followed at Weston Park and with the furnishings of the Tapestry Room at Hagley Hall in 1987. Another unprecedented sale was that of the Powderham bookcases, masterpieces by John Channon that were the first works of art ever bought by the Nation for cash and allowed to remain *in situ* in their original home.

There is hardly a major gallery in the country which has not been enriched by private sales negotiated through Christie's. Works of every category have been represented, from a Claude

Houghton Hall, The Saloon, with furniture designed by William Kent

for Cardiff to a Tinglit head-dress and the Cullen Armoury for Edinburgh, from the Londonderry silver for Brighton to Matthew Boulton's sidereal clock for Birmingham. The National Trust has been the beneficiary of a series of negotiations at Cotehele, Belton, Kedleston, Nostell, Knole and Coughton. There obviously have been cases where agreement has not been possible and where works of art offered to the Nation subsequently come up for sale due to lack of an agreement over price or terms. It is a cause of great pride to Christie's and great credit to Christopher Ponter that on not a single occasion has the asking price of a major work of art not been substantiated when it has been sold at auction.

A genuine willingness to enter into private negotiations and a realistic approach to pricing whereby both the owner and the national interest is safeguarded has characterised these sales.

It is Christopher Ponter's patience and unfailing courtesy which has made his advice so sought after, and made him such an invaluable member of the Board of Christie's for the last 22 years. Happily his retirement as a Director will not sever his connection with Christie's or his clients: he remains a consultant. The Taxation Department has been strengthened by the appointment of Edward Manisty, who as a partner in Stephenson Harwood developed a special interest in the heritage. He will be assisted by Nicholas Parnell – himself a recruit from the Revenue – who has been an Associate Director of Christie's for eight years. Christie's will continue to encourage clients to offer works of art to the Nation. We are extremely proud of our record in this respect and the best tribute that we can pay to Christopher Ponter is to continue his good work.

PORTRAITS FOR THE NATION

by Francis Russell

Portraits have a special place in our artistic patrimony. Portraiture was the major preoccupation of painting in this country for some three hundred years from the early sixteenth century. In recent decades, almost every year has yielded its quota of major portraits sold by negotiation to national institutions: this season has been no exception.

Surprisingly few picture collections have survived more or less as they were in the eighteenth century, as patterns of acquisition and sale have changed the character of almost every house. One of the rare exceptions is Knole in Kent, where the balance of portraits and old masters, although not their detailed arrangement, remains very much as it did at the death of its owner, Reynolds' patron, John Sackville, 3rd Duke of Dorset in 1799. Much of the furniture and silver for which the house is celebrated was the subject of negotiated sales in 1966 and is now owned by the National Trust. A number of pictures followed in 1988. These have now been joined by two notable family portraits which will remain *in situ* at Knole, the van Dyck of Lady Frances Cranfield, who married the 5th Earl of Dorset in 1638, and Sir Joshua's noble whole length of the 3rd Duke himself in his peer's robes. The portrait provides a telling comparison with another of the Duke's commissions, the Gainsborough of his mistress Giovanna Bacelli, itself the subject of a negotiated sale to the Tate Gallery in 1975. For it was intended to mark the climax of the long series of dynastic portraits in the house.

By coincidence, the sale of a second whole length by Sir Joshua Reynolds has also been recently arranged, that of John Drummond, 4th Earl of Dunmore (1730–1809), the last Governor of Virginia. The portrait is distinguished by being the artist's only such venture in highland dress, vying with such pictures as Copley's Major Hugh Montgomerie, and has now found an appropriate home in the Scottish National Portrait Gallery.

The National Portrait Gallery in London has been enriched by three remarkable portraits as a result of the efforts of our taxation department. The earliest is the picture by Pompeo Batoni of the young Frederick, Lord North (1732–1792), the future Prime Minister, from the collection of his descendant, the Earl of Guilford. North was in Rome in 1752–3, although the portrait was not delivered to him until four years later. The picture was apparently commissioned by his step-mother, Lady Guilford, at whose London house it was seen by Horace Walpole with three other Batonis of the same period. Evidence of *pentimenti* suggests the care with which the apparently effortless composition was resolved.

Very different in character is another of the National Portrait Gallery's acquisitions, the picture of the engineer Joseph Brindley (1716–1772) attributed to Francis Parsons. Brindley had a remarkable career. His expertise in allied fields brought him to the notice of the Duke of Bridgewater and this led to his becoming the foremost builder of canals in the first great era of canal construction. It was to such men that the Industrial Revolution was owed.

The Gallery's third purchase is a yet more compelling image, Lawrence's dynamic half-length of Lieutenant-General the Hon. Sir Charles Stewart, later 3rd Marquess of Londonderry (1778–1854). Stewart, who was the half-brother of Lord Castlereagh, the then Foreign Secretary, was a courageous soldier and is seen in Hussar uniform wearing the Peninsular medal awarded after the Battle of Talavera in 1809. He first sat to Lawrence in 1810; the prime version of the portrait is apparently lost, and the present picture was painted in 1812 for the sitter's uncle, the 1st Marquess Camden. It, or the superb canvas formerly at Londonderry House, was exhibited in 1813. Stewart's sittings to Lawrence led to a friendship which was to be extremely influential. In 1814 Stewart arranged that the Prince Regent should sit to the artist. Meyer's print of Stewart's portrait was shown to the Prince and was apparently to influence his decision to commission the heroic series of portraits now in the Waterloo Chamber at Windsor.

The energy with which the National Portrait Gallery has taken advantage of opportunities for negotiated sales ironically only serves to intensify its pressing need for more space. Its appeal which is now within sight of its target of £12,000,000 certainly deserves to succeed.

SIR JOSHUA REYNOLDS P.R.A. (British, 1723–1792)
Portrait of John Sackville, 3rd Duke of Dorset
oil on canvas
96 × 60 in. (240 × 150 cm.)
Accepted by the Commissioners of Inland Revenue *in lieu* of tax and allocated to the National Trust for preservation *in situ* at Knole

SIR THOMAS LAWRENCE P.R.A. (British, 1769–1830)
Portrait of Lieutenant-General the Hon. Sir Charles Stewart,
later 3rd Marquess of Londonderry
oil on canvas
56 × 44 in. (142 × 119 cm.)
Sold by private treaty to the National Portrait Gallery, London

AN ANTONELLO FOR THE LOUVRE

by Gregory Martin

When in 1863 the connoisseur and museum administrator John Charles Robinson acquired in Granada the *Christ at the Column*, by Antonello da Messina, only three other paintings thought to be Antonello's work were then known. In fact two years previously the National Gallery had acquired the signed and dated *Salvator Mundi* and it was presumably the relationship with this painting which confirmed the attribution for him. His discovery of the picture in Granada was thus a significant art historical and cultural event in that era of many discoveries, when the art of the fifteenth century was being classified and appreciated after well over two centuries of neglect.

At the time Robinson was Superintendent of the Art Collections at South Kensington (the fledgling Victoria and Albert Museum). He was the first to hold the post and made frequent trips to Italy, and especially Spain, buying works of applied art in vast quantities, thus laying the foundations for the incomparable holdings of the museum. It was presumably on one such buying trip that he came across the Antonello.

Robinson had the Antonello exhibited at the British Institution in 1865; three years later he published it and in that year it was purchased from him by Sir Francis Cook who had already embarked on amassing one of the most important collections of old masters of his time. Sir Francis' father, William, had established the family business – dealing in and manufacturing fabrics – and he was to take over the running of the firm in the following year. Coincidentally Robinson was to resign from his South Kensington post in the same year but was to continue acting as Sir Francis' advisor. One of Robinson's greatest coups was to be the acquisition for Sir Francis of the Jan van Eyck (he thought Hubert van Eyck) *The Three Marys at the Tomb* now in the Boymans-van Beuningen Museum.

Robinson's attribution of the Antonello was generally accepted until 1895 when Bernard Berenson was persuaded that it was a copy. Although Berenson had changed his mind and accepted the picture as autograph in his *Italian Pictures of the Renaissance* published in 1932, the picture's critical fortunes astonishingly remained mixed until quite recently. But certainly no doubts could have remained about its authenticity when it hung on temporary loan at the National Gallery. The picture had in fact previously been offered at auction by Brenda, Lady Cook in 1989, when it had failed to sell. Three years later it was sold by private treaty to the Louvre for a sum substantially in excess of the price it had been bought-in at in 1989.

That such an important institution as the Louvre should have bought the *Christ at the Column* would seem to make extraordinarily good sense. Indeed the acquisition may be said to be inspired, for not only is it a work of great beauty and expressiveness, but in addition it will form the perfect counterpart to the Antonello already there, *The Portrait of a Man (Il Condottiere)*.

That is signed and dated 1475 and is one of a group of masterpieces executed during Antonello's stay in Venice. Michiel, writing early in the following century, could well have had it in mind when he wrote of an Antonello portrait as having 'gran forza e gran vivacità e maxime in li ochi'. Indeed it is a portrayal of imposing directness; the sitter is very much of this world – active, tough and direct – and is minutely observed.

The same technique, inspired by Antonello's study of Netherlandish painting and, in particular, of Jan van Eyck, is evident enough in the *Christ at the Column*, which is thought to have been painted at about the same time or a little later. Such a work was executed to stimulate private meditation on Christ's suffering at the hands of Pilate before He was led away to be crucified.

The moment depicted is during or after the Flagellation. Christ is at the column crowned with thorns, blood falls from the wounds caused by them and tears are on His cheeks; the rope by which He will be dragged to Calvary is already round His neck. He lifts His head heavenwards to seek succour from His Father. The cult of this subject, which has no precise Biblical source, was perhaps stimulated by the presence in the church of Santa Prassede, Rome, of what was believed to be the actual column at which Christ had suffered in Pontius Pilate's *praetorium*. It had been brought from Jerusalem in 1223 by Cardinal Colonna.

Antonello had earlier treated the subject in the picture at Piacenza which is signed and dated 1473(?). Here Christ fixes the spectator with a pathetic yet iconic stare, and His mouth is turned down in an expression of despair and hopeless sadness. In the Louvre picture Christ is not depicted as seeking our sympathy though we can readily empathise as He lifts His head upwards.

Although the colour of the hair and head are similar the model is not the same; he appears however in what is probably the slightly later *Pietà*, that was acquired by the Prado in 1966. In it, the depiction of Christ's head shows a clear connection with the art of Giovanni Bellini, who like Antonello is first documented in the 1450s. This is not the place to analyse their relationship, but suffice it to state that the later art of Antonello is a unique synthesis of the style of van Eyck and the spirit of Giovanni Bellini.

In his treatment of *Christ at the Column* Antonello in fact introduced a new theme to Italian Renaissance painting and deepened the vocabulary of religious meditation. Thus now in the Louvre are juxtaposed two masterpieces – one brutally earthbound, the other spiritually uplifting – by the genius whose great reputation today rests on only a small corpus of extant paintings.

ANTONELLO DA MESSINA
(Italian, probably 1425/30–1479)
Christ at the Column
oil on panel
$11\frac{3}{4} \times 8\frac{1}{4}$ in. (30 × 21 cm.)
Sold by private treaty to the Musée du Louvre, Paris

OLD MASTER PICTURES

BERNARDO DADDI (Italian, active 1328–d.1348)
The Crucifixion
tempera on gold ground panel
$14 \times 7\frac{3}{8}$ in. (35.5 × 19.5 cm.)
London, 13 December 1991, £319,000 ($574,519)

This well-preserved panel is first recorded in the collection of James Dennistoun of Dennistoun, at whose sale at Christie's, 14 June 1855, it fetched $5\frac{1}{2}$ guineas.

DOMENICO BECCAFUMI, IL MECARINO
(Italian, c.1486–1551)
The Holy Family with the Infant Saint John the Baptist
oil on panel, circular
$35\frac{1}{4}$ in. (89.5 cm.) diameter
Sold by the J. Paul Getty Museum, Malibu
New York, 21 May 1992, $308,000 (£169,230)

Formerly in the Santini and Torrigiani collections, this was one of
a group of 31 pictures consigned by the J. Paul Getty Museum, all
of which were sold, for a total of $3,333,000 (£1,821,311)

A NEGLECTED VENUS AND ADONIS

by Charles Beddington

One of the highlights of a rich season in the field of Old Master Pictures was the sale in December 1991 of the *Venus and Adonis* painted by Titian, the greatest artist of High Renaissance Venice, with assistance from members of his workshop. It fetched £7,480,000 ($13,471,480), the highest price paid for any work of art at auction anywhere in the world in 1991. Although this result exceeded manifold unprinted pre-sale expectations of 'in excess of £1,500,000', it came as a surprise to few. While the sale included masterpieces by Jan van de Cappelle, Meindert Hobbema, Georges de La Tour, Bernardo Bellotto, Thomas Gainsborough, Bernardo Daddi and Adriaen Key, most of these establishing new record prices for the artists, it was already clear well in advance that the *Venus and Adonis* was drawing particular attention. No Venetian High Renaissance gallery picture of this quality had surfaced on the market for two decades and its illustrious provenance added significantly to its allure.

The painting is first recorded in the collection of Queen Christina of Sweden (1626–1689), one of the most extraordinary residents of Baroque Rome. Christina had inherited the Swedish crown at the age of five, on the death of her father Gustavus Adolphus at the battle of Lützen. She ruled from 1644 but a decade later, having been converted to Roman Catholicism, she abdicated and went to live in Rome. In March 1659 she took a lease on Palazzo Riario, now Palazzo Corsini, on the Lungara, where she was to live for the rest of her life, and where she installed her vast collection of predominantly Italian works of art. Based on the paintings which her father had looted in Prague, this Christina augmented energetically, despite her limited funds, until the end of her life. Although it is not known how she acquired this *Venus and Adonis*, it was certainly in her ownership by 1662, when it was recorded in detail in an inventory of her belongings. Her collection could be seen on appointment and legend has it that the queen would observe visitors to the *stanza dei quadri* through a secret peephole.

Christina bequeathed her collection of pictures to her devoted companion of more than three decades, Cardinal Decio Azzolino, who survived her by less than two months. Inherited by his nephew, it was sold in 1692 to the Odescalchi family, who resold it, still intact, to Philippe, Duc d'Orléans, in 1721. Christina's pictures subsequently formed the basis of the Italian section of the collection of the Ducs de Orléans at the Palais Royal in Paris, probably the greatest private collection of the eighteenth century. When the Orléans Collection was offered for sale by private treaty in London in 1798–9, Titian's *Venus and Adonis* was acquired by a Mr. Fitzhugh for £300. He sold it in 1844 to the 2nd Earl of Normanton and between then and the sale in December it was only seen in public once, in an exhibition at the Royal Academy in 1882. The painting's inaccessibility extended to the few scholars who saw it in recent decades, since it was hung too high to permit definitive judgement, and only after its consignment to Christie's did close study become possible.

Titian and his workshop executed no less than six large canvases of the subject. In these the poses of the protagonists remain constant but in other respects they are of two distinct compositions. The prime version of the type in which Cupid is shown awake was painted for the Farnese family, probably in the mid-1540s, and has been untraced since the early nineteenth century. It is known from derivations in the Metropolitan Museum of Art, New York, and the National Gallery of Art, Washington, both of which were classified by Professor Harold Wethey in his great catalogue of Titian's work as partially workshop productions executed in the first half of the 1560s. The undisputed prime version of the other type, showing Cupid asleep, is the famous picture painted for Philip II of Spain in 1553–4 and now in the Prado. The derivations from this were similarly regarded by Wethey as executed with studio assistance and dated *circa* 1555. Of these he lists the version in the London National Gallery before the picture sold at Christie's, of which he wrote: 'The quality of this item appears to be of superior workshop type, so far as one can judge considering its high position on the wall and its rather deteriorated condition in 1971.' While the condition of some parts of the picture, notably the figure of Venus, indeed impedes judgement of their quality, other areas are clearly far superior to the painting in the National Gallery, which was revealed by cleaning in 1973 to be no more than a workshop production with minimal intervention by the master himself. Indeed the quality of those parts of the picture sold at Christie's which differ most radically from the Prado prototype, notably the figure of Adonis, the landscape and the sky, leaves no room for doubt that they are the work of Titian himself. On the other hand, X-radiographs show that the main lines of the composition were firmly established before painting was begun; this is in contrast with the vivid and spontaneous blocking-in characteristic of available X-radiographs of autograph works by the master, and suggests that the early stages of the picture must have been delegated to assistants. Ultimately the question of the division of labour between Titian and his workshop had to be left to bidders to decide for themselves, and the spectacular result would seem to indicate a favourable verdict.

TIZIANO VECELLIO, called TITIAN (Italian, c.1490–1576)
and Workshop
Venus and Adonis
oil on canvas
$63 \times 77\frac{3}{8}$ in. (160×196.5 cm.)
London, 13 December 1991, £7,480,000 ($13,471,480)
Record auction price for a work by the artist
Now in the J. Paul Getty Museum, Malibu

SALVATOR ROSA (Italian, 1615–1673)
Portrait of the Artist, three-quarter length, in a doublet, a cap, a torn glove and with a sword
oil on canvas
$45\frac{1}{2} \times 37$ in. (115.5 × 94 cm.)
in the original carved and gilded 17th Century Florentine pierced and swept frame
Sold by the Executors of the late Lord Wolverton
London, 15 April 1992, £440,000 ($772,000)
Record auction price for a work by the artist

Previously unpublished, the picture is a major addition to a group of self-portraits generally dated, on stylistic grounds and from the apparent age of the subject, *circa* 1641, at the beginning of Rosa's Florentine period (autumn 1640-early 1649). Their identification as self-portraits is based on their resemblance to the only example documented as such, the head directly above the signature on the large *Battle* in Palazzo Pitti. Four other self-portraits of this period have hitherto been known. The earliest of these is probably the *Self Portrait as Silence* in the National Gallery, London, which was painted for Casa Niccolini in Florence and is of identical size to the present picture, while the latest may be the *Self-Portrait with the Attributes of a Satirical Poet* in the Uffizi.

Once in the Sciarra collection, Rome, this picture was acquired by the 1st Earl of Dudley, and was sold at Christie's, 16 June 1900, for 23 guineas.

LUCA CARLEVARIJS (Italian, 1663–1730)
Port Scene with a Frigate under repair
Signed with initials 'L.C.'
Oil on canvas
36⅝ × 49¼ in. (93 × 125 cm.)
Monaco, 20 June 1992, Fr. 2,700,000 (£275,510)

PIETRO FABRIS (Italian, active 1754–1792)
Peasants merrymaking on the Shore at Posillipo, the Bay of
Naples and Vesuvius beyond
Signed and dated 'Fabris.f.1777'
Oil on canvas
41 × 61⅞ in. (104.2 × 157.1 cm.)
New York, 16 January 1992, $495,000 (£281,250)
A record auction price for a work by the artist

CANALETTO'S *OLD HORSE GUARDS*

by Francis Russell

Until its sale was announced, Canaletto's *The Old Horse Guards from St. James's Park* was the least widely known of the masterpieces of his English period. Canaletto, who had for some two decades concentrated on work for English patrons, went to London for the first time in 1746: he was briefly in Venice in 1751, but was back in London by July that year: he was in Venice in the summer of 1753, but still seems to have been in London as late as 1755. The main achievements of Canaletto's later years in London were decorative canvases with reminiscences of Venice and elsewhere painted, among others, for Lord Chesterfield and a member of the King family. These are very different in character from the series of major London views that suggest how quick the artist was to respond to his initial experience of London. Three of these have long been widely known: the celebrated pair of views of 1746–7 from Richmond House which were commissioned by the 2nd Duke of Richmond and happily remain at Goodwood, and the large *Whitehall and the Privy Garden, looking North* of

1751–2, now at Bowhill. His friendship with the Richmond family may well have encouraged Prince Lobkowicz to acquire the pair of large Thames views, now in the National Gallery at Prague which, with the *Old Horse Guards*, are among Canaletto's major, but less generally familiar, achievements of the late 1740s.

Unlike the views of London from Richmond House which were specific commissions, the *Old Horse Guards* was taken up as a speculation, evidently in the early summer of 1749. The largest canvas of Canaletto's English period, this was completed by 25 July, when the artist advertised that it could be viewed in his lodgings near Golden Square. Canaletto clearly hoped to find a purchaser and seems to have done so in John Robartes, 4th Earl of Radnor: for in 1751 he would employ the same tactics when seeking to sell his panoramic view of the *Chelsea Hospital with Ranelagh and the Rotunda*. Radnor, on his death in 1756, bequeathed the *Old Horse Guards* and a view of the Tower of London, supplied as a pendant to this by Samuel Scott, to James

Harris, M.P., the author of *Hermes* and father of the 1st Earl of Malmesbury.

The Old Horse Guards building is flanked to the right by the Treasury and the houses at the end of Downing Street and to the left by the Admiralty, the spire of St. Martin's-in-the-Fields and houses on the Mall. The hour is late morning: footguards are being drilled and company gathers on the fringes of the park, servants beat a carpet, dogs play and ducks disturb the stillness of the water. Canaletto's decision to paint a London scene so different in type from his accustomed Venetian views may well have been determined by the impending demolition of the picturesque but relatively modest *Old Horse Guards*, which would make room for the new building designed by Kent, which he would show in a later, smaller version of the composition. Many Venetian artists of the eighteenth century worked for English patrons, but perhaps no other picture of the period by a foreigner captured the quintessential character of London and London life at the time with such sympathy and accuracy. The very reticence of the picture explains why Canaletto was to have so powerful an influence on the British topographical tradition.

As soon as the decision to sell the picture was taken, it was offered by private treaty to the National Gallery which, despite its magnificent holdings of works by Canaletto, lacks a major example of the English period. The gallery had other priorities and therefore the picture was included in our April sale. After this was announced, the Tate Gallery expressed a strong interest in the picture; subsequent negotiations proved abortive both because of a lack of public funds and because our estimate was questioned in some quarters. In the event this was fully vindicated in the saleroom and the picture was sold for £10,120,000. More gratifying still was the fact that although the underbidder was a foreign collector, the successful purchaser was Sir Andrew Lloyd-Webber, whose acquisition was widely heralded in the press and has since also been acclaimed in political quarters. He has already made generous arrangements for exhibiting what will now take its place as one of the most popular of all views of eighteenth-century London.

GIOVANNI ANTONIO CANAL, IL CANALETTO
(Italian, 1697–1768)
The Old Horse Guards, London, from St. James's Park, with numerous ladies and gentlemen and guards on parade
oil on canvas
46 × 93 in. (117 × 236 cm.)
London, 15 April 1992, £10,120,000 ($17,770,000)
Record auction price for a work by the artist

Opposite:
Detail showing the Old Horse Guards and buildings to the north

GIOVANNI ANTONIO CANAL, IL CANALETTO
(Italian, 1697–1768)
The Grand Canal, Venice, looking East from the Campo di S. Vio, with
the Palazzo Corner, barges and numerous gondolas, the dome of
S. Maria della Salute, the Dogana and the Riva degli Schiavoni beyond
oil on canvas
27 × 36¼ in. (68.7 × 92 cm.)
Sold by the Executors of the late H. J. Joel
London, 10 July 1992, £1,430,000 ($2,696,980)

This picture and the pendant, which fetched £990,000 ($1,867,140),
date from about 1735–40, and were owned by the sculptor Antonio
Canova by 1806. They subsequently entered the Bavarian royal
collection and were sold from the Alte Pinakothek, Munich in 1939.

Opposite:
BERNARDO BELLOTTO (Italian, 1721–1780)
A View of Vaprio and Canonica, looking North-West from the West
Bank of the Adda near the Confluence with the Brembo; and A View of
Canonica and Vaprio, looking South from Monasterolo on the West
Bank of the Adda
oil on canvas
18½ × 28 in. (47 × 71 cm.), a pair
Sold by the Abercorn Heirlooms Settlement
London, 13 December 1991, £2,090,000 ($3,764,090)

The twin towns of Vaprio and Canonica, at the confluence of the Rivers
Adda and Brembo and the Naviglio Martesana, were at a convenient
distance from Milan to provide summer residences for members of the
Milanese aristocracy. The villa of the Melzi family is seen in both
pictures.

THE PEREA MASTER (Spanish, active c.1490–1505)
The Last Supper
tempera on gold ground panel, in three sections
$104\frac{3}{4} \times 111\frac{3}{8}$ in. (266 × 283 cm.)
London, 29 May 1992, £308,000 ($559,328)

The present picture was originally the central section of an
enormous altarpiece devoted to the Eucharist. Its monumentality
and stark symmetry, as well as certain details, reveal the impact of
the great altarpiece of the same subject, in the Museo
Catedralicio, Segorbe (Castellón), ascribed to Jaime Baço
Jacomart (c.1410/17–1461) and datable about 1455.

Opposite:
DOMENIKOS THEOTOKOPOULOS,
EL GRECO (Spanish, 1541–1614)
The Disrobing of Christ
signed 'doménikos theoto/krès e'p' (in greek)
oil on panel
$22\frac{1}{4} \times 12\frac{5}{8}$ in. (56.6 × 32 cm.)
London, 29 May 1992, £1,870,000 ($3,395,920)
Record auction price for a work by the artist

This has a strong claim to be a preparatory study for El Greco's
earliest masterpiece, the *Espolio*, in the sacristy of Toledo
Cathedral, completed by 15 June 1579. Another small signed
version, also on pine panel and of almost identical size, is in the
Bearsted Collection at Upton House.

BARTOLOMÉ ESTEBAN MURILLO
(Spanish, 1617–1682)
The Madonna and Child
oil on canvas
$40\frac{5}{8} \times 32\frac{1}{2}$ in. (103.2 × 82.7 cm.)
London, 29 May 1992, £770,000 ($1,395,920)

This picture was dated *circa* 1660–5 by Professor Angulo.

BARTOLOMÉ ESTEBAN MURILLO
(Spanish, 1617–1682)
A laughing Boy, half length, wearing a plumed hat and
pointing with his right hand
oil on canvas
21¼ × 15⅞ in. (54 × 40.4 cm.)
Sold by the Trustees of the D. J. Robarts Marriage
Settlement
London, 13 December 1991, £715,000 ($1,287,715)

The banker Abraham Robarts, who acquired the
picture before 1856, was a notable collector of Dutch
masters. Professor Angulo proposed a dating 'around
1660 or slightly earlier' and pointed out that the model
for the boy would seem to have also been used for the
Family Group in the collection of Erin Berman,
Monroe, Michigan.

GEORGES DE LA TOUR (French, 1593–1652)
A blind Hurdy-Gurdy Player, seated three-quarter
length, in profile to the left
oil on canvas
$33\frac{3}{8} \times 24$ in. (84.7 × 61 cm.)
London, 13 December 1991, £1,870,000
($3,367,870)
Record auction price for a work by the artist
Now in the Museo del Prado, Madrid

Published by Pierre Rosenberg in 1990, the present
picture is the most important La Tour discovery since
the mid-1970s. La Tour painted a series of blind hurdy-
gurdy players which are generally regarded as early
works and dated to the 1620s. These include three full
length treatments of the subject, two (Musée Municipal,
Bergues, and Musée des Beaux-Arts, Nantes) showing
the hurdy-gurdy player frontally, respectively standing
and seated, while the third (Musée Charles-Friry,
Remiremont) represents him seated and in profile.

CHARLES-JOSEPH NATOIRE
(French, 1700–1777)
Hunters on Horseback conversing with a Shepherdess
spinning Wool and a young Woman at a Well
oil on canvas
$39\frac{5}{8} \times 33\frac{1}{4}$ in. (100.6 × 84.4 cm.), one of a pair
New York, 16 January 1992, $737,000 (£418,750)

This picture and its pendant were commissioned in
1737 by M. Orry, the *directeur des Bâtiments du Roi*, for
the large drawing room in the *petits appartements* of
Louis XV at the Château de Fontainebleau. The pictures
are last recorded at Fontainebleau in 1793 and have only
recently been discovered.

PIERRE-PAUL PRUD'HON (French, 1758–1823)
Portrait of Louise de Guéhéneuc, Duchesse de
Montebello (1782–1856)
signed 'P. P. Prud'hon'
oil on canvas
$21\frac{5}{8} \times 18\frac{1}{2}$ in. (55 × 47 cm.)
Monaco, 20 June 1992, Fr. 3,500,000 (£357,142)
Record auction price for a work by the artist

The sitter, Louise-Antoinette-Scholastique de
Guéhéneuc, who was born in 1782, married in 1800, as
his second wife, Jean Lannes, Duc de Montebello
(1769–1809).

LUCAS CRANACH I
(German, 1472–1553)
Portrait of a young Lady, seated three-quarter
length, in a red and orange dress and a wide-
brimmed plumed hat, holding a flower
signed with the serpent device
oil on panel
$33\frac{7}{8} \times 21\frac{7}{8}$ in. (86 × 55.6 cm.)
London, 15 April 1992, £506,000 ($888,536)

Friedländer and Rosenberg date the present
picture *circa* 1530; it was sold from the
Metropolitan Museum of Art, New York,
in 1988.

ADRIAEN THOMASZ. KEY (Flemish, apprenticed in
1558-active until 1589)
Group Portrait of a Gentleman aged 57, seated three-quarter
length, by a table with a skull, an hourglass and a book, with his
three Daughters, aged 30, 23 and 12, and his three sons, aged 19,
18 and 14
signed twice with monogram 'ATK', dated 1583 and inscribed
with the sitters' ages
oil on panel
$36 \times 45\frac{1}{4}$ in. (91.5 × 115 cm.)
London, 13 December 1991, £374,000 ($673,574)
Record auction price for a work by the artist
Now in the Museo del Prado, Madrid

This exceptional and remarkably well-preserved portrait group
was acquired by the outstanding nineteenth-century connoisseur,
Dr. Wilhelm von Bode, director of the Kaiser Friedrich Museum
in Berlin. It was subsequently in the possession of Sir George
Leon. Key, a pupil of his uncle, Willem, became a member of the
Antwerp painter's guild in 1568 and was for a generation a
leading portraitist there.

HENDRICK GOLTZIUS (Dutch, 1558–1617)
Christ on the Cross with Saint Mary Magdalen, the Virgin and
Saint John the Evangelist
signed with monogram 'HG.fe.'
oil on copper
17 × 11⅜ in. (43 × 28.8 cm.)
London, 15 April 1992, £341,000 ($598,796)

This unpublished work, untraced since 1758, is the earliest known
picture by the artist. Van Mander asserts that Goltzius took up
painting in the year 1600 and that his first work was this '*cleen
stucxken op coper*' [small piece on copper], executed for Gijsbert
Rijckersen of Haarlem, about whom nothing else is known save
for what presumably is a record of his burial on 2 January 1605.
Subsequently, however, Goltzius's friend and biographer states that
the artist had previously painted a now lost portrait of a certain
Tobias Swartsenburgh, leaving ambiguous the matter of which
picture came first. Van Mander noted the deathly character of
Christ and praises Goltzius for the figure's colouring, conception,
and execution.

PIETER BRUEGHEL II (Flemish, circa 1564–1637/8)
Peasants at Table
signed and dated 'P. BREVGHEL. 1625.'
oil on panel
$18\frac{5}{8} \times 26$ in. (47.3 × 66 cm.)
Amsterdam, 14 November 1991, Fl.966,000 (£295,503)

JAN BRUEGHEL II (Flemish, 1601–1678)
Entering into Noah's Ark
signed and dated 'BRVEGHEL 1625'
oil on panel
$23\frac{5}{8} \times 35\frac{3}{8}$ in. (60 × 90 cm.)
Monaco, 7 December 1991, Fr. 5,722,000 (£593,827)

GERBRAND VAN DEN EECKHOUT
(Dutch, 1621–1674)
Soldiers playing Tric-Trac in an Interior
signed with initials and dated 'G v E./A 1651'
oil on canvas
$17\frac{1}{4} \times 14\frac{7}{8}$ in. (43.8 × 37.8 cm.)
London, 15 April 1992, £374,000 ($656,744)
Record auction price for a work by the artist

Gerbrand van den Eeckhout is best known as a painter of
religious and historical subjects, in which his style comes closest
to that of Rembrandt, of whom he seems to have been a great
friend as well as one of the most talented pupils. An artist of great
versatility, he painted genre pictures, landscapes and portraits,
executed etchings and designs for gold and silverware and
occasionally wrote poetry. Peter Sutton, following Valentiner and
Gudlaugsson, has noted the significance of van den Eeckhout's
paintings in the development of the simplified form of genre
scene, with only a few figures in an upright format, first seen in
the years around 1650, which became so popular in Dutch art in
the following decades. The present picture would seem to be van
den Eeckhout's earliest dated genre painting and probably
antedates the first genre paintings of the new type by Pieter de
Hooch, such as his *Tric-Trac Players* in the National Gallery,
Dublin.

JAN VAN DE CAPPELLE (Dutch, 1625/6–1679)
Shipping in a Calm at Flushing with a States Yacht firing a Salute
signed and dated 'J. V. Capel 1645'
oil on panel
$27\frac{3}{8} \times 36\frac{1}{4}$ in. (69.7 × 92.2 cm.)
Sold by the Trustees of the D. J. Robarts Marriage Settlement
London, 13 December 1991, £2,640,000 ($4,754,640)
Record auction price for a work by the artist

This is the earliest known work by the artist, painted when he was only about twenty years old, an achievement made all the more remarkable by the fact that he was apparently self-taught. It is the first known example of what was to become a popular form in Dutch art, the so-called 'parade picture', a gathering of boats in a calm sea with luminous reflections. The locality depicted is identified by the porpoises as Flushing, as they do not visit anywhere else on the Dutch coast. The picture was originally purchased in the first half of the nineteenth century by Abraham Robarts, a friend of the connoisseur John Smith and in his day one of the foremost collectors of Dutch pictures.

MEINDERT HOBBEMA (Dutch, 1638–1709)
Cottages in a Woodland Clearing with a young
Fiddler arriving Home in a Cart greeted by his Family
signed 'Hobbema'
oil on canvas
$35\frac{1}{4} \times 41\frac{5}{8}$ in. (89.5 × 105.8 cm.)
Sold by the Trustees of the D. J. Robarts Marriage
Settlement
London, 13 December 1991, £1,600,000
($2,881,600)
Record auction price for a work by the artist

While Hobbema's work is admired for his perception of
the irregularities of nature, he seems to have worked
entirely in the studio and motifs frequently recur in his
pictures. Thus the cottage on the right in the present
painting is included in an otherwise completely different
composition in Berlin. More significantly, Hobbema
often re-arranged his own compositions. The present
picture is generally regarded as the final development in
a series of four variants which begins with a canvas in
Washington and continues with the small panel sold at
Christie's, 18 April 1980, lot 80, and now in the
Mauritshuis, and the large canvas in the London
National Gallery. The four pictures reveal an increasing
elaboration of the composition and opening up of the
centre which in the Washington painting is entirely
closed in by trees and in the present work allows a view
into considerable depth. The four pictures are generally
dated to the mid-1660s when the artist was at the height
of his powers. In 1668 he became one of the wine-
gaugers of the Amsterdam octroi and seems to have
painted little after that date.

The picture was acquired by Abraham Robarts by 1829.

OLD MASTER DRAWINGS

GIROLAMO FRANCESCO MARIA MAZZOLA,
IL PARMIGIANINO (Italian, 1503–1540)
Two Lovers
pen and brown ink
$5\frac{1}{4} \times 6$ in. (13.1 × 15.2 cm.)
London, 14 April 1992, £35,200 ($61,811)

This previously unknown drawing is a characteristic example of
Parmigianino's later manner, and must date from his second
Parmesan period (1530–40). It is a larger and more finished
development of a drawing at Budapest. A number of drawings
from this period, after Parmigianino's return from Rome, reveal a
similar taste for amorous subject matter: this certainly appealed to
patrons such as the Cavaliere Baiardo, for whom he painted his
Cupid, now in the Kunsthistorisches Museum, Vienna.

The drawing belonged to three celebrated painters and collectors:
Sir Peter Lely, Richard Cosway and Sir Thomas Lawrence. It was
sold at Christie's in 1887, catalogued as by Raphael for 4 guineas.

Opposite:
SIR PETER PAUL RUBENS (Flemish, 1577–1640)
The Dance of Death: an album of 44 drawings after Hans
Holbein II
pen and brown or grey ink, some with brown or grey wash
averaging 4 × 3 in. (10 × 7.5 cm.)
Amsterdam, 25 November 1991, Fl. 713,000 (£220,743)

These are generally regarded as the earliest known drawings by
Rubens, dating from *circa* 1591–2.

GERRIT BATTEM (Dutch, c. 1636–1684)
An extensive River Landscape with a Village
watercolour and bodycolour
$4\frac{3}{4} \times 8\frac{1}{2}$ in. (12.1 × 21.6 cm.)
Amsterdam, 25 November 1991, Fl. 92,000 (£28,483)

JEAN-ANTOINE WATTEAU (French, 1684–1721)
Three Ladies in profile to the right
red chalk
$6\frac{3}{4} \times 8\frac{5}{8}$ in. (16.7 × 27.4 cm.)
Sold from the collection of John A. Blum and the Estate of
Clara May Burns
New York, 15 January 1992, $154,000 (£85,555)

This was once part of Miss James' celebrated collection of drawings by
Watteau which was sold at Christie's in 1891; the present study fetched
32 guineas.

Opposite:
JEAN-ANTOINE WATTEAU (French, 1684–1721)
Studies of two Girl's Heads
black, red and white chalk
$5\frac{1}{8} \times 7\frac{5}{8}$ in. (13.2 × 19.4 cm.)
Sold from the collection of John A. Blum and the Estate of
Clare May Burns
New York, 15 January 1992, $242,000 (£134,444)

This drawing is probably of 1716: the head of a young girl wearing a
hat is related to a figure in *L'Embarquement pour Cythère* in Schloss
Charlottenburg, Berlin.

FRANÇOIS BOUCHER (French, 1703–1770)
Arion saved by the Dolphin
black chalk, pen and brown ink, brown wash heightened with white,
on blue paper
$8 \times 11\frac{5}{8}$ in. (20 × 29.5 cm.)
London, 10 December 1992, £44,000 ($79,464)

A preparatory study for the picture dated 1748 commissioned by King
Louis XV for the Château de la Muette, and now in the Art Museum,
Princeton.

La femme de m champagne —
peintre excellent en portraits
au naturel.

PHILLIPE DE CHAMPAIGNE (French, 1602–1674)
Portrait of Madame de Champaigne
with inscription 'La Femme de Mr. Champagne/
peintre excellent en portraits/au naturel'
black and white chalk with touches of red chalk on the
mouth
$8\frac{3}{4} \times 7\frac{3}{4}$ in. (22 × 19.6 cm.)
Monaco, 20 June 1992, Fr. 340,000 (£34,693)

The inscription on this exceptional drawing, evidently
taken from the life, has made possible the identification
of a related portrait in the Bowes Museum, Barnard
Castle as of the artist's wife. Formerly owned by Jean-
Pierre-Marie de Ruolz (1670–1726), the drawing was
part of the collection formed by M. Nicos Dhikéos.

ELISABETH-LOUISE VIGÉE-LE BRUN
(French, 1755–1842)
Portrait of Louisa, Princess Radziwill, bust length,
in a black velvet dress and lace collar
pastel
$22\frac{3}{4} \times 16\frac{1}{2}$ in. (59 × 42 cm.)
London, 14 April 1992, £50,600 ($88,853)

Princess Louisa Frederika von Hohenzollern married
Prince Radziwill, the head of one of the greatest Polish
families, in 1796.

This pastel was drawn in Berlin in 1801 and used for
the oil portrait Vigée-Le Brun later painted in Paris,
which was sold at Christie's in 1978.

A pastel from the same source, of the sitter's close
friend, Louisa, Queen of Prussia, was sold at the same
time for £37,400 ($65,450) and acquired for Schloss
Charlottenburg, Berlin.

OLD MASTER PRINTS FROM A GERMAN FAMILY OF TITLE

by David Llewellyn

The nineteenth and early decades of the twentieth centuries witnessed the formation of some remarkable collections of Old Master prints. Almost without exception these were dispersed, usually by auction, with many of the finest pieces passing initially from one generation of private collector to the next before finding their way gradually into the growing number of European and, later, American public institutions. The emergence of a nineteenth-century collection, unknown and untouched since it was assembled over a hundred years ago, is a rare and extraordinary occurrence in today's market.

The collection, sold in two parts on 10 December 1991 and 18 June 1992, had within it sufficient quantities of all periods and of different styles of printmaking to capture the many varied tastes of those that collect Old Master prints today. A handful of Italian prints from the sixteenth century contrasted well with a fine group of eighteenth-century Venetian prints. Early sixteenth-century Netherlandish prints and fine eighteenth-century French colour prints provided their own sections of interest. However, it was the works of Dürer and of Rembrandt in particular which provided the collection with its essential character and which contributed most significantly to its eventual overall value. A number of the engravings by Dürer were in exceptionally fine condition, the presence of unusually wide margins beyond some of the subjects helping to stimulate prices well in excess of expectation and previous auction precedent (two notable examples being *The Sudarium held by two Angels* and *Four naked Women* which sold respectively for £19,800 and £25,300).

However, the core of the collection was undoubtedly the large group of prints by Rembrandt, arguably the finest printmaker of all ages. Over 180 of his prints, the largest collection from a single source to appear at auction in the last twenty years, were offered for sale and contained examples of the many subjects that captured the artist's interest, including scenes from the Old and New Testaments, landscapes, beggars and portraits. The quality of the prints was generally of a high standard, a few pieces being of the greatest excellence and of the utmost rarity. Pre-eminent was the *Christ presented to the People*, a wonderful and unrecorded impression of the first state printed on Japanese paper, a masterpiece showing the artist at the height of his dramatic, emotional and technical powers. At £528,000 ($953,568) it realised the highest price for any print sold at auction in 1991, and in dollar terms was just a shade less than the record $990,000 paid for an impression of the pendant *Three Crosses* in New York early in 1990. Notable prices achieved for non-biblical subjects included £82,500 for a superb impression of *Beggars receiving Alms at the Door of a House*, a similar price for the exceptionally rare, sexually explicit but modestly titled *The Monk in the Cornfield*, £71,500 for the contemplative *Woman sitting half-dressed beside a Stove*, £51,700 for the *Landscape with three gabled Cottages* and £66,000 for the artist's only still-life in the printed medium, *The Shell* (*Conus Marmoreus*).

The greatest rarity among a sizeable group of portraits was the *Thomas Haaringh* ('*Old Haaringh*'), a civil servant who succeeded his father in 1617 as concierge at the City Hall in Amsterdam. One of the concierge's tasks was to supervise all sales under distress within the Court of Insolvents (*Desolate Boedelkamer*), a function which must have exposed him to many of the miseries of life. The portrait was executed in 1655 just a year before Haaringh was ironically obliged to initiate the series of sales of the distressed Rembrandt's own collection. Rembrandt's sensitive and sympathetic portrait contains no trace of rancour and instead imbues the elderly sitter with a quiet, wise and philosophical air.

The portrait is unique in being the only one in which the artist dispensed with the medium of etching and worked directly on the copper plate with drypoint and a few touches of engraving. The intention no doubt was to allow the 'burr' (the ridges of copper that hold a film of ink which surrounds and softens the incised lines) to capture the velvety textures of the sitter's dress and the drapery to the left. The fugitive nature of the medium of drypoint, where the burr tends to diminish rapidly with each successive impression, meant that only a small number of impressions of this print were made before the plate was presumably abandoned, since it could no longer produce an image close to the artist's original intention. As a result the '*Old Haaringh*' remains one of the rarest of Rembrandt's prints. A combination of its inherent rarity and the fact that this gem of a print had a lengthy and distinguished provenance that suggests it emanated from a collection initiated during Rembrandt's own lifetime helped it to achieve £308,000 ($556,248), over twice the higher end of the quoted estimate and a record auction price for a Rembrandt portrait print.

Overall the sales achieved an astonishing sold figure of over 96% and realised over £3,000,000, confirmation of both the excellent quality of the collection and of the continued and underlying strength of the market for Old Master prints.

REMBRANDT HARMENSZ. VAN RIJN
(Dutch, 1606–1669)
The Monk in the Cornfield (Bartsch 187)
etching with drypoint, 1646, an excellent impression,
from the Remy, Barnard and Weber collections
platemark $1\frac{7}{8} \times 2\frac{9}{16}$ in. (4.8 × 6.5 cm.)
London, 10 December 1991, £82,500 ($148,995)

REMBRANDT HARMENSZ. VAN RIJN
(Dutch, 1606–1669)
Thomas Haaringh ('Old Haaringh') (Bartsch 274)
drypoint, 1655, second (final) state, a magnificent
impression, from the Zoomer, Zanetti, Vivant-Denon,
Wilson, Baring, Verstolk, Brooke and Weber collections
platemark $7\frac{13}{16} \times 5\frac{7}{8}$ in. (19.8 × 14.9 cm.)
London, 10 December 1991, £308,000 ($556,248)
Record auction price for a portrait print by the artist

REMBRANDT HARMENSZ. VAN RIJN
(Dutch, 1606–1669)
Christ presented to the People:
oblong plate (Bartsch 76)
drypoint, 1655, the extremely rare first state
(of eight), a wonderful impression
platemark $15\frac{1}{6} \times 17\frac{5}{8}$ in. (38.2 × 44.7 cm.)
London, 10 December 1991,
£528,000 ($953,568)

REMBRANDT HARMENSZ. VAN RIJN
(Dutch, 1606–1669)
The Shell (Conus Marmoreus) (Bartsch 159)
etching with drypoint and engraving, 1650,
second state (of three), a very fine impression,
from the Linck collection
platemark $3\frac{5}{8} \times 5\frac{3}{16}$ in. (9.2 × 13.2 cm.)
London, 18 June 1992, £66,000 ($121,176)

LUCAS VAN LEYDEN (Flemish, circa 1489–1533)
The Emperor Maximilian I (Bartsch 172)
etching with engraving, 1520, a fine impression, from
the Zanetti, Vivant-Denon, Brooke and Weber
collections
sheet size $10\frac{1}{4} \times 7\frac{5}{8}$ in. (26 × 19.3 cm.)
London, 10 December 1991, £93,500 ($168,861)

BRITISH PICTURES

ROBERT WALKER (active 1641–1658)
Portrait of John Evelyn, half-length
oil on canvas
$34\frac{1}{2} \times 25\frac{1}{4}$ in. (87.9 × 64.1 cm.)
London, 10 April 1992,
£253,000 ($446,292)
Record auction price for a work by the artist
Now in the National Portrait Gallery,
London

John Evelyn (1620–1706), the celebrated *virtuoso* and diarist recorded in his diary on 1 July 1648 '(I) sate for my *Picture* (the same wherein is a *Death's Head*) to Mr Walker that most excellent painter'. Evelyn's diaries span more than sixty years and seven reigns and record daily events, thoughts and life at court. He was a politician, diplomat, horticulturalist and amateur scientist, and a founder member of the Royal Society for 'the promotion of experimental knowledge'. The painting had passed by direct descent from the sitter.

WILLIAM DOBSON (1611–1646)
Portrait of Sir Thomas Chicheley, half length
oil on canvas
40 × 30½ in. (101.5 × 80 cm.)
London, 10 April 1992, £101,200 ($178,516)

William Dobson was the only native English painter of significance to have studied the collection of King Charles I, and was profoundly influenced by the work of both Titian and his own contemporary, van Dyck. This portrait of an East Anglian Royalist, so obviously indebted to the work of van Dyck, is a characteristic example of Dobson's portraiture for the court of Charles I at Oxford. The portrait was sold by a descendant, through the female line, of the sitter.

GABRIELE RICCIARDELLI (active 1745–1777)
A Prospect of Stillorgan Park and Obelisk, with Dublin
and the Harbour beyond
oil on canvas
$14\frac{1}{4} \times 34\frac{1}{2}$ in. (36.2 × 82.5 cm.)
London, 10 April 1992, £33,000 ($58,212)

DAVID ALLAN (1744–1796)
A Portrait Group of three Boys, in Windsor uniform
oil on canvas
$47 \times 58\frac{1}{2}$ in. (119.5 × 148.5 cm.)
London, 10 April 1992, £68,200 ($120,304)

THOMAS GAINSBOROUGH, R.A. (1701–1788)
A wooded Landscape with rustic Lovers, a Herdsman,
Cattle and Sheep by a Pond
oil on canvas
$46\frac{1}{2} \times 58\frac{1}{2}$ in. (118 × 148.6 cm.)
London, 13 December 1991, £836,000 ($1,505,636)

This landscape can be dated to the artist's final period in London
(*circa* 1784–5) when the influence of Rubens' landscape paintings
can be seen in Gainsborough's works, for instance the darker palette
and breadth of handling. This picture relates most closely to *The
Harvest Waggon* (Art Gallery of Ontario, Toronto) painted in the
winter of 1784–5. A preparatory drawing for the present picture (in
a London private collection) does not show the two lovers on the
left, the inclusion of which completes the focus and composed
balance of the painting.

ANGELICA KAUFFMANN, R.A.(1741–1807)
Portrait of Lady Rushout and her daughter Anne
oil on canvas
$50\frac{1}{8} \times 40$ in. (127.5 × 101.5 cm.)
Sold by the Executors of the late Lord Lurgan
London, 17 July 1992, £132,000 ($254,628)

This extremely fine portrait dates from Kauffmann's stay in England and is one of a large number of paintings commissioned from the artist by the Bowles and Rushout families. Rebecca, Lady Rushout, *née* Bowles, was the sister and heiress of George Bowles who met Kauffmann in Venice and became her most dependable patron in England. This portrait was presumably commissioned by her husband Sir John Rushout, later 1st Lord Northwick. The portrait remains in the original frame.

SIR EDWIN LANDSEER, R.A.(1802–1873)
'Scarbro', the Old Cover Hack
oil on canvas
$48\frac{1}{4} \times 59\frac{3}{4}$ in. (122.5 × 151.8 cm.)
London, 10 April 1992, £143,000 ($252,252)

This picture of Scarbro, a grey hunter, was commissioned by the owner, Richard Heathcote, from Landseer and was exhibited at the Royal Academy in 1848. Ruskin, who had described an earlier work by Landseer as 'one of the most perfect poems or pictures which modern times have seen', objected to the use of shadow in this picture. Scarbro's tail, in a case inscribed with an old label 'Tail of Scarbro/The Old Cover Hack/dies about 1840 aged 25', was sold with the picture.

BRITISH DRAWINGS AND WATERCOLOURS

THOMAS GAINSBOROUGH, R.A. (1727–1788)
A Peasant Family going to Market
black and white chalk, stump, grey and brown wash extensively
heightened with white on brown paper
$16\frac{1}{8} \times 21$ in. (41 × 53.3 cm.)
Sold by the Trustees of Lord Clark's Settlement Trust
London, 14 July 1992, £352,000 ($672,672)

As Dr. Hayes has pointed out, this is 'an unusually elaborate
treatment (for a drawing) of the theme of travelling to and from
market, with which Gainsborough was particularly
preoccupied in the early 1770s'. The elaborate technique is also
characteristic of this period. The drawing depicts an idealised,
idyllic country life, akin to that described in James Thomson's
The Seasons of 1726–8 and Oliver Goldsmith's *The Deserted
Village* of 1770; but the composition also recalls the *Flight into
Egypt*. The drawing is therefore a particularly concentrated
example of the mixed sentiments and allusions that marked the
new appreciation of nature in eighteenth-century England.

SIR THOMAS LAWRENCE, P.R.A.
(1769–1830)
Portrait of Mrs. Ayscoghe Boucherett with her
two eldest Children, Emilia and Ayscoghe, and
her Half-Sister Juliana Angerstein, later Madame
Sabloukoff, in a garden
signed with initials and dated 1794
pastel
20 × 16¼ in. (50.7 × 41.2 cm.)
London, 7 April 1992, £82,500 ($142,972)

When Lawrence moved from Bath to London in
1787 he came with the reputation of a prodigy
who had made his name with small portraits in
pastel. His acquisition of the skills of painting in
oil as soon as he was settled was, however, so
phenomenally rapid that he abandoned pastel
almost entirely. This pastel was his last, his most
ambitious and his most successful effort in this
medium. It was exhibited at the Royal Academy
in 1795, no. 602, as *Portraits of a Family*. The
sitters were related by blood or marriage to John
Julius Angerstein, whose collection was to form
the nucleus of the National Gallery.

AN ALBUM OF DRAWINGS BY HENRY FUSELI, R.A.

by Martin Butlin

The appearance of an album containing 58 unrecorded drawings by Henry Fuseli, R.A. (1741–1825), also known by his original Swiss name of Johann Heinrich Füssli, was one of the excitements of the 1991–2 season. The album had been compiled by Miss Harriet Jane Moore, niece of the famous General Sir John Moore, hero of Corunna and a member of a family well acquainted with the artist, who knew both her grandfather Dr. John Moore, M.D., and her father James (later Carrick) Moore. When she was five years old, Fuseli had given her a copy of his friend William Blake's book *For Children: The Gates of Paradise*, and three of the drawings in the album were annotated by her as having been 'Given to me by Mr. Fuseli'. Similar inscriptions showed that other drawings had come from the collections of Fuseli's executor and biographer John Knowles, his friend the antiquary and scientific writer Sir Henry Englefield, Bt., and, tantalisingly, a 'Mrs Wainwright' whom it is tempting to identify as the wife of Fuseli's admirer the notorious Thomas Griffiths Wainewright, who was deported to Australia for forgery after poisoning his uncle, mother-in-law and half sister-in-law.

Harriet Moore owned a number of other works by Fuseli, including the large oil painting of *Titania and Bottom* now in the Tate Gallery and another album of drawings, all dating from the artist's Roman period, now in the British Museum, but the newly discovered collection was particularly interesting in that it covered all but the earliest years of Fuseli's career, and most aspects of his subject-matter.

The earliest group of drawings dated from Fuseli's years in Rome, 1770–8, or perhaps in some cases from even a year or so earlier. They included a masterly study in light and shade of *Macbeth and the three Witches showing him the armed Head*, the first version of a similar wash drawing from Harriet Moore's Roman Album in the British Museum (interestingly, the group of drawings included a number of versions of works from the Roman Album, in every case apparently the first to be executed). There was also a pen drawing of *The Massacre of the Innocents* with the dramatic figure of a wailing mother with arms outstretched inspired by Greek tragedy, and a similarly dramatic pen drawing of a woman slumped over a table with a threatening figure behind.

Also from this group were a number of studies inspired by Michelangelo's figures in the Sistine Chapel where Fuseli had

lain 'on his back day after day, and week succeeding week, with upturned and wondering eyes, musing at the splendid ceiling' so that 'He fulfilled the injunction of Reynolds – he ate and drank and slept and worked upon Michelangelo'. Such studies, several in long frieze-like compositions, led to the completely integrated and personal simplicity of the pen and wash drawing of *A young Woman with her Head resting on a Bolster,* as if in mourning. Also from this period were copies after Antique statues such as the famous *Dioscuri* and the Farnese *Hercules.* The influence of Michelangelo persists in a number of pen and wash drawings of single figures done after Fuseli's return to England, annotated with the date (17)89 and the capital letter 'L', apparently for London or, more likely, Liverpool, the home town of his patron William Roscoe. Also from these later English years were further composition sketches illustrating Aeschylus's *Prometheus Bound,* Chaucer's *Canterbury Tales* and Shakespeare's *Twelfth Night.* William Blake's influence is perhaps to be seen in the magnificent drawing of the airborne *Satan,* seen, as in Blake's watercolour in the Tate Gallery, in his original glory before his fall.

Fuseli's fascination with young girls, and in particular his fetishist preoccupation with exotic coiffeurs, was reflected in a number of studies, including the full-length *Lady walking.* A related interest was shown in his *Study of a Woman's gloved Arms,* while the eroticism of much of his art was seen in two exquisite studies of embracing lovers, mysteriously related in his mind (as is shown by the inscription on another version of one of the drawings) to the love of Siegfried and Kriemhild in the *Nibelungenlied.*

The sale of these drawings was a particularly striking success, making a total of £749,540 ($1,316,192).

JOHANN HEINRICH FÜSSLI, HENRY FUSELI, R.A. (1741–1825)
A young Woman with her Head resting on a Bolster
inscribed and dated, 'R [Rome]. 78.' and with inscription 'H. Fusili/From the Author' (*verso*)
pencil, pen and brown ink, grey and brown wash
$8\frac{1}{2} \times 10\frac{1}{4}$ in. (21 × 26.2 cm.)
London, 14 April 1992, £46,200 ($81,127)

Opposite:
JOHANN HEINRICH FÜSSLI, HENRY FUSELI, R.A. (1741–1825)
The Massacre of the Innocents
pencil, pen and brown ink, brown wash
$9\frac{7}{8} \times 14\frac{3}{4}$ in. (24.7 × 37.3 cm.)
London, 14 April 1992, £55,000 ($96,580)

JOHANN HEINRICH FÜSSLI,
HENRY FUSELI, R.A.
(1741–1825)
A Lady walking
pencil, pen and brown ink and
watercolour
$12\frac{3}{4} \times 8\frac{1}{4}$ in. (32.8 × 21.1 cm.)
London, 14 April 1992, £41,800
($73,400)

Below:
JOHANN HEINRICH FÜSSLI,
HENRY FUSELI, R.A.
(1741–1825)
A Frieze of Michelangelesque
Compositions (*recto*)
with inscription 'Fusili' twice and
numbered '42' and '43'
pencil, pen and grey and brown ink,
grey wash
$4\frac{3}{4} \times 15\frac{3}{4}$ in. (12.1 × 40.5 cm.)
London, 14 April 1992, £44,000
($77,264)

JOSEPH MALLORD WILLIAM TURNER, R.A.
(1775–1851)
The Splügen Pass
inscribed 'Bains'
pencil and watercolour with scratching out
$11\frac{1}{2} \times 17\frac{3}{4}$ in.(29.2 × 45.1 cm.)
London, 14 July 1992, £242,000 ($462,462)

This watercolour is the product of two schemes by Turner to produce finished watercolours, all but one of Swiss subjects, on commission from sketches given to his dealer Thomas Griffith, in 1842 and 1843. Turner also gave Griffith four finished works as examples of what he could do, including *The Splügen Pass*. Griffith succeeded in selling the four finished works and in getting orders for five more. Turner's friend H. A. J. Munro of Novar purchased five, including this watercolour. John Ruskin had also hoped to purchase at least

one watercolour in 1842, but his father was abroad on business and Ruskin had neither the money nor the authority to act on his own. As he wrote in 1878: 'The Splugen Pass I saw in an instant to be the noblest Alpine drawing Turner had ever till then made.' In his autobiographical *Praeterita* he amended this; 'I knew perfectly well that this drawing was the best Swiss landscape yet painted by man; and that it was entirely proper for *me* to have it, and inexpedient that anybody else should.' By the time Ruskin's father did return home *The Splügen Pass* had been sold to Munro. Ruskin was finally given the watercolour by a group of friends on his recovery from an illness. This was after the Munro sale at Christie's in 1878, when it fetched 1,000 guineas.

Ruskin pointed out that the composition is 'very remarkable as an example of Turner's occasional delight in a perfectly straight road seen for four or five miles in length at once'.

SIR EDWARD COLEY BURNE-JONES, Bt., A.R.A.
(British, 1833–1898)
The Annunciation ('The Flower of God')
signed and inscribed
watercolour and bodycolour
$23\frac{3}{4} \times 20\frac{3}{4}$ in. (60.3 × 52.7 cm.)
London, 12 June 1992, £82,500 ($156,750)

This watercolour was commissioned by the wood-engravers George and Edward Dalziel and conceived as a 'harmony in red', an interesting early example of 'aesthetic' values. The deliberately quaint style, which upset many when the *Annunciation* was first exhibited in 1864, betrays the influence of Burne-Jones's master Rossetti, as well as that of Carpaccio, whom he studied in Venice in 1859.

DANTE GABRIEL ROSSETTI
(1828–1882)
Portrait of Mrs. William J. Stillman, *née* Marie
Spartali, bust length
signed with monogram and dated 1869
coloured chalks on two joined sheets of
grey-green paper
$24\frac{1}{2} \times 18\frac{1}{2}$ in. (62.2 × 47 cm.)
Sold by descendants of the sitter
London, 12 June 1992, £88,000 ($167,200)

A celebrated Pre-Raphaelite beauty, Marie Spartali
belonged to the Anglo-Greek community which
played such a significant part in the history of later
Victorian art and taste. In addition to Rossetti, who
found her head 'about the most difficult I ever
drew', she sat to Burne-Jones, Madox Brown,
Julia Margaret Cameron and others. She was also a
talented artist herself.

EDWARD ROBERT HUGHES, R.W.S.
(British, 1851–1914)
Bertuccio's Bride
signed and dated 1895
pencil and watercolour with scratching out
$39\frac{1}{2} \times 30$ in. (100.3 × 76.10 cm.)
London, 29 October 1991, £88,000 ($148,720)
Record auction price for a watercolour by the artist

This watercolour is one of eighteen commissioned to illustrate the first English edition of *Le piacevole notte* by Gian Francesco Straparola, a collection of *novelle* resembling Boccaccio's *Decameron* published in Venice in 1550–3. E. R. Hughes, who was fascinated by obscure subjects from Italian literature, was the nephew of the Pre-Raphaelite painter Arthur Hughes and worked closely with Holman Hunt.

HELEN ALLINGHAM, R.W.S. (1848–1926)
Near Witley, Surrey
signed 'H. Allingham' and inscribed on the reverse
watercolour with scratching out
19 × 14¾ in. (48 × 37.5 cm.)
Sold by Marley Plc.
London, 19 September 1991, £46,200 ($76,461)

The Marley Collection of 55 watercolours by
Helen Allingham was formed between 1947 and 1970
by Sir Owen Aisher, former Chairman of Marley Plc.

Helen Allingham began her career as an illustrator but
her talent as a watercolourist was quickly recognised and
in 1875 she was elected the first female associate of the
Royal Society of Painters in Water-Colours; she became
the first female full member in 1890. Allingham's
watercolours of cottages were very popular and in 1886
and 1887 she held one-woman shows at the Fine Art
Society, both of which were sell-outs.

Helen Allingham's reputation stands as high today as it
did at the peak of her career; every watercolour in the
Marley Collection was sold and *Near Witley, Surrey*,
realised a new auction record for the artist. Allingham is
considered by many the supreme exponent of the rustic
idyll in Victorian watercolour painting. She is also
thought of as a painter of an idealised picture of country
life, but her drawings of cottages were not merely
escapist. She was actively involved in the Society for the
Protection of Ancient Buildings, and her watercolours
have an underlying seriousness of purpose as she sought
to capture a way of life and a type of vernacular
architecture that were disappearing even as she painted.
Allingham's work was so accurate that it was possible to
identify many of the cottages recorded in the Marley
Collection including that in *Near Witley, Surrey*, with the
result that some of the watercolours were bought by the
cottages' current owners.

ARCHIBALD THORBURN (1860–1935)
Clearing after Rain; Red Grouse among Heather
signed and dated 'Archibald Thorburn/1920.'
pencil, watercolour and bodycolour
21 × 29¾ in. (53.3 × 75.6 cm.)
London, 25 February 1992, £44,000 ($76,648)

One of a group of 33 Thorburns included in Christie's
fourth annual sale of Watercolours and Pictures of Birds.

VICTORIAN PICTURES

DADD'S 'CONTRADICTION: OBERON AND TITANIA'

by John Christian

Two pictures by Richard Dadd are in a class of their own: *Contradiction: Oberon and Titania* and *The Fairy Feller's Master-Stroke*, which Siegfried Sassoon gave to the Tate Gallery in 1963. Dadd is the only artist one can readily think of whose work was produced under conditions of latent or declared madness. It is therefore invariably interesting, and often rises to heights of poetic intensity. But in no other pictures did he give such complete expression to his lyrical, obsessive and often tortured vision. Ostensibly they belong to the familiar genre of Victorian fairy painting, but such is the power of imagination displayed that they transcend the limitations of fairy painting and have no meaningful parallel in the whole of Victorian art.

Contradiction, the earlier of the two, was painted in Bethlem Hospital (now the Imperial War Museum) in 1854–8. In 1842 Dadd had set out with Sir Thomas Phillips on a tour of the Middle East. The visual excitement and physical hardship of the journey had precipitated a long impending crisis, and ten months later he had returned insane. In August 1843 he murdered his father at Chatham, believing that he was acting as the agent of the Egyptian god Osiris (the tour had included Egypt) who had commanded him to destroy the devil. He then fled to France, where he attempted another murder and was arrested. His behaviour left no doubt of his disturbed state of mind, and in August 1844 he was committed to Bethlem Hospital.

Dadd was to remain there for twenty years, moving in 1864 to the newly-built Broadmoor in Berkshire. Conditions had improved since the bad old days when it had been a fashionable pastime to 'view the lunatics' in 'Bedlam', but they were still grim enough in the criminal department to which Dadd was confined. Although he resumed painting almost immediately, his output was small for the first eight years. However, a change occurred in 1852 when Dr William Charles Hood became the hospital's first resident superintendent at the age of 28. A man of compassion, culture and industry, Hood introduced a more enlightened regime, enlarging the windows and furnishing the wards with aviaries of birds, flowers, pictures and books. He was ably assisted by a new steward, George Henry Haydon, and both men encouraged Dadd with his painting. Hood was to acquire over thirty examples, *Contradiction* being the most important. Impressed by the picture, Haydon commissioned something similar; the result was *The Fairy Feller's Master-Stroke*, begun about 1857 and not quite finished when Dadd left Bethlem in 1864.

During his early career Dadd had specialised in fairy subjects, earning a reputation as their leading exponent. Many of these pictures and illustrations had been inspired by *A Midsummer Night's Dream*, and in *Contradiction* he returned to the play, showing Oberon and Titania quarrelling over Titania's refusal to give up her Indian changeling boy to be Oberon's page (Act II, Scene 1). Demetrius and Helena, one of the two pairs of human lovers, appear on the right, while fairies, gnomes and goblins lurk among the dew-laden undergrowth or cavort across the curious platforms that fill the middle distance.

The only known photograph of Dadd in Bethlem shows him working on the picture, painstakingly filling in the design, detail by detail, from the lower right corner upwards. Technically it is a *tour de force*, all the more astonishing for its superb condition. However 'mad' Dadd may have been, it in no way confused his drawing or handling of paint. On the contrary, the picture has a gem-like precision of form and a superabundance of detail which, in combination, give it a positively surreal quality. The visual memory behind it is phenomenal, and when brought to bear on natural phenomena results in an almost mystical involvement, deeply moving in view of Dadd's surroundings in Bethlem – cell, crowded gallery, and bleak exercise yard. Despite Hood's reforms, an account of Dadd at work in the 1850s describes him 'weaving his fine fancies on the canvas amidst the most revolting conversation and the most brutal behaviour'.

Iconographically, the picture echoes some of Dadd's earlier fairy paintings, while certain details seem to have been suggested by his Middle Eastern travels. Oberon, for instance, recalls his description, in a letter written at the time to W. P. Frith, of a Syrian sheikh, with a 'black grizzly beard', whose band of Arab tribesmen had captured his party at Jericho. Dadd was probably also aware of other treatments of his theme. Henry Howard, who had been Professor of Painting when he was a student at the Royal Academy schools in the late 1830s, had painted a *Contention of Oberon and Titania*, and more recently J. Noel Paton's paintings of the *Quarrel* and *Reconciliation* of the fairy monarchs (1847–50; National Gallery of Scotland) had been much acclaimed. Dadd, who eagerly seized on information about his profession from the outside world, may well have known of these pictures, and they certainly make a fascinating comparison with his own. While they are charming but essentially 'thought up', Dadd, so to speak, has 'been there'. It is a classic demonstration of Coleridge's distinction between Fancy and Imagination.

The picture remained in Hood's possession until his death in 1870, and was not exhibited until 1930. Laurence Binyon praised it in 1937, but it was only with the revival of interest in Victorian art in the 1960s, and in particular the Dadd exhibition at the Tate in 1974, that its significance was fully appreciated. In 1983 it realised £550,000 at auction, a world record for a Victorian painting which evoked widespread comment in the press. Four years later the record was eclipsed when Rossetti's *Proserpine* was sold at Christie's for £1.3 million, but now *Contradiction* has regained its saleroom supremacy, setting a new record which is likely to be held for some time. There is poetic justice in the fact that these laurels have been bestowed on Dadd, whose madness caused him to be shut away and forgotten by his contemporaries.

RICHARD DADD (1817–1886)
Contradiction: Oberon and Titania
signed and dated 1854–1858
oil on canvas, oval
$24 \times 29\frac{3}{4}$ in. (61 × 75.5 cm.)
London, 12 June 1992, £1,650,000 ($3,135,000)
Record auction price for a work by the artist and for a Victorian
picture

DAVID ROBERTS, R.A. (1796–1864)
Jerusalem from the South
signed and dated 1860
oil on canvas
$48\frac{1}{4} \times 72\frac{1}{4}$ in. (122.5 × 183.5 cm.)
London, 25 October 1991, £418,000 ($713,108)
Record auction price for a work by the artist

Before its recent rediscovery, this picture was the only missing
work among the six large views of Jerusalem that Roberts
painted. The artist set out for the East in August 1838. After
wintering in Egypt, he paid two visits to Jerusalem the following
March and April, finally returning to England in October 1839.
He had long looked forward to seeing Jerusalem, and was bitterly
disappointed. 'There cannot be any city more wretched', he
wrote. Its monuments were 'of such a paltry and contemptible
character that no artist could render them interesting.' Distant
views were equally unpromising, and the Sirocco blinded him
with sand.

Despite all this, Roberts managed to make enough drawings not
only for the six large oils he was later to paint but the eighteen
lithographs by Louis Haghe – fourteen subjects inside the walls
and four external views – which were published in *Egypt, Syria
and the Holy Land* in 1842–9. *Jerusalem from the South* was painted
in 1860, more than twenty years after Roberts' return from the
East – a remarkable tribute to his powers of recall and the
traditional method of painting landscapes in the studio from notes
made on the spot. The picture was bought by the dealer Ernest
Gambart, and passed through several English collections in the
nineteenth century. Discovered by one of our staff in Sweden, it
made an auspicious start to our London sale of important
Victorian pictures on 25 October 1991.

FREDERIC, LORD LEIGHTON, P.R.A. (1830–1896)
Lady Sybil Primrose
oil on canvas
48 × 34¼ in. (121.9 × 87 cm.)
London, 13 March 1992, £231,000 ($392,238)

Born in 1879, Lady Sybil was the eldest child of Archibald Primrose, 5th Earl of Rosebery, and his wife Hannah de Rothschild. Her younger sister Peggy was painted at the same time by Millais, the two portraits being exhibited as pendants at the Royal Academy of 1885. When Rosebery succeeded Gladstone as Prime Minister in March 1894, the portrait of Lady Sybil hung in the drawing room at 10 Downing Street. A dazzlingly stylish performance, painted at the height of Leighton's career as President of the Royal Academy, the picture remained in the sitter's family and was not exhibited between 1885 and its recent reappearance.

CHARLES EDWARD HALLÉ (1846–1919)
Paolo and Francesca
oil on canvas
73½ × 48¾ in. (186.7 × 123.8 cm.)
London, 13 March 1992, £110,000 ($186,780)
Record auction price for a work by the artist

The son of the famous conductor Sir Charles Hallé, C. E. Hallé trained as an artist but is chiefly known as a director of the Grosvenor Gallery, flagship of the Aesthetic Movement, and the New Gallery, which succeeded it. This picture, which he showed at the opening exhibition at the New Gallery in 1888, is by far his most impressive work. The subject of Paolo and Francesca, the lovers whom Dante encounters in the second circle of Hell, was a favourite with nineteenth-century artists; Flaxman, Ingres, Blake, Delacroix, Dyce, Rossetti and Watts were also among its exponents.

ARTHUR HUGHES (1832–1915)
Silver and Gold
signed
oil on canvas
39 × 26½ in. (99 × 67.3 cm.)
London, 25 October 1991, £220,000 ($375,320)
Record auction price for a work by the artist

Exhibited at the Royal Academy in 1864, the picture combines two of Hughes's favourite themes: the passage of time, represented not only by the figures but such details as the sundial and scythe; and love, the subject of the girl and her companion's confidences and again embodied in a wealth of imagery, not least the purple lilac, symbol of 'the first emotions of love' in the Victorian 'language of flowers.' *Silver and Gold* was one of some twenty works acquired by Hughes's patron John Hamilton Trist, a Brighton wine merchant.

Opposite:
JOHN ATKINSON GRIMSHAW (1836–1893)
Dulce Domum
signed and dated 1885
oil on canvas
$32\frac{3}{4} \times 48\frac{1}{4}$ in. (83 × 122.5 cm.)
London, 12 June 1992, £159,500 ($303,050)
Record auction price for a work by the artist

One of Grimshaw's finest works, *Dulce Domum* was the last and most significant of the series of domestic subjects which he painted to celebrate his life at Knostrop Old Hall, the seventeenth-century manor house near Leeds where he settled in 1870. Two girls, believed to be his daughters Enid and Elaine, are seen in the dining-room, surrounded by fashionably 'aesthetic' bric-a-brac. Indeed, with its 'Queen Anne' setting, musical theme and 'greenery yallery' colouring, the picture is a microcosm of the Aesthetic Movement. Warmly received when exhibited at the Royal Academy in 1885, it was acquired by Walter Battle, the Leeds solicitor who was Grimshaw's most consistent patron.

SIR SAMUEL LUKE FILDES, R.A. (1843–1927)
The Village Wedding
signed and dated 1883
oil on canvas
$59\frac{3}{4} \times 100\frac{1}{2}$ in. (151.7 × 255.3 cm.)
London, 12 June 1992, £275,000 ($522,500)
Record auction price for a work by the artist

The Village Wedding is one of the outstanding examples of Victorian genre, remarkable for its subtlety of interpretation no less than its immense scale. Begun at Aston Tirrold, near Wallingford, in August 1881, it was completed in time for the Royal Academy exhibition of 1883, where it scored a great success. The picture marked a distinct concession to popular taste after the works of social realism with which Fildes had made his name in the 1870s.

Right:
EVELYN DE MORGAN, née Pickering (1855–1919)
Clytie
signed and dated 1886–7
oil on canvas
$41 \times 17\frac{1}{2}$ in. (104 × 44.5 cm.)
London, 25 October 1991, £99,000 ($168,894)

Clytie was a sea-nymph who loved Apollo, god of the sun; when he rejected her, she was turned into a sunflower whose head would always follow the sun's course. Although signed with the initials of the artist's maiden name, the picture was completed the year she married the potter William de Morgan, and is painted in a special technique which he invented. It was bought in 1907 by Canon George Tugwell of Lee, near Ilfracombe. When he asked her to remove 'two leaves of the sunflower' she politely but firmly refused.

CORNELIS SPRINGER (Dutch, 1817–1891)
The Rokin, Amsterdam
signed and dated 1854
oil on panel
$23\frac{1}{2} \times 30\frac{1}{2}$ in. (59.7 × 77.5 cm.)
London, 29 November 1991, £165,000 ($289,080)
Record auction price for a work by the artist

Urban topography was a major preoccupation of the painters of the Dutch Romantic Movement, 'The Second Golden Age'. The leading Dutch exponent of this genre was Cornelis Springer, whose works are characterised by their topographical accuracy, which owes much to the example of his predecessors Jan van der Heyden (1637–1712), Gerrit Berckheyde (1638–1698) and Isaac Ouwater (1750–1793). Springer specialised in views of Dutch and German towns. This picture shows the Rokin in the heart of Amsterdam.

NDRIES SCHELFHOUT (Dutch, 1781–1870)
inter: Peasants by a Booth and Skaters on a frozen Canal
ned and dated '57'
on panel
$\frac{13}{16} \times 30\frac{7}{8}$ in. (58 × 78.5 cm.)
nsterdam, 22 April 1992, Fl.431,250 (£135,549)
ecord auction price for a work by the artist

AREND CORNELIS KOEKKOEK (Dutch, 1803–1862)
Winter Landscape with Figures skating on a frozen River
ned and dated 1839
on canvas
$\frac{3}{4} \times 33$ in. (68 × 83.8 cm.)
ondon, 19 June 1992, £121,000 ($225,850)

GUGLIELMO CIARDI (Italian, 1842–1917)
Laguna veneziana
signed
oil on canvas
$17\frac{3}{4} \times 29\frac{7}{8}$ in. (45 × 76 cm.)
Rome, 24 March 1992, L.230,000,000 (£106,000)

PEDER SEVERIN KRØYER (Danish, 1851–1909)
The Departure of the Fishing Fleet
signed and dated '94'
oil on canvas
$53\frac{1}{2} \times 88\frac{1}{2}$ in. (155.9 × 224.8 cm.)
London, 29 November 1991, £154,000 ($269,808)
Bought by the Aarhus Kunstmuseum, Denmark

IGNACIO ZULOAGA Y ZABALETA (Spanish,
1870–1945)
Baile Gitano: En una Terraza de Granada
signed
78 × 78¾ in. (198 × 200 cm.)
London, 29 May 1992, £242,000 ($439,472)

Zuloaga painted a number of gypsy compositions in
Seville in 1902–4. *Baile Gitano* was the only large scale
work of this subject. Two of the *gitanos* are the artist's
cousins. The picture was purchased by Alvan M. Fuller
from the artist on his visit to Boston in 1925. It was sold
by the Alvan M. Fuller Foundation at Christie's on
1 December 1961 for 2,200 guineas.

GUSTAVE BAUERNFEIND (German, 1848–1904)
Praying at the Western Wall, Jerusalem
signed and inscribed
oil on canvas laid down on board
$51 \times 39\frac{1}{2}$ in. (129.5 × 100.3 cm.)
London, 20 March 1992, £220,000 ($371,800)

Formerly an architect, Bauernfeind took up painting in his native Stuttgart in the early 1870s. He first travelled to the Middle East in 1880–1. Two further trips to Palestine in 1884 and 1888 established his reputation, especially in England, as an orientalist painter. He finally settled in Jerusalem in 1896. It was in this latter period that *Praying at the Western Wall, Jerusalem* was painted.

FERNAND KHNOPFF (Belgian, 1858–1921)
Portrait of Jeanne de Bauer
signed and dated 1890
oil on panel
$20\frac{7}{8} \times 13\frac{3}{4}$ in. (53 × 35 cm.)
London, 29 November 1991, £231,000 ($400,471)

The wistful look in the sitter's face, the subtle colours and the
timeless setting of this portrait relates to other portraits of
Khnopff's oeuvre, such as the *Portrait of the Artist's Sister*, sold at
Christie's in New York, 28 February 1991, bought by the

Fondation Roi Baudoin and now on permanent loan to the Musées
Royaux des Beaux-Arts, Brussels, and *Madame Rothmaler* (Galleria d'Arte
Moderna, Venice). The studied distancing of the sitter from the spectator
underlines the meditative and symbolic atmosphere frequently found in
Khnopff's work, such as *Blue Wing* and *Silense* (Musées Royaux des Beaux-
Arts, Brussels). The monochrome colour and the absence of space in this
portrait reflect the influence of Whistler (for example *Arrangement in Black,
no. III*) and parallels can be drawn with Burne-Jones's female portraits that
Khnopff so admired. It is, of course, significant that Khnopff chose to
exhibit this portrait in 1891 at the New Gallery in London, of which
Burne-Jones had been the 'star' since its opening in 1888.

GUSTAVE COURBET (French, 1819–1877)
Flowers on a Bench (*Fleurs sur un banc*, also known as *Fleurs au
pied d'un arbre* and *Gerbe de fleurs au soleil couchant*)
signed and dated '62'
oil on canvas
28 × 42½ in. (71.1 × 107.9 cm.)
Sold from the Estates of Palmer and Charles Ducommun
New York, 27 May 1992, $1,540,000 (£856,507)
Record auction price for a work by the artist
Bought by the Fondation Jean-Louis Prevost, Musée d'Art
et d' Histoire, Geneva

Flowers on a Bench is one of the largest of some two dozen flower
paintings created by Courbet during a year of unusually intense
work in the small provincial city of Saintes in south-western
France. Prior to the visit to Saintes in 1862, still life painting had
held little interest for Courbet, and *Flowers on a Bench* marks an
important new direction in his work for the growing market of
private collectors.

Flowers on a Bench was included in a large exhibition mounted in
the city hall of Saintes by Courbet and several local painters in
January 1863. During the 1880s, the painting belonged to
Jean-Baptiste Faure, a popular and successful operatic singer
who became one of the foremost early collectors of Impressionist
and avant-garde painting.

JEAN-FRANÇOIS MILLET (French, 1814–1875)
Return from the Fields
stamped 'J. F. Millet'
oil on canvas
32 × 39½ in. (81.3 × 100.4 cm.)
New York, 16 October 1991, $2,145,000 (£1,261,764)
Record auction price for a work by the artist

This late masterpiece by Millet, lost to public view since 1921, offers a powerful new glimpse of Millet's thinking on the eve of his death.

Throughout his career, Millet frequently returned to favoured themes, studying a subject anew, then altering or recomposing it to fit the artistic or social concerns that occupied his attention at the moment. *Return from the Fields* of 1873, the last productive year of Millet's life, is the final version of a subject that had held his attention since his earliest explorations of the countryside around Barbizon at the end of the 1840s.

Return from the Fields brings together the interests in monumental figure compositions and landscape painting that dominated Millet's last decade. Where the earliest versions of the theme had emphasized details of costume and locale, in *Return from the Fields* Millet simplified his figural subject and landscape setting to their essential components. Drawing his peasant man and woman into a single dramatically silhouetted unit strengthened the suggestion of a family relationship between the figures and gave their stately passage home an aura of timelessness and solemnity. Dropping the horizon to the lowest quarter of the composition not only gave grandeur to the couple and their animals; it also offered Millet a vast sweep of sky in which to explore the evanescent colours of the fading day.

IMPRESSIONIST AND MODERN PICTURES

EDOUARD MANET (French, 1832–1883)
Les Travailleurs de la Mer
signed
oil on canvas
25 × 31¼ in. (63 × 79.3 cm.)
Sold by the Victoria Nebeker Coberly Family Trust
New York, 12 May 1992, $1,980,000 (£1,093,922)

This work was painted in 1873, the year Manet achieved the approval of the establishment with the acceptance by the Salon of his Frans Hals-like canvas, *Le Bon Bock* (Philadelphia Museum of Art). Manet's official success was echoed commercially when, in November 1873, the baritone Jean-Baptiste Faure of the Paris Opéra bought five of his paintings including *Le Bon Bock* and *Les Travailleurs de la Mer*.

Also entitled *Pêcheurs en Mer*, this canvas was the chief product of three weeks spent by Manet and his family at Berck-sur-Mer. It is likely that in order to capture the sensation of wind, speed and foaming sea Manet took to the ocean with fishermen in a *sardinier*. The artist was, in fact, originally destined for a life at sea and at the age of 16 sailed to Rio de Janeiro and back on a merchant vessel prior to taking, for the second time, his naval examinations which, perhaps fortunately, he failed.

Opposite:
CAMILLE PISSARRO (French, 1830–1903)
Le Printemps, L'Eté and L'Hiver: from Les Quatre Saisons
each signed
oil on canvas
21⅞ × 51⅞ in. (55 × 130 cm.)
New York, 5 November 1991, $6,820,000 (£3,875,000)

In 1872, for the first time in his career as an artist, Pissarro became financially independent of his mother.
The commission he received from Achille Arosa for the *Four Seasons* undoubtedly contributed to this development. The sale of these four pictures could be hailed as a turning point in Pissarro's career, and as the initial break that prompted broader recognition for the artist and the beginning of financial success. In the *Four Seasons*, Pissarro rid pictorial language of all its cumbersome clichés – a task analogous to that conducted by Flaubert in literature. These paintings contributed in bringing Camille Pissarro's work to the limelight in 1891, when the Arosa collection was sold, and thus have a privileged place in the history of Impressionism.

PIERRE-AUGUSTE RENOIR
(French, 1841–1919)
La Loge
signed
pastel on paper laid down on board
22 × 17 in. (55.9 × 43.2 cm.)
Sold by the Estate of Elsie Cassatt Stewart Simmons, Philadelphia
New York, 5 November 1991, $990,000 (£556,179)

The sitter for this portrait was Renoir's favourite model (and perhaps mistress), Marguerite Legrand, known as Margot. Few models teased Renoir's patience as much as Margot. She would deliberately miss a prearranged sitting, just when the painter needed her the most.

Before her tragic death from smallpox in 1879, when even the homeopathic ministrations of Dr Gachet could not save her, Renoir made her the subject of a number of his most important works, including *La sortie du Conservatoire* (The Barnes Foundation, Merion, Pennsylvania) and *Au Café* (Rijksmuseum Kröller-Müller, Otterlo).

MARY CASSATT (American, 1844–1926)
Elsie Cassatt holding a big Dog
pastel on paper
$25\frac{1}{4} \times 20\frac{1}{2}$ in. (64.2 × 52.1 cm.)
Sold by the Estate of Elsie Cassatt Stewart Simmons,
Philadelphia
New York, 5 November 1991, $1,540,000 (£865,168)

The subject of this pastel is Mary Cassatt's niece Elsie,
the daughter of her brother Alexander, an executive of
the Pennsylvania Railroad. Born in 1875, Elsie was five
years old when she sat for this portrait in 1880. She also
appears at the same age, listening to her grandmother
reading fairy tales, in a large multiple portrait by Cassatt,
La Lecture (private collection).

ADOLPHE MONTICELLI (French, 1824–1886)
Grande Nature Morte au Pichet
oil on panel
$17\frac{1}{2} \times 25\frac{1}{2}$ in. (44.5 × 64.7 cm.)
Sold on behalf of Cancer Relief, Macmillan Fund
London, 29 June 1992, £319,000 ($603,548)
Record auction price for a work by the artist

Adolphe Monticelli's handling of paint and understanding of colour set him apart as one of the great innovators of late nineteenth-century painting. Among his greatest admirers was Vincent van Gogh who acknowledged his debt to Monticelli and, like Oscar Wilde and the Burrell brothers, owned several paintings by the artist, who he described as the 'only painter to perceive the chromatism of things with such intensity'.

This painting was the most important work by Monticelli to come on the market in recent years. Besides being rare, few of these large still-lifes are still in private hands. Others are in the Rijksmuseum, Amsterdam, the Musée d'Orsay, Paris, and the National Gallery, London. As a consequence the present painting attracted particular interest and achieved a world record price for the artist at auction.

CAMILLE PISSARRO (French, 1830–1903)
La Gelée blanche, Femme cassant du Bois
signed and dated 1890
oil on canvas
49¾ × 50½ in. (126.4 × 128.3 cm.)
London, 2 December 1991, £1,870,000 ($3,291,200)

La Gelée blanche, Femme cassant du Bois demonstrates Pissarro's pre-occupation with producing well-resolved, large-scale compositions for exhibition purposes. The larger of two impressive renderings of the subject executed in the late 1880s, the painting was prepared specifically as the focal point for a major one-man exhibition arranged by Vincent van Gogh's brother Theo at Boussod & Valadon in Paris in March 1890. It took Pissarro the better part of eight months to paint, and was frequently the cause of fretful correspondence between Theo and Pissarro before the exhibition. Described by Pissarro as *'ma grande toile'*, this shimmering *tour de force* of colour, texture and brushwork was offered at 3,000 francs and remained unsold. Despite encouragement to offer it to the Palais de Luxembourg, which sought to acquire a major work by him, Pissarro kept the painting until his death in 1903.

CLAUDE MONET (French, 1840–1926)
Charing Cross Bridge, La Tamise
signed and dated 1903
oil on canvas
28¾ × 39⅜ in. (73 × 100 cm.)
London, 29 June 1992, £2,145,000 ($4,058,000)

Monet's Thames series paintings are unquestionably the work of an artist completely at ease, both with his subject and with his technique. Begun in the 1890s, some thirty years after Monet had first visited London as a refugee from the Franco-Prussian war, his Thames views follow his extremely successful Rouen cathedral and haystack series. Like many of his mature paintings, the present work is the product of both his observation and his imagination. Begun *in situ* from his window at the Savoy Hotel in 1900, the painting was finished in his studio at Giverny three years later, only shortly before the whole series was exhibited to great acclaim at Durand-Ruel in Paris in 1904. The present painting is undoubtedly among the most important works from the Thames series to come on the market in recent years.

PAUL CÉZANNE (French, 1839–1906)
Baigneuses
oil on canvas
$11\frac{1}{2} \times 9\frac{1}{4}$ in. (29.2 × 23.5 cm.)
London, 29 June 1992, £792,000 ($1,498,464)

Unpublished works by the artist are in themselves a rarity, but to find a previously unrecorded study for one of the icons of twentieth-century painting, Cézanne's *Les Grandes Baigneuses*, was indeed a startling and unexpected pleasure both to ourselves and to the innumerable collectors who examined and admired it. Unusually full and well-resolved, the painting almost doubled its lower estimate after ferocious competition in the saleroom.

THE TREMAINE COLLECTION

by Michael Findlay

I probably collect art for the same reason I buy books –
for enjoyment, education, amusement, self-knowledge.

Emily Hall Tremaine

From 1936, when the then Baroness von Romberg (born Emily Hall, in Butte, Montana) purchased *The Black Rose* by Georges Braque, until her death in 1987 (while planning a trip to visit the studios of new, young Los Angeles artists) the Tremaine Collection was a constantly evolving celebration of the very best in Modern and Contemporary art in both the United States and Europe. Comprising over seven hundred and fifty major pieces it was, however, never static. Works were given to friends and relatives, traded with dealers and, most often, donated to museums. It was simply the best of its kind in private hands in America. Most remarkable is that it was equally the product of two intellects: one platonic (Emily Hall Tremaine) and one Apollonian (Burton Tremaine Jr.). Emily Tremaine wrote: 'if, as Alfred Barr suggested, works of art are inherently either masculine or feminine, then Burton's taste in art appreciates the feminine, mine the masculine. Burton is also more daring than I am.'

They married in 1945; he was an amateur painter and head of the Miller Lighting Company in Connecticut, a family business, she had been widowed by Baron von Romberg and divorced from Adolph B. Spreckels II, a sugar magnate. The daughter of a mining executive, she had been tutored at home and sent to Italy at the age of twelve where she assembled a collection of postcards of works she intended to acquire, from Donatello to van Gogh. Just before they were married they made the acquisition which would become the standard-bearer of the collection: *Victory Boogie-Woogie* by Piet Mondrian. Emily Tremaine recalled: 'I will never forget the impact. I don't think anything has hit me as hard as that painting did.'

She bought it from Valentine Dudensing, a pioneer New York dealer of Modern art. Then, in the first three years of her marriage to Burton, they bought some thirty works including examples by Picasso, Juan Gris, Theo van Doesburg, Wassily Kandinsky, Paul Klee, Ben Nicholson and Alexander Calder. At the time few American museums gave these artists any attention. By 1948 a core group of major works had been assembled including *Le Petit Dejeuner* by Fernand Léger, *Still Life with Pears* by Juan Gris and *Still Life* by Le Corbusier. These were to constitute the first important exhibition of Modern European works of art to tour American museums. Throughout their lifetimes the Tremaines enjoyed a symbiotic relationship with one of the country's oldest institutions, the Wadsworth Atheneum in Hartford, Connecticut. By the late 1940s A. Everett Chick Austin Jr. had been Director for over twenty years and had been responsible for the first International Style structure in the United States, the Avery Building. He and the Tremaines endlessly debated Modernism and in 1948 he persuaded Alfred Barr (the founder of the Museum of Modern Art in New York) and noted scholar Henry-Russell Hitchcock to create a landmark exhibition drawn entirely from the Tremaine Collection: *Painting Toward Architecture*. Robert Rosenblum, one of today's most distinguished critics, was a first year graduate student when he stumbled on the catalogue: 'What lay inside had, for me, almost the character of a thrilling manifesto, a sweeping overview that, with the help of discussions of specific works of art, summed up the most adventurous and progressive feeling and thinking of the first half of our century.'

Although purchased by Emily and Burton the collection was in fact the property of Burton's lighting business, the Miller Company, of which Emily was Art Director. It constituted the first 'corporate' art collection of any significance probably anywhere in the world and, under that banner *Painting Toward Architecture*, toured almost thirty major American museums from 1948 until 1952 with additions being made as they were acquired. The tour ended just as the Tremaines purchased a work that was almost as much of a landmark of modernism as their Mondrian: *Premier disque* by Robert Delaunay, the very first abstract painting in France, dated 1912 and bought from the artist's widow Sonia. As advertising, this exhibition was an extemely clever and novel concept because the principal specifiers of lighting equipment were the architects that the exhibition appealed to in particular. On a personal level also, the Tremaines involvement with architects was constant. Oscar Niemeyer designed their beach house in Santa Barbara; Frank Lloyd Wright consulted for a project on their Arizona ranch; Buckminster Fuller for a modular home on their New York City rooftop and Phillip Johnson designed their apartments in New York and the executive offices and factory additions for the Miller Company in Connecticut and Tennessee. During the 1950s Emily and Burton gradually turned their attention to what was being created by new American painters. They were the first to buy a work by Barnett Newman, *Euclidian Abyss*. While many of today's collectors of cutting edge art make their choices at their desks from transparencies hand-delivered by the minions of mogul-like dealers, to find this work in 1947, the Tremaines took the train to Chicago to see *Abstract and Surrealist Art in America* at the Art Institute of Chicago and then searched to discover how they could acquire the relatively small gouache on canvasboard from a totally obscure artist.

In the 1950s they patronised the gallery of a man with an incredible eye for new talent, former shirt manufacturer Sydney Janis. From him they bought *Frieze* and *Silver and Black* by Jackson Pollock, *Lehigh* by Franz Kline and *Yellow Woman* and *Villa Borghese* by Willem de Kooning. In the same decade they acquired major works by Rothko as well as by Riopelle and the 'new' Europeans: Agam, Appel and Jorn. I met the Tremaines in the early Sixties when they would attend virtually every gallery exhibition in New York, often very discreetly (and shrewdly, to get first choice) preferring to come in while the exhibition was being installed. I sold them works by Bridget Riley, who was having her first New York exhibition at the Richard Feigen Gallery. By then they were best known as the first collectors of Pop Art. As Emily Tremaine wrote: 'About 1961 a comet flashed across this dark scene with a blazing light and we saw objects we

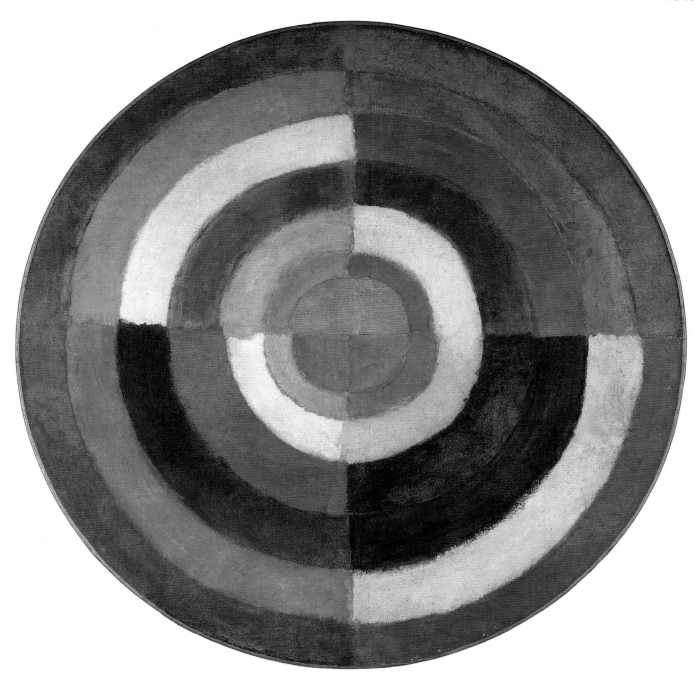

had really not seen before – This was Pop Art and it painted the wonderful, vulgar, jazzy, free and crazy New York.'

In 1958 they purchased *White Flag* by Jasper Johns and a year later visited the artist's studio to buy *Three Flags* (now in the Whitney Museum of Art) even before it was finished. In 1961 they bought four Oldenburgs, three Rosenquists, three Wesselmans and in 1962 six Dines, five Lichtensteins (including *I Can See the Whole Room . . . and There's Nobody in It!*) and fifteen works by Andy Warhol.

Far more important than the numbers, however, was the quality of their choices and the level of their commitment. Although within a couple of years *Time* magazine would christen Pop art and declare it a Movement, when the Tremaines were buying, it was from disparate young painters with various dealers who shared a common vision but were by no means in touch with each other. Jim Rosenquist and Roy Lichtenstein met for the first time in the Tremaine's living room well after their work entered the collection! The magnificent Warhol in the Tate Gallery is in part a creation of Emily's since she suggested to the artist that two paintings she wanted to buy, both of Marilyn Monroe (one in colour, one in black and white) be made into the *Marilyn Monroe Diptych*. Usually when the Tremaines purchased the work of artists now so heralded their accomplishments are obvious, they were, if

ROBERT DELAUNAY (French, 1885–1941)
Premier Disque
oil on canvas
53 in. (134.6 cm.) Diameter
New York, 5 November 1991, $5,170,000 (£2,904,494)

known at all, generally denigrated. Whether it was Frank Stella's *Luis Miguel Dominguez* bought the year it was made (1961) from the 25 year-old painter or Rauschenberg's early silkscreen painting *Windward* (1963) the Tremaines were never guided by popular taste, only by their need for the challenging and rewarding. They continued to travel constantly and in Paris and Rome bought works as they were being made by Manzoni (1958) and Fontana (1961) and the Pomodoro brothers (1981).

Pop, however, was just a new beginning and Emily and Burton went on to discover, ahead of the herd: Sol LeWitt, Agnes Martin, Richard Artschwager, Walter de Maria and the arcane work of light manipulator and conceptualist, Robert Irwin. Sculpture by Andre, Heizer and Flavin joined their Calders, Giacomettis and

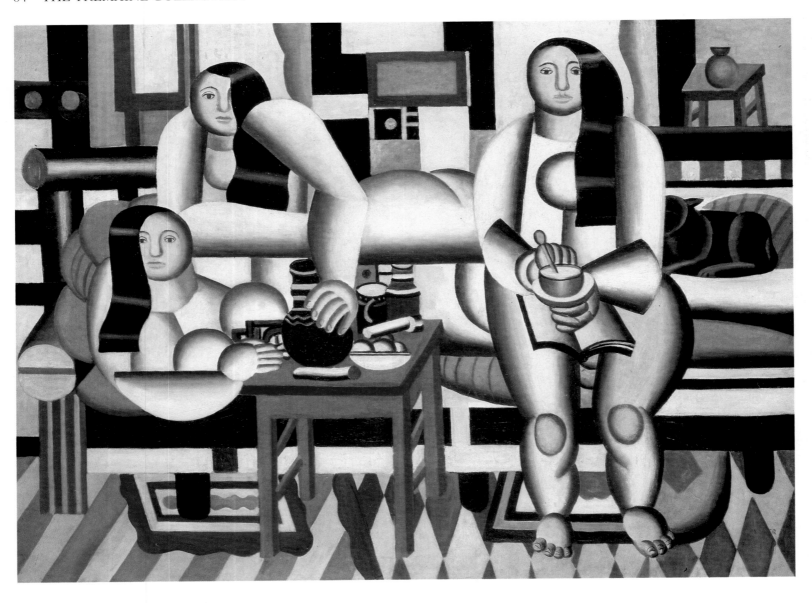

Chamberlains and by 1984 the Tremaine Collection was ready for its second major exposure as *The Spirit of Modernism* under the auspices of the then Director of the Wadsworth Atheneum and subsequently curator of the Tremaine Collection, Tracy Atkinson. The catalogue was written by Robert Rosenblum and the show organised by Chief Curator Gregory Hedberg. As well as exhibiting works of the previous fifty years many of which had become icons, this incarnation of the Tremaine Collection presented new work by Brice Marden, Robert Mangold, Richard Tuttle and other younger New York artists.

As a couple Emily and Burton's interests went far beyond collecting modern art and included their dual management of the Miller Company, cattle breeding, Planned Parenthood, population control and various nationwide architectural projects. Nevertheless their lives revolved around their passionate patronage of new art and with typical candour Emily commented, at the time of the 1984 exhibition:

> A collector has one of three motives for collecting: a genuine love of art, the investment possibilities, or its social promises. I have never known a collector who was not stimulated by all three. For the full joy and reward the dominant motivation must be the love of art but I would question the integrity of any collector who denies an interest in the valuation the market puts on his pictures . . . . The social aspect is another never-ending reward. From Rome to Tokyo, our art interest has brought unexpected and unbelievable experiences, and friends as full of vitality, imagination and warmth as the art they collect.

FERNAND LÉGER (French, 1881–1955)
Le petit Déjeuner
signed and dated '21'
oil on canvas
38 × 51 in. (96.5 × 129.5 cm.)
New York, 5 November 1991, $7,700,000 (£4,325,842)

Opposite:
GEORGES BRAQUE (French, 1882–1963)
La Rose noire
signed and dated '27'
oil on canvas
19¾ × 36½ in. (50.2 × 92.1 cm.)
New York, 5 November 1991, $1,100,000 (£617,977)

JUAN GRIS (Spanish, 1887–1927)
Poires et Raisins sur une Table
signed and dated '13'
oil on canvas
21½ × 28¾ in. (54.5 × 73 cm.)
New York, 5 November 1991, $3,300,000 (£1,853,332)
Record auction price for a work by the artist

Guitare sur une Table, a work by the same artist from the McCarty-Cooper collection, was sold in New York on 11 May 1992, for $1,485,000 (£829,608).

THE McCARTY-COOPER COLLECTION

by Christopher Burge

As has been widely and appositely noted elsewhere, Billy McCarty-Cooper's collecting verve, his percipient eye and talent for challenging visual confrontations culminated in the virtuoso eclecticism of the stunning interiors of his house in the Hollywood Hills. The successful sales at Christie's New York this Spring of his collections of Art Deco furniture and silver, of books and of Tribal Art were testament to the depth and discernment of his interests and enthusiasm. The superb modern works of art he owned however, were, with few exceptions, inherited from the renowned art historian and collector, Douglas Cooper, who had adopted Billy McCarty in 1972.

The sale in New York on 11 May, following Billy McCarty-Cooper's untimely death last year, saw the dispersal of the last section of one of the most remarkable accumulations of modern art assembled in the twentieth century. The core of Cooper's collection was formed in the 1930s – from 1933 to 1939 – as a result of the young art historian's decision to devote a portion of his inheritance to collecting modern art. As he explained much later: 'it was a favourable moment for a collector to buy because the earlier boom had turned into a terrible and long-lasting slump, with the result that the prices for paintings by the four masters of Cubism had again fallen . . . I took advantage of the situation . . . and in 1932 [at the age of 21!] began to buy true cubist paintings with the intention of forming a substantial collection of my own. The pursuit became the adventure of a lifetime . . . '

Cooper's early association with Fred Mayor – he was a director of the Mayor Gallery from 1933 until around 1937 – gave him the entrée he needed to the art world of the time. Soon he was corresponding with D. H. Kahnweiler, who clearly had a profound and formative effect on his collecting aesthetic, and was buying from Kahnweiler's friend and colleague Alfred Flechtheim, who became a major source for the young collector, as did Léonce Rosenberg a year or two later. Cooper also bought directly from other collectors including Earl Horter in Philadelphia and the influential G. F. Reber in Lausanne, who had, among other things, amassed, according to Flechtheim, the 'decisive Picasso collection'. By 1939 Cooper's collection was largely shaped, for although many works of art were bought and sold (and given to the collector) over the next forty years, the character and direction of this incredible assemblage of contemporary art was essentially decided before the Second World War.

After the war, possibly in emulation of Reber's Château de Béthusy at Lausanne, as Dorothy Kosinski has noted, Cooper bought the Château de Castille at Argilliers in the South of France which was to house the collection for the next 25 years and to become a salon to a wide artistic and social circle. Cooper now directed his energies more to the renovation of the Château and to his activities as art historian and curator than to collecting, although major works were still added and commissions undertaken, particularly as a result of his close association with Picasso, Léger and Braque. The latter's *Atelier VIII* of 1952–5 for example, seen by Cooper as a summation of the artist's achievements, was bought from the artist shortly after it was finished in 1955.

The theft in 1977 of 27 works from the Château prompted Cooper's move to Monte Carlo. He sold a number of works before his death in 1984: another large group was sold shortly thereafter and in 1985 Christie's held a wildly successful sale of lesser works from the collection in London. However the 91 lots offered at Christie's New York on 11 May still represented a sparkling cross-section of the original holdings and fully documented the collector's method and scope.

Some of Cooper's earliest purchases were still on hand: his first Picasso, an early cubist drawing of 1909 bought from the Haskell Gallery in London in 1933 for £8; a stunning late cubist Picasso pastel of 1912–3, and a powerful 1916 Gris oil, bought from Reber in 1939. In 1935 Cooper exchanged his only Cézanne *La Préparation du banquet* with Paul Rosenberg for Picasso's majestic *Compotier et guitare* of 1932.

The range and depth of the collection was still forcefully demonstrated by the large and uniformly high quality group of Picasso, Léger and Gris drawings and watercolours and the early Braque prints and drawings. Although the 'true' cubists were at the core of the collection, Cooper also devoted individual rooms at the Château de Castille to Klee and Miró. Most of these had been sold later to enrich the cubist collection but one fine example by each artist remained in the sale, the Miró having been given to Cooper as early as April 1934. The sale also included works by Laurens and Giacometti, Hockney and Sutherland and an assortment of ephemera, ceramics, prints and watercolours by various artists in Cooper's circle, menus decorated by Dalí and Marini, greeting cards designed by Braque, photographs, and sculpture.

This extraordinary collection came about as a consequence of an unrepeatable conjunction; Cooper's highly developed eye, his collecting drive and passion, his scholarly attainments (and his money) allied to the availability of works of art in large quantity at reasonable prices. We will not see its like again.

Opposite:
PABLO PICASSO (Spanish, 1881–1973)
Compotier et Guitare
signed and dated '13.2.32'
oil on canvas
$38\frac{1}{4} \times 51\frac{3}{16}$ in. (97.1 × 130 cm.)
New York, 11 May 1992, $3,850,000 (£2,162,921)

GEORGES BRAQUE (French, 1882–1963)
Atelier VIII
signed
oil on canvas
$52 \times 77\frac{1}{2}$ in. (132.1 × 196.9 cm.)
New York, 11 May 1992, $7,700,000 (£4,325,842)

PABLO PICASSO (Spanish, 1881–1973)
Homme à la Sucette
signed and dated '23.7.38'
charcoal on paper
$26\frac{1}{2} \times 17\frac{1}{2}$ in. (67.5 × 44.5 cm.)
New York, 11 May 1992, $968,000 (£543,820)

Above, left to right:
ODILON REDON (French, 1840–1916)
Tête suspendue, coiffée, par une chaîne
signed
black chalk on paper
$18\frac{1}{8} \times 15$ in. (46 × 38 cm.)
Amsterdam, 11 December 1991, Fl.379,500 (£118,243)

OTTO DIX (German, 1891–1969)
Sadisten gewidmet
signed and dated '22'
watercolour, pencil, pen and black ink on paper
$19\frac{5}{8} \times 14\frac{3}{4}$ in. (49.8 × 37.5 cm.)
London, 29 June 1992, £110,000 ($208,120)

Left:
OSKAR SCHLEMMER (German, 1888–1943)
HK 1926
watercolour and pencil on paper
$21\frac{3}{4} \times 17\frac{5}{8}$ in. (55.3 × 40.4 cm.)
London, 3 December 1991, £143,000 ($245,960)
Record auction price for a work on paper by the artist

Considered by the government to be a prime example of
'decadent art', this watercolour was removed from the walls of
the *Nationalgalerie* in Berlin in 1938. Ironically the work is now
considered amongst Schlemmer's finest watercolours of his
Bauhaus years. Executed in 1926, this unusually large and finely
constructed composition fittingly achieved a record auction
price for a work on paper by the artist.

PIET MONDRIAN (Dutch, 1872–1944)
Composition avec rouge, gris, bleu et jaune
signed and dated '22'
oil on canvas
$21\frac{1}{4} \times 21$ in. (54 × 53.4 cm.)
Sold by the Estate of Henri-Georges Doll, New York
New York, 12 May 1992, $2,585,000 (£1,428,176)

The Doll Mondrian reflects a finely tuned colour
harmony utilizing the triad of primary colours that was
the artist's final conclusion. The most notable feature of
this painting is the scale and dominance of the red
square creating Mondrian's classic equilibrium.

According to Joop M. Joosten, this painting was one of
four bought by Antony Kok from the artist in 1921 and
1922. Antony Kok was one of the founding members of
De Stijl. Kok owned four paintings by Mondrian: one
was sold to John Senior which is now in the Museum of
Modern Art, New York; one to a private collection in
Texas; and the present work which Petronella van
Doesburg sold to Henry-Georges Doll on 21 May 1952
for $4,000. The fourth was sold by Jan Streep and is
now in the Galleria Nazionale in Rome.

PAUL KLEE (Swiss, 1879–1940)
Mondauf-Sonnenuntergang
signed and dated 1919
oil on board
16 × 13⅝ in. (40.5 × 34.5 cm.)
London, 2 December 1991, £814,000 ($1,432,640)

Mondauf-Sonnenuntergang was given by Klee to his friend and fellow artist, Heinrich Campendonk in 1919. Pre-war oils by Klee are relatively rare and it was only on moving into new studios in Munich in 1919 that Klee truly committed himself to painting in oil. In the present work one can measure the artist's unbounded enthusiasm for the medium in the dynamism of the composition, the vigour of his brushwork and the strengths and contrasts of his colours. Previously unexhibited, Campendonk considered the painting among his prized possessions and refused to part with it during his lifetime.

MARC CHAGALL (Russian, 1887–1985)
Bouquet de Fleurs
signed and dated '937'

oil on canvas
39 × 28 in. (99 × 71 cm.)
New York, 12 May 1992, $2,860,000 (£1,606,741)

MARC CHAGALL (Russian, 1887–1985)
La Grande Parade
signed
oil on canvas
47¼ × 52 in. (120 × 132 cm.)
London, 29 June 1992, £1,012,000 ($1,912,680)

Chagall's interest in the circus began as a boy when he watched jugglers and acrobats performing in Vitebsk, but it was not until he moved to France that this boyish interest developed into an artistic fixation. Ambroise Vollard commissioned Chagall to produce a large series of circus gouaches and etchings based on the performances of the Cirque d'Hiver in the late 1920s. *La Grande Parade* includes many of the characters from these early paintings as well as Chagall himself and is a celebration of the colour, movement, music and spectacle of the circus.

JACK BUTLER YEATS, R.H.A. (Irish, 1871–1957)
The Minister
signed
oil on panel
14 × 9 in. (35.5 × 23 cm.)
London, 6 March 1992, £49,400 ($84,325)

The Minister is from a series of twelve oils painted in 1913 by Yeats as illustrations to the novel *Irishmen All* by George Birmingham. Yeats provided a portrait for each of the twelve chapters which describe an Irish-type official, exile squireen, politician, shop assistant and so on. George Birmingham was the pseudonym of Canon James Owen

Hannay (1865–1950), himself a priest of the Church of Ireland, and sometime Rector of Westport, Co. Mayo. His humorous, often satirical novels about Irish life were not always well received. He found a sympathetic illustrator in Jack Yeats, who had already provided black and white drawings for several of George Birmingham's stories in the magazine *A Celtic Christmas* over the years. Yeats seems to have received a list of chapter headings, with perhaps a summary of the author's intentions, and that was all. Neither saw the other's work beforehand, yet the novelist wrote to the artist to express his delight at how well the illustrations and the text complemented each other.

SIR WILLIAM ORPEN, R.A., R.H.A.
(Irish, 1878–1931)
In Dublin Bay
signed
oil on canvas
$41\frac{1}{2} \times 32\frac{3}{4}$ in. (105.5 × 83 cm.)
London, 6 March 1992, £137,500 ($264,550)

This picture dates from 1909. Between 1902 and 1914 Orpen had a part-time teaching post at the Metropolitan School of Art in Dublin. From about 1907, he made twice yearly visits to Ireland to teach and in August he would rent a house at Howth Head for a family summer holiday. These idyllic months resulted in a series of magnificent portraits conceived and drawn out of doors on the cliffs and beaches near Howth. The sitter in this portrait is the artist's wife, Grace.

ROBERT BEVAN (1865–1925)
Horse Dealers at the Barbican
signed
oil on canvas
21¾ × 25½ in. (55 × 64.5 cm.)
London, 5 June 1992, £104,500 ($190,085)
Record auction price for a work by the artist

This picture dates from about 1918. Sickert encouraged Robert Bevan to paint the things he saw around him that interested him in the City of London. This resulted in 1907 or 1908 in the first of a series of cab-yard pictures which Bevan painted until 1912 when motorised cabs took over from horses. At about the same time he began to paint the London horse-sales. In a memoir, his son, R. A. Bevan, recalled: 'As children we were very conscious of the importance of the horse in our father's life. We were allowed to go with him when he was making drawings for cab-yard and horse-sale pictures. In earlier years he took us, of course, by horse-bus, and we sat on the front seats on top so that he could talk horses to the driver. At Tattersall's and Aldridge's, the Barbican and Ward's Repository, there would always be a word or two with dealers and with handlers – and even with the bearded top-hatted auctioneer – who all seemed rather surprised that anyone should think they were worth drawing. The sales at the Barbican specialised in van-horses and hacks and a friend of Bevan's once remarked that: "It was the not very good horses that Bevan is so good at." '

GLYN WARREN PHILPOT, R.A. (1884–1937)
Penelope
oil on canvas
$53\frac{1}{2} \times 36\frac{1}{8}$ in. (136 × 91.8 cm.)
London, 7 November 1991, £101,200 ($178,112)

Daisy Philpot, the artist's sister, records that the present painting
was begun in Florence, where Philpot rented a studio for some
months in the summer of 1922. It was completed in his studio at
33 Tite Street, Chelsea in time for inclusion in the 1923 Summer
Exhibition at the Royal Academy, where it was one of only two
paintings by Philpot hanging when he was elected Royal
Academician at the early age of thirty-eight.

LUCIAN FREUD, O.M. (b. 1922)
Portrait of a Man
oil on canvas
$9\frac{1}{2} \times 7\frac{1}{2}$ in. (24 × 19 cm.)
London, 8 November 1991,
£126,500 ($222,513)

The subject of this painting of June 1946 is the artist John Craxton, with whom Lucian Freud toured Greece in that year. They exhibited together at the London Gallery in October to November 1947.

RIDGET RILEY (b. 1931)
êng-tung
ned and dated 1974
ylic on canvas
× 90 in. (96.5 × 288.5 cm.)
ndon, 11 June 1992, £33,000 ($60,225)

TRICK HERON (b. 1920)
ree Squares (Ceruleum, Naples, Ochre) January 1962
on paper laid on board
$\frac{1}{4}$ × 17$\frac{1}{4}$ in. (69 × 44 cm.)
ndon, 11 June 1992, £12,100 ($22,082)

riting about his use of colour in 1978, the artist observed:
have found myself increasingly indulging, since about 1962, in
r sharper and more complex linear frontiers between my
our-areas – because I had already raised those colours to an
diluted maximum chromatic intensity by that date: yet despite
s fact – that by 1962 my colours were as bright and as strong in
mselves as it was physically possible to make them – my works
ce then have appeared to get steadily more brilliant in hue
again.'

THOMAS BAINES (English, 1820–1875)
The Mosi-o-a-Tunya (Smoke resounding) or Victoria Falls,
Zambesi River
signed, inscribed and dated 1874
oil on canvas
20 × 26 in. (50.8 × 66.1 cm.)
Sold by members of the Dawnay family
London, 22 October 1992, £66,000 ($112,530)

Thomas Baines, who had accompanied Livingstone on his Zambesi expedition of 1858 as artist and storekeeper, reached the Victoria Falls for the first time on James Chapman's expedition in 1862 and, like Livingstone, reported on the spectacle of the Falls 'presenting to the eye, long wearied of sere and yellow moganie leaves, dry rocks, burnt grass, and desolated country, the most lovely and refreshing "coup d'oeil" the Soul of artist could imagine'. Remarkably, Baines managed to produce watercolour sketches of the Falls (now in the Africana Museum, Johannesburg) from the drenched rain forest opposite the chasm. In a break on the return trip at Otjimbengue, Baines was able to work on a first group of oils of the Falls, and these images were copied, elaborated on and engraved over the next ten years.

In the early 1870s Baines was in financial straits following the failure of various ambitious speculations in Matabeleland. He accepted many commissions to raise capital. The present picture is one of a group of fifteen oils produced for the sportsman, Cuthbert Guy Dawnay, between 1872 and 1874, and was the thirteenth to be sold for the Dawnay family by Christie's in recent years.

CONRAD WISE CHAPMAN
(American, 1842–1910)
Mexico from 'Hacienda de los Morales'
signed, inscribed and dated 1892
oil on panel
$5\frac{1}{4} \times 9\frac{13}{16}$ in. (13.3 × 24.9 cm.)
London, 22 May 1992, £17,600 ($31,486)

THOMAS JACQUES SOMERSCALES
(English, 1842–1927)
Rio Aconagua, Chile
signed and dated 1911
oil on canvas
23 × 36 in. (58.4 × 91.4 cm.)
London, 22 October 1992, £24,200 ($41,261)

AUSTRALIAN PICTURES

RUPERT CHARLES WULSTEN BUNNY
(1864–1947)
Mrs Herbert Jones and her Daughters, Hilda and Dulce
signed
oil on canvas
$42\frac{1}{8} \times 54$ in. (107 × 138 cm.)
Sold by Dallhold Investments Pty. Limited (in liquidation)
Melbourne, 28 July 1992, Aus.$440,000 (£170,940)

This portrait of 1903–4 shows the artist's sister Annette, with two
of her three daughters by her marriage to Walter Cooke;
Hilda, the eldest seated casually on the edge of the couch and
Dulce, the youngest, with the Schipperke dog, 'Jekka', named
after a famous Zulu chief.

The setting is the drawing room at the family's home, The Priory,
Huntingdon, England, where Bunny spent the summer of 1904.

Opposite:
EUGENE VON GUERARD (1811–1901)
Sydney Heads
signed and dated 1866
oil on canvas
$28\frac{3}{8} \times 48\frac{1}{2}$ in. (72 × 123 cm.)
Sold by Dallhold Investments Pty. Limited (in liquidation)
Melbourne, 28 July 1992, Aus.$715,000 (£277,777)
Record auction price for a work by the artist

FREDERICK McCUBBIN (1855–1917)
Feeding Time
signed and dated 1893
oil on canvas
30 × 50 in. (76 × 127 cm.)
Sold by Dallhold Investments Pty. Limited (in liquidation)
Melbourne, 28 July 1992, Aus.$462,000 (£179,487)

SIR GEORGE RUSSELL DRYSDALE
(1912–1981)
The Camp
signed
oil on canvas
30 × 36¼ in. (76 × 91.5 cm.)
Sold by Dallhold Investments Pty. Limited (in liquidation)
Melbourne, 28 July 1992, Aus.$660,000 (£256,410)
Record auction price for a work by the artist

A trip to the Cape York Peninsula in 1951 inspired new
developments in Drysdale's technique and imagery. Arthur Boyd
visited the Northern Territory in the same year and the two
journeys inspired the first paintings of Aborigines.
This picture is of 1953.

Opposite:
JOHN PETER RUSSELL (1858–1930)
Cruach en Mahr, Matin, Belle Ile en Mer
signed
oil on canvas
24 × 29 in. (60.4 × 73.5 cm.)
Melbourne, 28 April 1992, Aus.$407,000 (£188,251)

After studying in Paris at the Academie Cormon in the 1880s
with fellow students Lautrec, van Gogh, Bernard, Anquetin,
Laval and Hartrick, Russell moved to Belle Ile with his family in
1888. He had first been to the island in the summer of 1886 when
his visit coincided with Monet's working sojourn there from
September to November. The two artists met in September and
the present painting clearly shows Monet's influence. Apart from
four pictures which Russell included in Durand Ruel's 1895
exhibition of works by Cormon's pupils, it was the only work
exhibited by him in France.

ARTHUR MERRIC BLOOMFIELD BOYD (b.1920)
Frightened Bridegroom II
signed
oil and tempera on muslin on board
54 × 72 in. (137 × 183 cm.)
Melbourne, 28 April 1992, Aus.$286,000 (£132,284)

AMERICAN PICTURES

THOMAS MORAN (1837–1926)
In the Teton Range
signed and dated 1899
oil on canvas
42 × 30 in. (107 × 76 cm.)
New York, 6 December 1991, $572,000
(£317,777)

Thomas Moran, perhaps more than any other artist, made the West familiar to Easterners with his panoramic views of the Yellowstone, Yosemite, Zion, Grand Canyon and Teton Mountain regions. Moran's first journey to the West was in 1871 on the United States Geological Expedition to the Yellowstone area. In 1873, the artist travelled to survey the Grand Canyon and the Rocky Mountains. Painted in 1899, *In the Teton Range* captures the vastness of this western American landscape.

FITZ HUGH LANE (1804–1865)
Beached for Repairs, Duncan's Point, Gloucester
oil on canvas
$16\frac{1}{4} \times 22\frac{1}{8}$ in. (41 × 56.2 cm.)
Sold from the collection of Mr. and Mrs. Eddy G.
Nicholson
New York, 28 May 1992, $330,000 (£183,333)

ARTHUR FITZWILLIAM TAIT (1819–1905)
Trappers following the Trail: At Fault
signed and dated 1851
oil on canvas
36 × 50 in. (91.5 × 127 cm.)
Sold from the collection of Mr. and Mrs. Eddy G.
Nicholson
New York, 28 May 1992, $605,000 (£336,111)

THOMAS BIRCH (1779–1851)
Commodore Perry leaving the *Lawrence* for the *Niagara*
at the Battle of Lake Erie
oil on canvas
18⅜ × 23⅜ in. (46.7 × 59.4 cm.)
New York, 28 May 1992, $264,000 (£146,666)
Record auction price for a work by the artist

JAMES E. BUTTERSWORTH (1817–1894)
Racing off Sandy Hook
signed
oil on canvas
26 × 40 in. (66.2 × 101.8 cm.)
New York, 6 December 1991, $187,000 (£103,888)

HENRY F. FARNY (1847–1916)
An Indian Encampment
signed and dated '92'
gouache on paper
$8\frac{1}{2} \times 14\frac{1}{4}$ in. (21.5 × 36.2 cm.)
New York, 6 December 1991,
$148,500 (£82,500)

WILLIAM ROBINSON LEIGH
(1866–1955)
Ready to Shoot
signed
oil on canvas
40 × 30 in. (101.8 × 76.1 cm.)
New York, 6 December 1991,
$159,500 (£88,611)

MARTIN JOHNSON HEADE (1819–1904)
Still Life with an Orchid and a Pair of Hummingbirds
signed
oil on canvas
16 × 14 in. (40.5 × 35.3 cm.)
New York, 28 May 1992, $286,000 (£158,888)

Heade's fascination with orchids began while he was studying hummingbirds in Brazil in 1863–5, although he did not paint the flower until 1870. The artist combined the two for the first time in 1871. This picture is probably of the 1890s.

WINSLOW HOMER (1836–1910)
Three Boys in a Dory
signed and dated 1873
oil on panel
$5\frac{7}{8} \times 10$ in. (15.1 × 25.3 cm.)
Sold by the Victoria Nebeker Coberly Family Trust
New York, 28 May 1992, $935,000 (£519,444)

WILLIAM JAMES GLACKENS (1870–1938)
Summer Hotel
signed and dated 1909
oil on canvas
26 × 31 in. (66 × 87.7 cm.)
Sold from the Estate of Mr. and Mrs. A. E. Staley, Jr.
New York, 28 May 1992, $330,000 (£183,333)

JOHN SINGER SARGENT, R.A. (1856–1925)
The Green Parasol
pencil, watercolour and bodycolour
18¾ × 13¾ in. (47.5 × 35 cm.)
London, 5 June 1992, £286,000 ($520,234)
Record auction price for a watercolour by the artist

A similar but less finished watercolour of the same title
was exhibited at the New English Art Club in 1910.
W. H. Downes describes that work and the small group of
similar sketches also in the exhibition as 'a most amusing
and charming series of figure pieces in which the doings
of two or three ladies on a vacation among the Alps are
reported . . . This set might be called the Adventures of
the Green Parasol, as that article of use and adornment
appears and reappears from time to time in these playful
sketches from Switzerland.'

EDWARD HOPPER (1882–1967)
The Yellow House
signed and dated 1923
watercolour on paper
$11\frac{3}{4} \times 18$ in. (30 × 47 cm.)
New York, 26 September 1991, $220,000 (£127,168)

MILTON AVERY (1893–1965)
Adolescence
signed and dated 1947
oil and pencil on canvas
30 × 40 in. (76 × 101.5 cm.)
Sold from the collection of Ruth B. Haft
New York, 6 December 1991, $352,000 (£195,555)

LATIN AMERICAN PICTURES

DIEGO RIVERA (Mexican, 1886–1957)
Paisaje de Toledo
signed and dated 1913
oil on canvas
$20\frac{1}{4} \times 24\frac{1}{8}$ in. (51.4 × 61.2 cm.)
New York, 18 May 1992, $1,210,000 (£664,105)

This early Cubist work is the first of three known paintings of the subject. It shows a view near Toledo, looking down into a gorge with the bend of the Tagus, lined on both sides by geometricized rock formations; in the background, the groves of carefully cultivated olive trees can be seen, punctuated on the upper right by an equally geometrically simplified group of farm houses above the steep gorge. The painting was executed in the autumn of 1913, and was originally in the collection of Rivera's close Parisian friend, the Russian emigré sculptor Oscar Miestchanninof.

DIEGO RIVERA (Mexican, 1886–1957)
Vendedora de Flores
oil on masonite
48 × 48 in. (122 × 122 cm.)
New York, 19 November 1991, $2,970,000
(£1,659,217)
Record auction price for a Latin American work of art

Calla lilies are commonly associated with funerals, but Diego Rivera invested those he painted with a sense of life, energy and more personality than the people shown selling them. Painted in 1942, *Vendedora de Flores* (*Calla Lily Seller*) is the most successful of a series of paintings with calla lilies – a theme of interest to Rivera since the early 1920s when he included the flowers in a mural depicting Good Friday traditions. The painting exhibits something of the solemn, hieratic feeling inspired by characteristics of the pre-Hispanic sculpture Rivera so admired. The female figure is block-like and still, caught at the moment she is about to rise with the heavy basket of flowers strapped to her back. Aiding her is a man who is virtually unseen except for the top of his head and his bare feet. There is an implied melancholy in this, an ironic contrast between the beauty of the calla lilies and the woman's demanding labour. Through his distinctive style, the artist created an image of delicate grace and charm, and at the same time paid homage to the perennially downtrodden people of his country, the workers struggling to earn a minuscule wage by performing often herculean tasks.

FRIDA KAHLO (Mexican, 1907–1954)
Recuerdo
oil on canvas
15¾ × 11⅛ in. (40 × 28.3 cm.)
New York, 18 May 1992, $945,000 (£518,660)

Painted in 1937, this self-portrait depicts the artist as a recipient of a fusion of profane with religious love, paralleling her passion to that of the sixteenth-century Spanish saint, Santa Teresa. The various symbols in the painting refer to Kahlo's predicament upon learning of her husband Diego Rivera's affair with her sister Cristina: the schoolgirl outfit on the left beckons, while the arm of the Mexican dress pulls the heartbroken, ambivalent Kahlo to the uncertainty of the ocean that represents Rivera's dangerously unpredictable love.

JUAN O'GORMAN (Mexican, 1905–1982)
Los Mitos
signed and dated 1944
tempera on panel
48 × 35¾ in. (122 × 91 cm.)
New York, 19 November 1991, $330,000 (£184,357)

The underlying theme of *Los Mitos* is the artist's belief that reality itself is a human myth. He demonstrates some of the religious and political concepts with which mankind has deceived itself throughout the ages – from the notion of progress and development to the idea of an inferno peopled by demons and devils. In the upper left of the painting, men on a scaffold paint a mountainous scene, thus indicating that reality itself is a myth created by man.

LEONORA CARRINGTON (British, b. 1917)
The Temptation of Saint Anthony
oil on canvas
$47\frac{1}{2} \times 35\frac{1}{8}$ in. (120.5 × 89 cm.)
New York, 18 May 1992, $440,000 (£241,492)
Record auction price for a work by the artist

Carrington herself said that 'the picture seems pretty clear to me, being a more or less literal rendering of St. Anthony complete with pig, desert and temptation. Naturally one could ask why the venerable holy man has three heads – to which one could always reply, why not?' Explaining some of the iconography, the artist points out that the girl in red denotes female charm and the delights of the table, but that the intention of the Queen of Sheba on the right is ambiguous.

REMEDIOS VARO (Spanish, 1900–1963)
Microcosmos (or Determinismo)
signed
tempera on masonite
$37\frac{1}{4} \times 35\frac{1}{4}$ in. (94.5 × 89.5 cm.)
New York, 19 November 1991, $605,000 (£337,988)

In writing about this painting of 1954 to her brother, Dr Rodrigo Varo, the artist comments: 'this painting is part of the *project* I planned when they commissioned those murals for the Cancer Pavilion, which, in the end I did not want to do. On the upper portion of the picture we can see part of the zodiac circle . . . Scorpio, Sagittarius and Capricorn, each in its little ship (it is to be assumed that the rest of the zodiac remains outside the painting). As you can see, they are tugging with their hands at celestial substances which then come out of the ships' exhaust pipes. Each of these pipes is shaped like the corresponding zodiac sign. The celestial substances then fall into a kind of temple where, after convenient spiritual and chemical transformation, diverse creatures are produced. The creatures leave the temple and go into the world. When they leave, they are all white and all wrapped in the same white cloth, as if it were a celestial placenta. When the creatures detach themselves from each other they take on colour.'

JASPER JOHNS (American, b. 1930)
Device Circle
signed, titled and dated '59' on the reverse
encaustic, oil, newspaper collage, wooden arm and
metal screw on canvas
40 × 40 in. (101.7 × 101.7 cm.)
Sold from the Tremaine Collection
New York, 12 November 1991,
$4,400,000 (£2,485,875)

Jasper Johns's *Device Circle*, painted in 1959, marks the
artist's first use of the circle together with a movable
object that functions both as a demarcating compass and
the hands of a clock (a symbolic reference to change
through time). It set a precedent for a group of other
works (1959–63) combining a painted circle with the
object or tool that created it, including *Diver* (1962)
which we sold in 1988. *Device Circle* is also Johns's
earliest work to examine the process of making a
picture and the possibilities of painting with the primary
colours red, yellow and blue. Like Johns's flags and
targets, it creates a balance between the concepts of
image and reality.

WILLEM DE KOONING (American, b.1904)
Villa Borghese
signed
oil on canvas
80 × 70 in. (203.3 × 177.7 cm.)
Sold from the Tremaine Collection
New York, 12 November 1991,
$2,090,000 (£1,180,700)

Willem de Kooning's *Villa Borghese* reveals the artist's desire to explore the pure and basic qualities of nature, a desire bred of his sense of new-found freedom upon packing up his New York studio and moving permanently to the Springs on Long Island in 1960. The painting reflects the colours and surfaces of his summer surroundings there, with their flat, sunny terrain, green grass, yellow beach, green water, blue sky and brown earth. Slathering on these colours with free-flowing, massive six-inch brushstrokes, de Kooning created a monumental landscape that marks the transition from his more urban and explosive *Parkway Landscapes* of 1957–60 to the more lyrical and contemplative *Pastorale Landscapes* of 1960–3.

FRANZ KLINE (American, 1910–1962)
Henry H II
signed, titled and dated '59–60' on the reverse
oil on canvas
$79\frac{1}{2} \times 60$ in. (201.9 × 152.4 cm.)
New York, 12 November 1991, $1,650,000
(£932,203)

Opposite:
HANS HOFMANN (American, 1880–1966)
The Ocean
signed and dated '57'
oil on canvas, $59\frac{7}{8} \times 71\frac{7}{8}$ in. (152 × 182.5 cm.)
New York, 5 May 1992, $550,000 (£287,958)

ERNST WILHELM NAY (German, 1902–1968)
Gabelungen
signed and dated '53'
oil on canvas, $39\frac{3}{8} \times 47\frac{1}{4}$ in. (100 × 120 cm.)
London, 5 December 1991, £115,500 ($204,435)

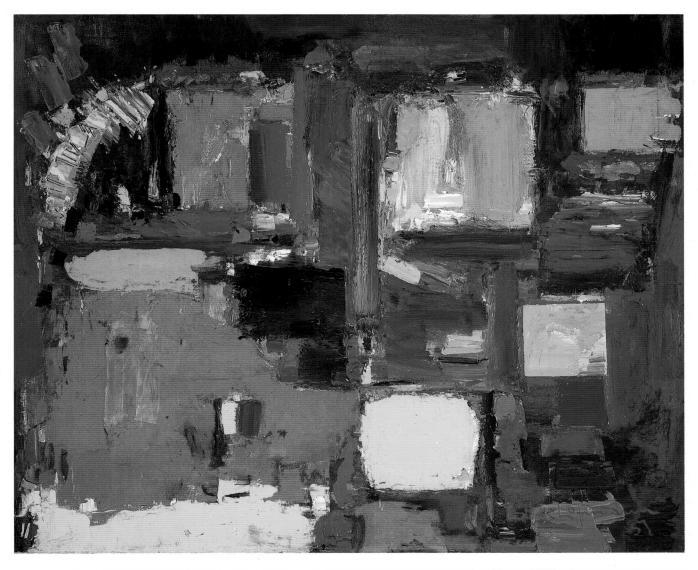

ANDY WARHOL (American, 1928–1987)
210 Coca-Cola Bottles
signed and dated '62'
silkscreen ink, synthetic polymer and graphite on canvas
82½ × 105 in. (209.6 × 266.7 cm.)
New York, 5 May 1992, $2,090,000 (£1,094,240)

Created in 1962, two years after Warhol began his career as a Pop artist with hand-painted images of mass media comic strips and advertisements, *210 Coca-Cola Bottles* is the largest and most complex of Warhol's series of Coke bottle paintings. The work was characteristically executed, Warhol selecting an image, then sending it to a commercial silkscreen shop to be transferred to a stencil. At the factory, the artist and his assistants applied stencil to canvas, assembly line style, creating orderly rows of images suggestive of supermarket shelves. The finished product is a prime example of differentiated repetition, where the Coke bottles appear to be mass produced but actually represent three different views with no regularly repeated pattern.

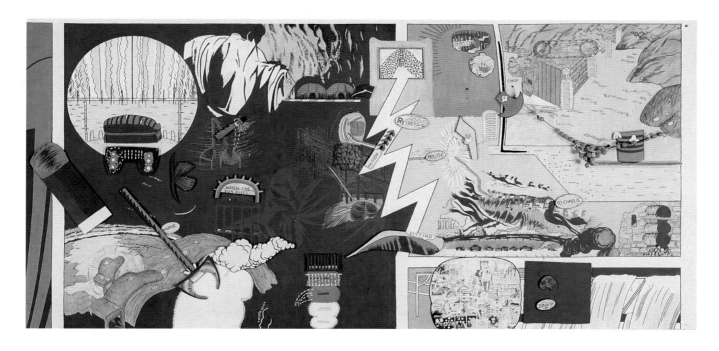

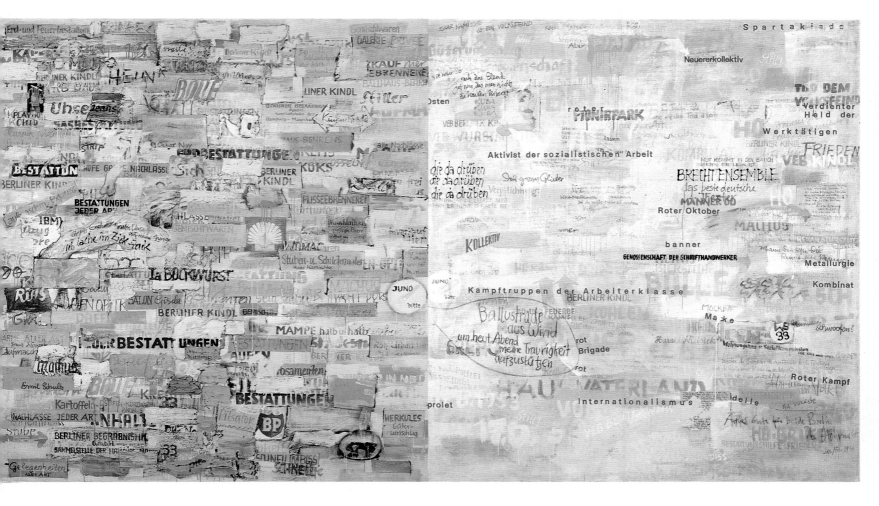

Top:

ÖYVIND FAHLSTRÖM (Swedish, 1928–1976)
Sitting . . . Six Months later
signed and dated 1963
oil, gouache and collage with magnets, nylon threads, beads,
wire and composition on canvas mounted on metal
22 × 45⅝ in. (55.9 × 116 cm.)
Sold from the Estate of Fredrik Roos
London, 2 July 1992, £37,000 ($70,263)

Above:

GERHARD HOEHME (German, 1920–1989)
Berliner Brief
signed, inscribed with title and dated 1966
acrylic, pencil and canvas collage on canvas
diptych, overall 78¾ × 141¾ in. (200 × 360 cm.)
London, 5 December 1991, $154,000 ($272,580)

Opposite:
ANSELM KIEFER (German, b.1945)
Säulen
signed and dated '83'
oil, shellac and straw on canvas
$110\frac{1}{4} \times 110\frac{1}{4}$ in. (280 × 280 cm.)
Sold from the Estate of Fredrik Roos
New York, 5 May 1992, $638,000 (£334,031.50)

ALBERTO BURRI (Italian, b.1915)
Rosso e Nero
signed and dated on the reverse '54'
mixed media on board
$18\frac{7}{8} \times 42\frac{1}{8}$ in. (107 × 48 cm.)
London, 2 July 1992, £104,500 ($198,445)

LUCIAN FREUD (British, b.1922)
Man in a Sports Shirt
oil on canvas
$20\frac{1}{16} \times 16$ in. (50.9 × 40.7 cm.)
London, 2 July 1992, £275,000 ($522,225)

ALEXANDER CALDER
(American, 1898–1976)
Bougainvillea
standing mobile-painted sheet
metal and rod, wire and stone
height: 78¼ in. (198.5 cm.)
span: 86 in. (218.4 cm.)
Sold from the Tremaine
Collection
New York, 12 November
1991, $935,000 (£528,248)

ROBERT GOBER
(American, b. 1954)
Untitled (Bed)
signed, titled and dated 1988
enamel, wood, cotton and wool
44 × 71 × 39 in.
(112 × 180.3 × 99 cm.)
Sold from the Estate of Fredrik
Roos
New York, 5 May 1992,
$198,000 (£103,664)

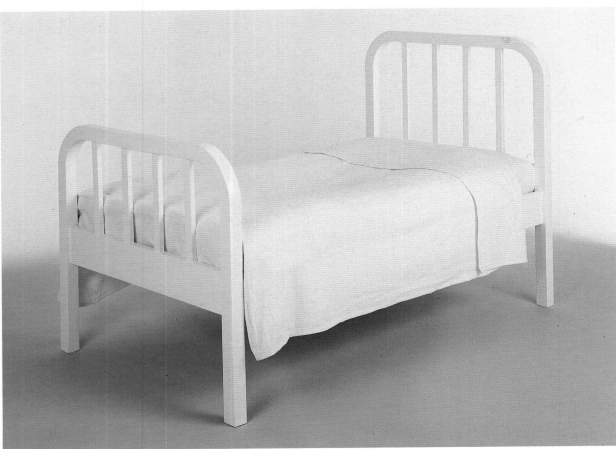

Opposite:
MARCEL BROODTHAERS
(Belgian, 1924–1976)
Armoire Blanche et Table
Blanche
wood, oil and egg-shells
cabinet 33⅞ × 32¼ × 24½ in.
(86 × 82 × 62 cm.)
table 41 × 39⅜ × 15¾ in.
(104 × 100 × 40 cm.)
London, 2 July 1992, £396,000
($752,004)

The collection of nine works sold at Christie's on 2 July 1992 by the Belgian artist, Marcel Broodthaers, was acquired during the 1960s by a European collector who was a friend of the artist. There was tremendous interest from prospective private, trade and museum buyers. Never before had a group of such exceptional quality appeared on the auction market and the sale total was £1,141,800 (US$2,158,000) over three times the high estimate total of £331,000 ($625,000)

Broodthaers was already forty when, in 1964, he consciously opted for a 'career as an artist'. As a young poet he had practised virtually every profession to make a living – including journalism. He had his first one man show in July 1964 which was virtually unprecedented for an artist with no formal training. In the following years he executed several works, using elements from everyday life in an original manner: mussels, eggshells, bottles, coal, bricks. The panels

and pots with mussels have probably become his most famous images in which Broodthaers plays with the complex ways of interpreting 'la moule' (the mussel) and 'le moule' (the mould). The work titled *Triomphe de Moule I (Moule Casserole)* which realised £176,000 ($332,640) also demonstrates the physical relationship between objects and their common practical usage. *Armoire Blanche et Table Blanche* is one of his most impressive monumental compositions, unforgettable in its disconcerting absurdity. Sold for £396,000 ($752,004), a world record auction price for the artist, it more than trebled its high estimate.

Marcel Broodthaers remains one of the most important post-war artists whose prices soared to spectacularly high levels at our recent auction. However, it may take some time before we can truly appreciate the importance of his ideas, as well as the revolutionary way in which he created the images we are now familiar with.

HENRI DE TOULOUSE-LAUTREC
(French, 1864–1901)
La grande Loge (Delteil 204)
lithograph printed in colours, 1896–7, an extremely rare
trial proof, inscribed
sheet size $20\frac{1}{4} \times 15\frac{11}{16}$ in. (51.4 × 39.9 cm.)
London, 11 December 1991, £231,000 ($411,180)
Record auction price for a print by the artist

EDVARD MUNCH (Norwegian, 1863–1944)
Mondschein (Schiefler 81c)
woodcut printed in colours, 1896, signed
subject $15\frac{7}{8} \times 18\frac{7}{16}$ in. (40.3 × 46.8 cm.)
London, 3 July 1992, £60,500 ($115,071)

JAN MATULKA (American, 1890–1972)
Arrangement – New York (Flint 31)
lithograph, circa 1925, signed
subject $16 \times 12\frac{1}{2}$ in. (41.2 × 31.8 cm.)
New York, 26 September 1991, $25,300 (£14,624)
Record auction price for a print by the artist

Above, from left:
MAX BECKMANN (German, 1884–1950)
Grosse Brücke ('Eiserner Steg' in Frankfurt am Main)
(Hofmaier 234B)
drypoint, 1922, signed, from the edition of 50
platemark $16\frac{13}{16} \times 10\frac{1}{16}$ in. (42.7 × 25.5 cm.)
London, 3 July 1992, £26,400 ($50,212)

GEORGES BRAQUE (French, 1882–1963)
Bass (Vallier 7)
etching, 1911, signed, numbered from the edition of 50
platemark $18\frac{1}{4} \times 13$ in. (46.5 × 33 cm.)
New York, 12 May 1992, $30,800 (£17,111)

BARNETT NEWMAN (American, 1905–1970)
Untitled
lithograph, 1961, signed and dated, numbered from the
edition of 30
sheet size $30\frac{1}{8} \times 22\frac{1}{4}$ in. (76.3 × 56.3 cm.)
New York, 4 November 1991, $49,500 (£27,808)

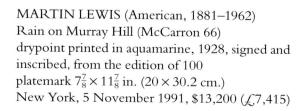

MARTIN LEWIS (American, 1881–1962)
Rain on Murray Hill (McCarron 66)
drypoint printed in aquamarine, 1928, signed and
inscribed, from the edition of 100
platemark $7\frac{7}{8} \times 11\frac{7}{8}$ in. (20 × 30.2 cm.)
New York, 5 November 1991, $13,200 (£7,415)

JASPER JOHNS (American, b. 1930)
Fall and Winter: from The Seasons
etchings with aquatint printed in colours, 1987,
the set of four, all signed and dated, numbered from
the edition of 73
sheet size $26\frac{3}{8} \times 19\frac{1}{2}$ in. (67 × 49.5 cm.)
New York, 11 May 1992, $165,000 (£91,666)

SCULPTURE

Attributed to ANDREA DELLA ROBBIA
(Italian, 1435–1525)
Portrait of a young Man surrounded by a Wreath
glazed terracotta
24¼ in. (61.5 cm.) diameter
London, 7 July 1992, £85,800 ($163,620)

A similar della Robbia medallion is in the Metropolitan
Museum of Art in New York. This example was in the
Borghese Collection in Rome until 1893.

ALESSANDRO ALGARDI (Italian, 1595 or
1602–1654)
The Pietà
bronze
12¾ × 12⅚ in. (32.4 × 32 cm.)
Sold by the Estate of Victor D. Spark, New York
New York, 14 January 1992, $154,000 (£85,698)
Now in the Frick Collection, New York

This rare composition is documented in a payment from
Cardinal Francesco Barberini (25 August 1657) for
polishing, gilding, mounting and framing an octagonal
relief of the *Pietà* by Algardi. The plaster mould is also
noted in the posthumous inventory of the sculptor
Ercole Ferrata (1686), 'Cavo di una Pieta del Langardi (sic)'.

This finely worked relief is technically superior to, and
more refined in detail than, the other known versions.
It is considered the best and most authentic cast of
Algardi's relief of the *Pietà*.

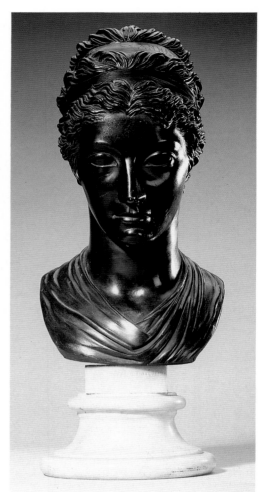

Attributed to FRANCESCO FANELLI (Italian, 17th Century)
Cupid on Horseback
bronze, 6⅜ in. (16.2 cm.) high
London, 10 December 1991, £23,200 ($41,899)

Cast from a model by ANNE SEYMOUR DAMER
(English, 1749–1828)
Portrait of Mary Berry
bronze, 18¼ in. (46.3 cm.) high
London, 10 December 1991, £17,600 ($31,785)

From a design by JOHN BACON R.A. (English, 1740–1799)
A River Goddess
coade stone
68¼ in. (173.5 cm.) wide; 43 in. (109.3 cm.) high
London, 12 May 1992, £28,600 ($47,476)

Attributed to GÉRARD RICHIER (French, 1534–1600)
A carved Chimneypiece
limestone
156 in. (397 cm.) high, 84 in. (214 cm.) wide
New York, 14 January 1992, $660,000 (£367,278)

The chimneypiece is from the Salle des Séances du Tribunal des Grands Jours in the Maison de la Prévôté, Saint-Mihiel, Lorraine. This meeting hall, where the sovereign held court and the principal assize court convened, was re-designed in 1571. Ligier Richier (whose name is inscribed on the later cartouche in the fireplace) had died by 1566. An attribution to his son Gérard is convincing. Not only was he his father's assistant, but his known sculpture (all in Lorraine) is similar in style and technique to the present carving. Although the figures and scenes relate to the benefits of law and order conferred on the populace by the court, the iconographic programme has yet to be deciphered.

This superb chimneypiece is important, not only because its provenance can be determined and its authorship attributed, but also as an impressive and rare example of architectural ornamentation from the second school of Fontainebleau.

HIRAM POWERS (American, 1805–1873)
Bust of Proserpine
signed 'H. POWERS. SCULP.'
white marble
21 in. (53.5 cm.) high
London, 21 May 1992, £35,200 ($63,888)

A. CIPRIANI (Italian, 19th Century)
Venus in Vulcan's Net
signed 'A. CIPRIANI'
marble
88¾ in. (225.5 cm.) high
New York, 30 April 1992, $170,500 (£97,095)

AUGUSTUS SAINT-GAUDENS (American,
1848–1907)
Diana of the Tower
bronze
21⅝ in. (55 cm.) high from top of head to toe, 36⅞ in.
(93.7 cm.) total height including bow and tripod base
New York, 6 December 1991, $242,000 (£134,444)

A monumental figure of *Diana* was originally conceived
in 1886 as a weathervane for the tower of Stanford
White's Madison Square Garden. The eighteen foot
figure proved unwieldy and imbalanced and was
removed in 1892. Two years later, a second version was
placed atop the tower. This thirteen foot *Diana* is now
in the collection of the Philadelphia Museum of Art.
This landmark sculpture became so popular that Saint-
Gaudens immediately copyrighted the model and
produced an edition of hand-modelled reductions in
two sizes with variations in details such as the base,
sphere, bow and hair. The present example is of the
smaller figure on the most elaborate base.

FURNITURE

One of a Pair of Louis XV *Chenets*
17$\frac{3}{8}$ in. (44 cm.) high; 22$\frac{1}{8}$ in. (56 cm.) wide
Monaco, 20 June 1992, Fr.1,221,000 (£124,592)

The exuberantly sculpted form of these *chenets*, in the
Louis XV manner, recalls the type of *fantaisie* cartouche
invented by Jacques de Lajoue (d.1761). Surmounted by
Cupid and Psyche, these *chenets* are related in design and
quality to the work of Jacques Caffieri (d.1755), the
celebrated *fondeur-ciseleur*.

BERNARD II VAN RISAMBURGH (French,
1696–1766)
A Louis XV ebonised, kingwood and Chinese lacquer
Commode
$63\frac{1}{2}$ in. (161 cm.) wide; $36\frac{1}{2}$ in. (90 cm.) high;
$27\frac{1}{2}$ in. (70 cm.) deep
Sold by the Luton Hoo Foundation
London, 11 June 1992, £660,000 ($1,202,200)

In B.V.R.B.'s *oeuvre* this commode represents a transitional
phase between the earliest group of commodes of around
1737 and those dating from the later 1740s, when he had
evolved a more richly sculptural style.

JEAN-FRANÇOIS LELEU (French, 1729–1807)
A Louis XVI amaranth *Bureau Plat*
72 in. (183 cm.) wide; 31½ in. (80 cm.) high;
38½ in. (98 cm.) deep
Sold by Mrs Barbara Piasecka Johnson
London, 11 June 1992, £1,210,000 ($2,202,200)

This ormolu-enriched bureau plat, with fluted 'herm' legs and
'poetic' frieze of laurel-wreathed 'Apollo' sunflowers within
acanthus-flowered ribbon *guilloche*, epitomises the elegant Louis
XVI Grecian style of the 1770s. It bears the brand of the *Maître
Ebéniste*, Jean-François Leleu, who provided the Prince de Condé
with a related suite of furniture at the Palais Bourbon, including a
bureau with acanthus-wrapped 'vase' capitals in 1771. Acquired
by the Comte (1785–1870) and Comtesse de Flahaut
(1788–1867), in the mid-nineteenth century, this bureau plat
passed into the Lansdowne family through their eldest daughter,
Emily Jane, wife of the 4th Marquis of Lansdowne (1819–1895).
It was sold by the 8th Marquis of Lansdowne at Christie's,
3 December 1981 for £330,000 ($646,800).

Opposite:
Attributed to ADAM WEISWEILER (French, 1744–1820)
A Louis XVI *Console-Desserte*
66¼ in. (168 cm.) wide; 37½ in. (94.5 cm.) high;
22¾ in. (57 cm.) deep
Monaco, 20 June 1992, Fr.3,441,000 (£351,122)

JEAN-BAPTISTE LELARGE (French, 1711–1771)
A Canapé from a Suite of Louis XVI Seat-Furniture, comprising
six *Fauteuils* and two *Canapés*
Monaco, 21 June 1992, Fr.3,774,000 (£385,102)

Attributed to PIERRE GOUTHIÈRE (French,
1732–1813)
A Pair of Louis XVI ormolu Candlesticks
13½ in. (34.25 cm.) high
London, 11 June 1992, £79,200 ($144,144)

These princely candlesticks, designed in the French Grecian
manner and adorned with antique lion-masks, triumphant
laurel collars and classical drapery are almost certainly by
Pierre Gouthière, the celebrated *doreur ciseleur* who became
maître in 1758 and *doreur ordinaire des Menus-Plaisirs* in 1767.

One of a Pair of Louis XIV Pots and Covers
13¾ in. (35 cm.) high; 13 in. (33 cm.) wide
Monaco 20 June 1992,
Fr.1,554,000 (£158,571)

PIERRE GOUTHIÈRE (French, 1732–1813)
The Duc d'Aumont's alabaster Vases
A Pair of Louis XVI ormolu-mounted Vases of
Egyptian Alabaster
16¼ in. (41 cm.) wide; 16½ in. (42 cm.) high
Sold by the Meikleour Estate Trust
London, 11 June 1992, £286,000 ($520,520)

These vases, of the finest *alabastro egiziano* (lapis
onyx) and embraced by triumphant bifurcated
laurel mounts, were commissioned by the 5th
Duc d'Aumont, *circa* 1770–5, from Pierre
Gouthière. They were probably designed by
François-Joseph Balanger, who like Gouthière
was employed in the Duc's workshop at the
Hôtel des Menus-Plaîsirs. Originally
surmounting a pair of *verde antico* columns, the
vases were purchased on behalf of Louis XVI in
the legendary sale of the Duc d'Aumont's
collection (12–21 December 1782, lot 7).
They were subsequently acquired by the
Comte and Comtesse de Flahaut in the 1820s or
early 1830s.

A Venetian rococo parcel-gilt
and polychrome-painted
Commode
mid-18th Century
62 in. (155 cm.) wide;
$36\frac{1}{2}$ in. (92 cm.) high;
25 in. (63 cm.) deep
New York, 6 March 1992,
$176,000 (£102,080)

A Neapolitan rosewood and
palisander *bombé* Commode
circa 1780
$53\frac{1}{8}$ in. (135 cm.) wide;
$36\frac{7}{8}$ in. (93.5 cm.) high;
24 in. (61 cm.) deep
Rome, 20 November 1991,
L.253,000,000 (£116,375)

PIETRO PIFFETTI (Italian, 1700–1777)
The Ashburton Cabinet
An ormolu-mounted ivory-inlaid kingwood and
parquetry Bureau-Cabinet
Turin, circa 1770
33½ in. (85 cm.) wide; 90¾ in. (230.5 cm.) high;
18½ in. (47 cm.) deep
London, 11 June 1992, £770,000 ($1,401,400)

This serpentined, scalloped and scroll-pedimented
bureau-cabinet, embellished with the shell and
rose emblems of Venus, with trellised parquetry
panels enriched with golden rosettes and ribbon-
bandings of ivory and ebony, is a masterpiece of
the Turin cabinet-maker, Pietro Piffetti.
Originally fitted with mirrors to the *cartonnier*
section and cabinet door, it is related closely to the
celebrated cabinet supplied for the Palazzo
Chiabeles, Turin in 1767 by Piffetti, who was
ebanisto to Vittorio Amadeo III (1726–96) and has
been described as 'the best cabinet-maker of the
Italian eighteenth century'. Its flowered trellis
parquetry related to Parisian furniture provided for
the French court after about 1770. This bureau-
cabinet is thought to have been acquired by
Francis, 3rd Lord Ashburton (1806–1868), who,
after his marriage in 1833 to Hortense Eugènie
Claire, daughter of the Duc de Bassano, resided in
the Place Vendôme, Paris, and, with a pair of
Piffetti commodes, is likely to have formed part of
the furnishing of the 'Italian Room' created at the
Grange, Hampshire.

Opposite:
A Spanish Colonial mother-of-pearl inlaid tortoiseshell Cabinet
Meuble Encochado
Mexican, 18th Century
85½ in. (213.7 cm.) wide; 113 in. (282.5 cm.) high;
26 in. (65 cm.) deep
London, 27 September 1991, £126,436 ($220,000)

A South German Renaissance sycamore, fruitwood, parquetry
and marquetry Travelling Cabinet
Augsburg, circa 1560
21½ in. (53.7 cm.) wide; 15½ in. (38.7 cm.) high;
16 in. (40 cm.) deep
New York, 14 January 1992, $55,000 (£30,555)

ABRAHAM ROENTGEN (German, 1711–1793) and
DAVID ROENTGEN (1743–1807)
An amaranth and marquetry *Bureau de Dame*
Neuweid, circa 1765–70
44 in. (112 cm.) wide; 40 in. (102 cm.) high;
23 in. (58.5 cm.) deep
London, 11 June 1992, £253,000 ($460,460)

This serpentined and ormolu-enriched *bureau de dame*, in the
Louis XV style is thought to have been commissioned by Johann
Philipp von Walderdorff, Elector of Trier (d.1768). Its florid
marquetry of flower-strewn and open-scrolled brackets with
birds and butterflies, combined with its ingenious craftsmanship,
represent the qualities that earned the Neuweid cabinet-making
business of Abraham Roentgen and his son David international
renown in the 1760s.

THE SAMUEL MESSER COLLECTION OF ENGLISH FURNITURE, BAROMETERS AND CLOCKS

by Anthony Coleridge

Samuel Messer had a great love for English furniture. He always sought the best possible advice and bought the best. In addition, he made sure that what he bought gave him, and others, pleasure. He not only received great satisfaction from sharing his collection with those who appreciated it, but also loved to wind his clocks and to polish his furniture or silver himself, gaining great pleasure from the actual feel of the piece. Patination, colour, the quality and crispness of carved ornament and the proportion of a piece all ranked highly when he made his choice. In later years, he attached due importance to research, literature and provenance. He was a man of great taste with a discerning eye and this was reflected not only by his collection of English furniture, clocks and barometers but also by his gardens at Pelsham, set in hilly country behind Rye in Kent.

Soon after he started to collect, Messer sought the help of R.W. Symonds, one of the most respected authorities on the subject. Symonds was adviser to a select few of the great collectors of English furniture at the time, including Percival Griffiths, Herbert Rothbarth, James Thursby-Pelham, Fred Skull, Geoffrey Blackwell and S. Sykes. Sam Messer joined this illustrious band. Symonds died in 1958, but Messer continued to collect: his many friends in the English furniture and clock trade gave him their advice and much enjoyed his friendship, as did many of us at Christie's. When he died in June 1991 he left a collection which included pieces which had been acquired by fellow collectors, tutored by Symonds, and others with prestigious primary source provenances such as St. Giles's, Tythrop, Lumley Castle and Serlby.

The Messer Collection deserved, and indeed required, a catalogue which would serve not only as a memorial to its creator but also as a magnet to all those who might be interested in bidding when it was offered on 5 December last year − an auspicious day as it was the 225th anniversary of James Christie's first auction of 5 December 1766. I have already stressed that, in later years, Sam Messer paid great attention to scholarship and provenance but this was not necessarily so in his earlier collecting years. Christopher Gilbert, a noted furniture historian himself, emphasises this in his short article *A supreme piece of English Furniture* which was recently published in our International Magazine. He writes:

> Sam Messer's connoisseurship, his personal system of values that perceived excellence in furniture, was, judged by modern standards, slightly old-fashioned and unadventurous. Today, great emphasis is placed on establishing the provenance and identifying the maker of furniture, however, he regarded dynastic origins as being of less importance than fluent design, illustrious quality and authenticity. Accordingly, many of Messer's undocumented pieces, while displaying elegance and style, were felt by some to lack genuine art historical significance; in fact John Hardy and Charles Cator did uncommonly well in the time available to illuminate the ancestry of several distinguished lots.

The challenge which faced my colleagues in our furniture department was to produce a scholarly catalogue in a limited time.

Since Robert Symonds and his contemporary Ralph Edwards started to write serious books on furniture history between and after the wars, English furniture has been the subject of increasing scholarly research which has materially affected the value of individual examples. This explains why the auction houses and furniture trade alike aim to publish erudite catalogues of the auctions and exhibitions which they mount.

More research was necessary into Messer's earlier purchases than his later ones. Fresh information was being unearthed until the last minute. This enabled the George III commode (p. 151) to be identified as one supplied in about 1766 to Chippendale's great patron, Sir Rowland Winn, for his London House in St. James's Square. Prior to Christopher Gilbert's research, it had only been possible to attribute the commode to Chippendale on stylistic grounds with the backing of an unpublished drawing in the Metropolitan Museum. The pre-sale estimate for the commode was £250,000–£350,000 and it sold for £935,000 − a fitting tribute to Sam Messer's connoisseurship. It was also a timely reassurance that, if it can be demonstrated that a piece of furniture is indeed from the workshop of a great English cabinet-maker, those who vie for the possession of the finest examples of our furniture will reach even deeper into their pockets in order to secure the object of their choice.

The Messer Chippendale commode was the last of the 130 lots in this sale. On the day the Great Rooms here in St. James's were packed to overflowing and the result of the sale proved to be a major tonic for the market. It was a very exciting morning and all that an auction should be. When Charles Allsopp stepped out of the rostrum, he had notched up a total of £7.7 million − a record for a collection of English furniture, clocks and barometers. Every lot was eagerly snapped up. Those brave enough to fend off the very considerable opposition included buyers from the United States and Canada and a strong European showing from Switzerland, Germany, Spain, Italy and Belgium − for fine English furniture has a very wide appeal. I am confident that the proud new possessors of these pieces will get as much pleasure from them as did Sam Messer, and am sure that this would have been his wish.

The sale got off to an excellent start with Sam Messer's library of furniture books and then we were into the serious business with the barometers and clocks. Two of the barometers were head and shoulders above the others, the silver-mounted example by Daniel Quare and the Daniel Delander barometer (p. 159). The former, mounted with the royal cypher of William III, and probably made for Kensington Palace, tripled its estimate at £341,000, a record for a barometer: the latter, the only known barometer made by this fine clock-maker, its silver mounts contrasting with its ebony veneered case, fetched £220,000, four times the low estimate. Among five clocks by Thomas Tompion, the Barnard Tompion led the field (p. 161). It is believed to have been made for Queen Anne and given by George II to his private secretary, Andrew Stone, whose sister married into the Barnard family and took the

clock with her. It was sold for £572,000, a record for any bracket clock. Fine clocks by Joseph Knibb, Johannes Fromanteel, George Graham and John Ellicott also fetched high prices.

Then it was the turn of the furniture. Apart from the Messer commode which he wrote 'made me feel weak at the knees', Christopher Gilbert singled out three lots for special praise. These three 'masterpieces' as he described them were 'the wonderfully inspired' St. Giles's House chairs (p. 156), the Tythrop wine cistern (p. 154), and the Cusworth Hall dining-table. They were sold for £275,000, £165,000 and £187,000, the latter two prices being exceptional sums for pieces of English dining room furniture. I often feel that, without seeing pieces, or at least photographs of them, that lists of prices become almost meaningless, and so my selection will be brief. The pair of George III *bombé* commodes from Henbury Mansion near Bristol (p. 154) fetched £374,000, more than doubling their high estimate, and the same price was paid for the George III library bookcase (p. 158). Sam Messer had paid £6,500 for the commodes in 1955 and £5,500 for the bookcase two years later – not a bad return after some 35 years. A pair of George II 'dolphin' armchairs which were a joy to sit on (p. 157), sold for £286,000 and a mahogany bedside cupboard attributed to Thomas Chippendale, a man for whom I harbour much respect, was sold for £33,000. What pleasure it would be to have this standing by one's bed!

Take the best advice, buy the best, love what you have bought, carry out research on it, give others great pleasure in your possession of it, no man can do more than that. Sam Messer did so and his many friends will for many years remember him for this.

THOMAS CHIPPENDALE (English, 1718–1779)
A George III mahogany Commode
62¼ in. (158 cm.) wide; 23¼ in. (59 cm.) deep; 35¼ in. (89 cm.) high
London, 5 December 1991, £935,000 ($1,654,950)

The design relates to a pattern published in Chippendale's *Gentleman and Cabinet-maker's Director* of 1762. The commode, whose medallioned doors and 'Etruscan' ebony-ribbon inlay reflect the neo-classical style introduced in the 1760s by Robert Adam (1728–1792), can be identified with one listed at the St. James's Square house of Sir Rowland Winn, 5th Bt., who was among Thomas Chippendale's first and most important patrons.

The commode was included in Christie's sale of the Winn's London house on 9 April 1785, as 'A large mahogany commode chest of drawers', but was retained by the family.

A George II mahogany and needlework cheval Fire-Screen
32 in. (81 cm.) wide; 22½ in. (57 cm.) deep;
49¾ in. (126.5 cm.) high
London, 5 December 1991, £60,500 ($107,085)

Almost certainly commissioned by George Lee, 2nd Earl of
Litchfield (1689–1741) for the drawing room at Ditchley Park,
Oxfordshire, this needlework panel depicts Pluto's abduction of
Proserpine as described in Ovid's *Metamorphoses*.

A Pair of George II walnut and parcel-gilt Candle-Stands
13¾ in. (35 cm.) diameter; 42½ in. (108 cm.) high
London, 5 December 1991, £99,000 ($175,230)

These stands with fretted tray tops and baluster stems
incorporating strigil fluting emerging from an acanthus bulb
relate to pedestals in the Franco–Italian style published in James
Gibbs's *Book of Architecture* of 1728 (reissued in 1739).

Opposite:
One of a Pair of George III mahogany Commodes
49 in. (124.5 cm.) wide; 34¼ in. (87 cm.) high; 27 in. (68.5 cm.) deep
London, 5 December 1991, £374,000 ($661,980)

These ormolu-enriched commodes in the French manner are likely
to have been commissioned in the 1760s by Thomas Farr, Lord
Mayor of Bristol (d.1791) for Henbury Mansion, near Bristol. Their
serpentined and *bombé* frames and bowed and scrolled apron typify
the concept of elegance expressed by William Hogarth in his *Analysis
of Beauty* of 1753.

A George II mahogany Wine-Cooler
27¾ in. (70.5 cm.) wide; 16¼ in. (41 cm.) high; 19¾ in. (50 cm.) deep
London, 5 December 1991, £165,000 ($292,050)

This oval cistern wine-cooler, supported by bacchic panther feet, and
enriched with gilt brass mounts in the manner of Gaetano Brunetti
(d.1758), was commissioned by James Herbert, Member of
Parliament for Oxford, for the Palladian banqueting room, which he
created at Tythrop House, Oxfordshire in the 1730s.

Above:
One of a Pair of George II mahogany Commodes
31¼ in. (79.5 cm.) wide; 32 in. (81 cm.) high; 20 in. (51 cm.) deep
London, 5 December 1991, £253,000 ($447,810)

These serpentined chest of drawers with bacchic panther feet
emerging from Roman foliage are mounted with acanthus-scrolled
handles used by Thomas Chippendale in the 1750s. They have been
associated with the 'Pair of Mahogany drawers' noted in the 'Best bed
chamber' at Serlby Hall, Yorkshire in the inventory taken after the
death of William Monckton Arundell, 2nd Viscount Galway
(1718–1772).

One of a Pair of George II mahogany open Armchairs
the seats 20½ in. (52 cm.) wide; the backs 36 in. (91.5 cm.) high
London, 5 December 1991, £275,000 ($486,750)

These richly carved parlour chairs, with bacchic enrichments designed in the French picturesque manner, were commissioned by Anthony Ashley–Cooper, 4th Earl of Shaftesbury (1710–1771), and are thought to have been provided by William Hallett (1707–1781), the celebrated cabinet-maker of Great Newport Street, for the banqueting pavilion at St. Giles's House, Dorset, which was built in the 1740s by the architect Stephen Wright (d.1780).

One of a Pair of George II mahogany Library Armchairs
the seats 27½ in. (70 cm.) wide; the backs 41 in. (107 cm.) high
London, 5 December 1991, £286,000 ($506,220)

These chairs, with sporting-dolphin feet, relate to a 'French Chair' pattern published by Thomas Chippendale in his *Gentleman and Cabinet-Maker's Director* of 1754, and were formerly in the collection of The Hon. Lady Baillie, Leeds Castle.

Attributed to THOMAS CHIPPENDALE (English, 1718–1779)
A George III mahogany breakfront Library Bookcase
79 in. (199.5 cm.) wide; 99 in. (251.5 cm.) high;
24½ in. (62.5 cm.) deep
London, 5 December 1991, £374,000 ($661,980)

The Messer bookcase, lent to the Victoria & Albert Museum in the
1950s, is a masterpiece of the neo-classical style which Thomas
Chippendale helped to establish through the 1762 edition of his
Gentleman and Cabinet-Maker's Director. With its immaculate
construction, ingeniously fitted desk-drawer and 'antique' ebony
enrichments it relates to the furniture that he supplied for
Pembroke House, London, and Nostell Priory, Yorkshire.

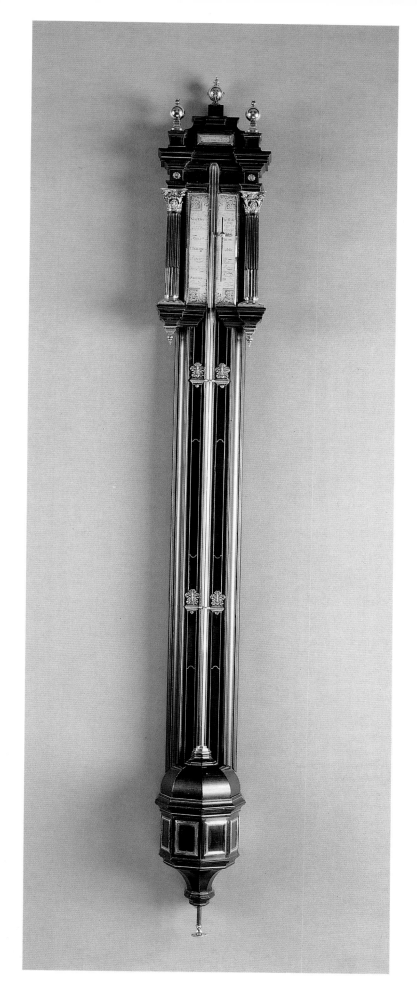

DANIEL QUARE (English, 1649–1724)
A William III silver-mounted ebonised siphon tube Barometer of
royal provenance
London, circa 1700
39 in. (99 cm.) high
London, 5 December 1991, £341,000 ($603,570)
Record auction price for a barometer

DANIEL DELANDER (English, 1674–1733)
A George I ebony and silver-mounted stick Barometer
London, circa 1725–30
43½ in. (110.5 cm.) high
London, 5 December 1991, £220,000 ($389,400)

Purchased by Thomas Pelham-Holles (1693–1768), 1st Earl of
Clare, later 1st Duke of Newcastle

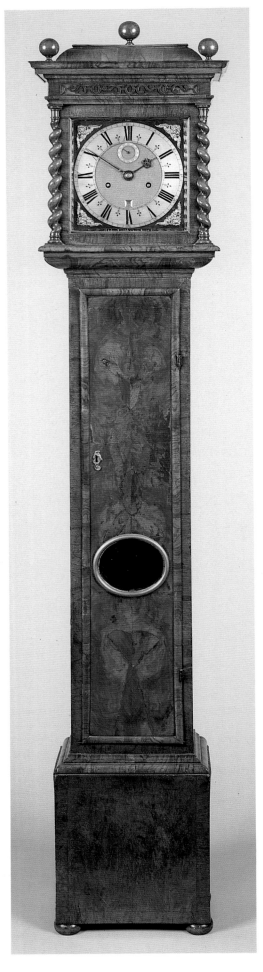

JOSEPH KNIBB (English, 1640–1711)
A Charles II ebony miniature
Longcase Clock
London, circa 1682–5
64 in. (162.5 cm.) high
£137,500 ($243,375)

JOHN KNIBB (English, 1650–1722)
A Charles II walnut Longcase Clock
Oxford, circa 1685
78 in. (198 cm.) high
£52,800 ($93,456)

THOMAS TOMPION (English, 1639–1713)
A Charles II gilt-bronze mounted ebony
Roman striking month-going Longcase Clock
London, circa 1675
79 in. (200.5 cm.) high
£132,000 ($233,640)

THOMAS TOMPION (English, 1639–1713) and
EDWARD BANGER (English, c. 1668–1720)
The Barnard Tompion: a small ebony silver-mounted striking
Bracket Clock, No. 460
London, circa 1708
9 in. (23 cm.) high; 7¾ in. (19.5 cm.) wide; 5½ in. (14 cm.) deep
£572,000 ($1,012,440)
Record auction price for an English bracket clock

The Barnard Tompion was reputedly made for Queen Anne
and given by King George II to Andrew Stone, who served as
his private secretary and was tutor to his grandson, George,
Prince of Wales. It was then inherited by his sister Anne, wife
of William Barnard, Bishop of Londonderry and passed by
family descent.

Many of Tompion's greatest clocks were enriched with silver
mounts on ebony or giltmetal cases; their ornament reflecting
the fashionable French taste popularised by the Huguenot
ornamentalist Daniel Marot. The Barnard Tompion is a more
refined version of the similar, but smaller, silver-mounted
clock, No. 222, now in the Victoria and Albert Museum,
which itself may be of royal provenance.

A George II walnut Mirror
51 × 26¾ in. (130 × 68 cm.)
Sold by members of the Blackwell family
London, 9 July 1992, £93,500 ($178,585)

Designed in the Palladian style and embellished with flowered scroll pediments, oak festoons and a scallop-shell, this mirror together with the dressing table, formed part of the celebrated furniture collections assembled, under the guidance of R. W. Symonds, by Percival Griffiths (1861–1935) and Geoffrey Blackwell (1884–1943).

A George II burr and figured walnut kneehole Dressing-Table
41¼ in. (105 cm.) wide; 30½ in. (77.5 cm.) high, closed; 23¼ in. (59 cm.) deep
Sold by members of the Blackwell family
London, 9 July 1992, £137,500 ($262,625)

Designed in the Palladian style, this compass-fronted pier dressing-table with drawers flanking an arched recess is fitted with a hinged top concealing a mirror and lidded toilet compartments. It bears an engraved plaque stating that it belonged to George Gordon, 6th Lord Byron (1788–1824), the poet and hero of the Greek War of Independence, who is also said to have owned the mirror, and was probably commissioned by William Byron, 5th Lord Byron (1722–1798) for Newstead Abbey, Nottingham.

Opposite top:
SAMUEL DIXON (Irish, active 1743–1755)
Four from a complete Set of twelve Irish George II embossed Bird Pictures
averaging 13⅜ × 17⅜ in. (34 × 44.2 cm.)
Sold by Lady Olivia Waldron
London, 9 April 1992, £115,500 ($200,277)

Opposite:
An Irish George II mahogany Side Table
66¼ in. (168.5 cm.) wide; 32¾ in. (83 cm.) high
London, 9 July 1992, £48,400 ($92,444)

This sideboard table, in the Palladian style, with bacchic lion feet and mask cartouche accompanied by garlands framing a scallop-shell, was photographed about 1900 in the banqueting hall at Castle Morres, Co. Kilkenny, and is likely to have been supplied to Harvey Morres (1706–1766), created Baron Mount Morres in 1756 and Viscount in 1763.

One of a Pair of early George III giltwood Mirrors
$94\frac{1}{2} \times 46$ in. (240 × 177 cm.)
London, 9 April 1992, £110,000 ($190,740)

These flower-festooned and acanthus-wreathed pier-glasses with mirrored borders capped by a foliate spray escutcheon are designed in the Louis XV 'picturesque' style, expressed by Thomas Chippendale in his *Gentleman and Cabinet-Maker's Director* of 1754, and were previously in the collection of the Hon. Mrs. Aileen Plunket, Luttrellstown Castle, Co. Dublin.

THOMAS CHIPPENDALE (English, 1718–1779)
One of a Pair of George II giltwood Mirrors
40 × 27¾ in. (101.5 × 69 cm.)
London, 9 July 1992, £104,500 ($199,595)

These 'girandoles', with their rams' masks and Grecian palmette frames in the antique manner of Robert Adam (1728–1792), were supplied by Thomas Chippendale *circa* 1770 to Edwin Lascelles, later 1st Lord Harewood (1713–1775), almost certainly for the corner window piers of the dining room at Harewood House, Yorkshire.

MATTHEW BOULTON (English, 1728–1809)
A Pair of George III ormolu, bronze and white marble three-light Candelabra
14¼ in. (36 cm.) wide; 26¾ in. (68 cm.) high
London, 5 December 1991, £79,200 ($140,896)

Designed in the Louis XVI 'antique' style and depicting Apollo and Diana, these candelabra feature in the pattern books of Matthew Boulton of Birmingham, and have been identified with lot. 124 in his sale held at Messrs. Christie & Ansell on 18 May 1778.

Opposite top:
Attributed to THOMAS VARDY (English, active 1751–1788)
A pair of George III walnut Side Tables
62½ in. (159 cm.) wide; 35 in. (89 cm.) high; 32½ in. (82.5 cm.) deep
Sold by Lord Bolton
London, 5 December 1991, £319,000 ($567,501)

Commissioned by Charles Powlett, 5th Duke of Bolton (1718–1765), Lord Lieutenant of Hampshire and Lieutenant of the Tower of London, for the banqueting hall at Hackwood Park, Hampshire, these sideboard tables with gold flecked 'Portor' marble slabs were designed in the Palladian style with 'Bolton' falcon feet by the architect John Vardy (d.1765) and are attributed to his brother Thomas, cabinet-maker of Park Street, Mayfair.

Above:
Attributed to JOHN MAYHEW (English, 1736–1811) and
WILLIAM INCE (English, d. 1804)
A George III satinwood and marquetry semi-elliptical Commode
72½ in. (184 cm.) wide; 36¾ in. (93.5 cm.) high;
29¼ in. (74 cm.) deep
Sold from the Barbara Piasecka Johnson Collection
London, 9 July 1992, £660,000 ($1,260,600)

The design of this ormolu-enriched marquetry commode,
formerly in the collection of Alexander Baring, 1st Lord
Ashburton (1774–1848), was inspired by the architect Robert
Adam's Derby House commode, executed in the 'Etruscan'
style and illustrated in his *Works in Architecture* of 1779.
Attributed to Messrs. Mayhew & Ince, cabinet-makers of
Golden Square, Soho, the commode has painted medallions
representing Venus and Cupid, and Diana and Endymion.

Top:
A Regency simulated rosewood and parcel-gilt Settee
77½ in. (197 cm.) wide; 34½ in. (87.5 cm.) high; 25 in. (63.5 cm.) deep
London, 9 July 1992, £46,200 ($88,242)

This tripartite-back settee with *bergère* sides in the Louis XVI 'antique' manner was previously in the collection of Lord Gerald Wellesley, later 7th Duke of Wellington (1885–1972), a leading figure in the revival of popularity for Empire and Regency furniture.

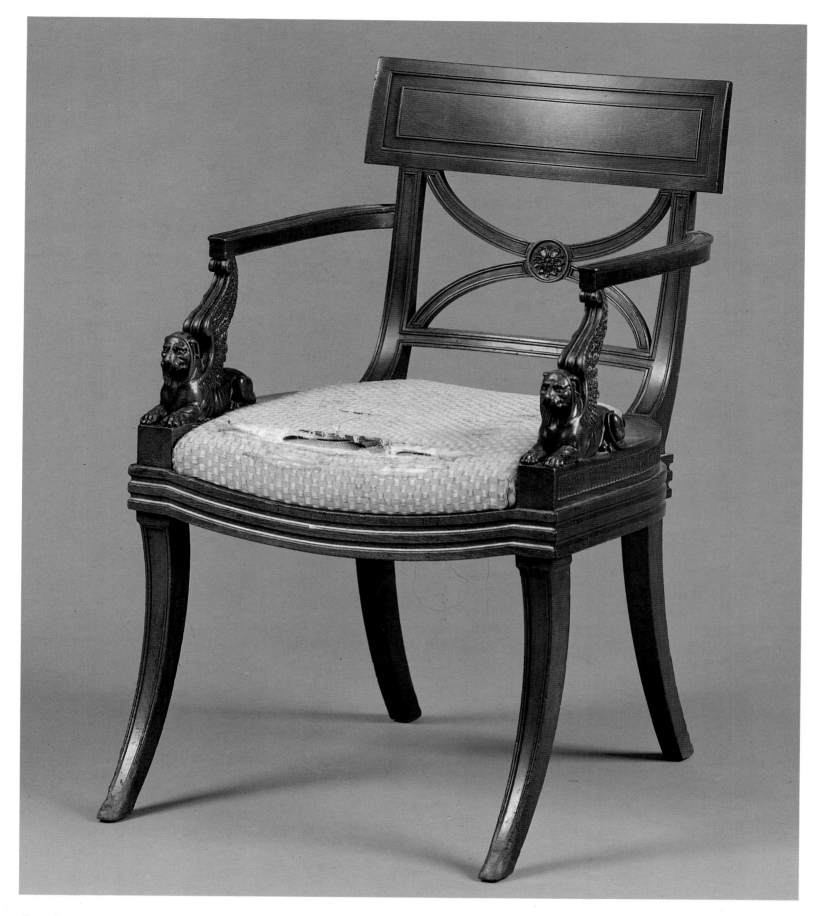

Opposite:
WILLIAM TROTTER (Scottish, 1772–1833)
One of a Pair of Regency rosewood Side Tables
75 in. (146 cm.) wide; 37¼ in. (94.5 cm.) high;
31 in. (79 cm.) deep
Edinburgh, 29 April 1992, £101,200 ($179,124)

Commissioned in 1813 by George Home (d.1839) for the saloon at
Paxton House, Berwickshire, this pair of console tables with their
richly carved 'trusses with plinths and balls' were designed by William
Trotter, cabinet-maker of Princess Street, Edinburgh and charged at
£41.10.0 in his account of August 1814. They were designed to
harmonise with the room's Grecian architecture and support Italian
marble slabs with sunflower 'mosaic' patterns, which Home's uncle
had acquired on his Grand Tour in the 1770s.

Above:
Attributed to WILLIAM MARSH (English, active 1774–1808) and
THOMAS TATHAM (English, 1763–1818)
A Regency mahogany Armchair
Sold from the collection of the late Mrs. Marjorie Beatrix Fairbarns
London, 9 July 1992, £31,900 ($60,929)
Bought by the Fitzwilliam Museum, Cambridge

This early nineteenth-century chair, incorporating the Egyptian lioness
of the Campidoglio, Rome was designed by the connoisseur Thomas
Hope (1769–1831) for his Duchess Street mansion and illustrated in his
Household Furniture and Interior Decoration of 1807. It reflects the romantic
neo-classical style that he partly adopted from his friend Charles Percier's
Receuil de décorations Intérieures of 1801 and is attributed to the specialist
carver Peter Bogaert.

Opposite:
The Bispham Family Chippendale carved walnut
Dressing-Table
1755–60
33 in. wide; 30½ in. high; 20½ in. deep (84 × 77.5 × 52 cm.)
Sold from the collection of Mr. and Mrs. Eddy G. Nicholson
New York, 17 June 1992, $165,000 (£89,100)

A Chippendale carved mahogany Chest of Drawers
1750–5
32 in. wide; 16½ in. deep (81 × 42 cm.)
New York, 17 June 1992, $220,000 (£118,800)

Above:
One of a Set of four Federal white painted and
parcel gilt Armchairs
circa 1790
36 in. (91.5 cm.) high
New York, 19 October 1991, $49,500 (£28,779)
Bought by Yale University

A Brussels Tapestry
117 × 182 in. (297 × 462 cm.)
London, 11 June 1992, £60,500 ($110,412)

Opposite:
A shaped Axminster Carpet (detail)
240 × 175 in. (609 × 442 cm.)
Sold from the Estate of the late R. B.W. Clarke
London, 11 June 1992, £52,800 ($96,360)

This was the first time that this carpet had been sold since it was
commissioned in around 1795 by the Clarke family of Bridwell,
Devon, from the local carpet workshops in Axminster.
Unfortunately the original bill of sale has not survived.

A Charles X Savonnerie Carpet
213 × 168 in. (540 × 427 cm.)
London, 11 June 1992, £68,200 ($124,465)

The design of this carpet draws heavily on the work of Louis
Saint-Ange-Desmaisons (1780–1831), the most prolific designer
working for the Savonnerie in the Empire and early restoration
periods.

JOHANNES CLAUSS (German, c.1605–1671)
A silver-gilt mounted Nautilus Cup and Cover
Nuremburg, circa 1630
18½ in. (47 cm.) high
New York, 30 October 1991, $286,000 (£164,367)

Seashells, particularly of the nautilus and turban variety were used extensively by sixteenth and seventeenth-century goldsmiths to produce exotic, but often impractical pieces. The silver mounts were normally gilded and the shells heavily polished.

CHRISTOPH JAMNITZER (German, 1563–1618)
A silver-gilt Beaker
Nuremburg, circa 1600
$4\frac{1}{8}$ in. (10.5 cm.) high
(6 ozs.)
New York, 30 October 1991, $104,500 (£60,057)

Christoph Jamnitzer was the most talented descendant of Wenzel Jamnitzer (1508–1585), founder of the Mannerist school of goldsmithing in Nuremburg. Wenzel established Nuremburg as the centre of silver design in the sixteenth century, leading the movement away from pure Renaissance forms toward Mannerist and Gothic revival styles. This beaker, by his grandson, Christoph, continues the Gothic revival tradition introduced by Wenzel in the 1560s.

Top, right:
ANDREAS KAUXDORF (German, c.1595–1669)
A parcel-gilt covered Baker's Guild *Münzbecher*
Leipzig, circa 1645
$10\frac{5}{8}$ in. (27 cm.) high
(42 ozs.)
Geneva, 19 May 1992, S.Fr.154,000 (£57,678)

Right:
Attributed to GERRIT VALCK (Dutch, 1613–1663)
A Marriage Cup
Amsterdam, 1641
$7\frac{1}{8}$ in. (20 cm.) high
(7 ozs.)
Geneva, 19 May 1992, S.Fr.110,000 (£41,199)

Opposite:
CHRISTIAN WINTER (German,
c.1670–1737) or
CHRISTOPH WARMBERGER
(German, c.1680–1746)
A Pair of silver-gilt circular Dishes
and Covers
Augsburg, 1730
dishes, $18\frac{3}{4}$ in. (47.5 cm.) diameter
(184 ozs.)
covers, 17 in. (43 cm.) diameter;
$10\frac{1}{4}$ in. (26 cm.) high
(190 ozs.)
Geneva, 19 May 1992, S.Fr.715,000
(£282,609)

Each dish and cover is engraved with the
coat-of-arms of Augustus II, King of
Poland, frequently referred to as Augustus
the Strong on account of his physical
strength and prowess. These pieces formed
part of a dinner service which originally
comprised 270 vessels and 98 pieces of
flatware and was commissioned to
celebrate the wedding of the Crown
Prince in 1719. The service was
subsequently added to in 1730 and again
in 1733.

JACQUES-CHARLES MONGENOT
(French, c.1735-c.1795)
A Louis XVI Tureen and Stand
Paris, 1783–4
15 in. (38 cm.) high;
18 in. (46 cm.) diameter
(300 ozs.)
Geneva, 19 May 1992, S.Fr.308,000
(£121,740)

A Pair of Louis XVI Wine-Coolers
Paris, 1784–5
$11\frac{1}{2}$ in. (26.5 cm.) high
(150 ozs.)
Geneva, 19 May 1992, S.Fr.264,000
(£104,348)

Above:
JEAN-BAPTISTE-CLAUDE ODIOT
(French, 1763–1827)
A Pair of silver-gilt Tureens and Covers from the
Branicki Service
Paris, 1819
16 in. (40.1 cm.) high
(630 ozs.)
New York, 28 April 1992, $550,000 (£308,988)

The Branicki Service is one of the most
celebrated of the great early nineteenth-century
dinner services from the workshops of Odiot and
Biennais. It was commissioned by the recently
widowed Countess Branicki in 1819. The
subsequent history of this remarkable service is
shrouded in mystery.

JAMES PLUMMER (British, c. 1595–1663)
A Charles I silver Tankard
York, 1648
6 in. (15 cm.) high
(16 ozs.)
New York, 30 October 1991, $137,500 (£79,022)

Silver of the reign of Charles I is extremely rare, and the fascinating verses and admonitions engraved on this tankard make it unique in English silver. Owned for many years by the Frank family of Yorkshire, Judith Bannister has shown that it was decorated to commemorate the wedding of John Frank to Mary Harbred. The cover is inscribed: 'When this yow se remember, whom God joynes together Let no man separate.'

ANTHONY NELME (British, c.1660–1723)
Two from a Set of Four Queen Anne Wall Sconces
London, 1704
11¾ in. (29.8 cm.) high
(99 ozs.)
London, 8 July 1992, £275,000 ($529,210)

Each back plate is engraved with the arms of Bligh, for
John, 1st Earl of Darnley (1683–1728), with those of his
wife, Baroness Clifton, in pretence. Designed in the
Louis XIV 'Antique' or 'Arabesque' manner, each
sconce is embellished with the garlanded mask of the
nature-goddess wearing her triumphal, scallop-shell
headdress. This ornament derives from the goldsmiths'
pattern book which was published in the early
eighteenth century by Daniel Marot in his *Nouveau
Livre D'Orfevrerie Invente par Marot Architecte du Roy.*

THE ROCKINGHAM EWER AND BASIN

by Stephen Clarke

The ewer and sideboard dish, or basin as it is more generally known, were indispensable adjuncts to every formal dining-room before the introduction of the table fork to England from Italy in the sixteenth century. They developed from purely functional pieces in the middle ages into magnificent objects used to display their owner's superior wealth and rank by the end of the seventeenth century. With the importance that such articles carried, their makers were often allowed full license to produce stunning objects of which their owners would be justifiably proud. The Rockingham rose-water ewer and basin are unquestionably amongst the finest produced by either Huguenot or native craftsmen.

Commissioned by Sir Thomas Watson-Wentworth, later 1st Marquess of Rockingham (1693–1750), they formed part of a group of ceremonial plate made to celebrate his nomination as a Knight of the Order of the Bath. In 1725, King George I, with encouragement from Sir Robert Walpole, his first Prime Minister, revived this ancient military order. Sir Thomas was among those who attended the inaugural banquet at Westminster. The dubbing of water, a symbol of cleansing, was part of the ceremony and therefore a ewer and basin were eminently suitable to commemorate such a celebration.

The goldsmith chosen for this important commission was David Willaume the elder and the ewer and basin exemplify the extraordinary heights that certain London goldsmiths attained during the reign of George I. Arthur Grimwade in *London Goldsmiths, 1697–1837*, discusses Willaume's work at length and states: 'among so many outstanding pieces it is difficult to select any pre-eminent masterpiece, when all display the highest qualities of rich design and impeccable execution.' He does however go on to list several important pieces, including the Rockingham ewer and basin.

The antique silver collector's palate is never more acutely excited than by a remarkable piece making its maiden appearance at auction. Although the Rockingham ewer and basin had been exhibited twice before, at the celebrated *Queen Charlotte's Loan Exhibition of Old English Silver*, at Seaford House in 1929, and in *Heritage of England, Silver Through Ten Reigns*, in New York in 1983, this was the first time collectors had been given the opportunity to acquire this historically important and superlatively well preserved set.

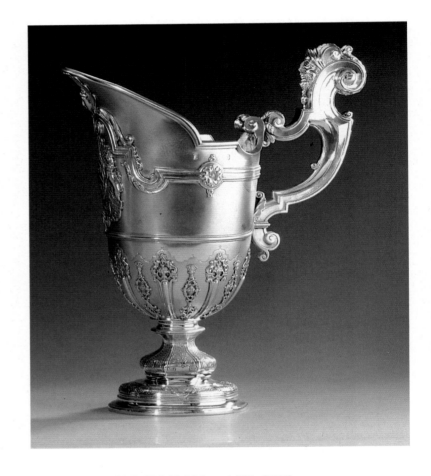

DAVID WILLAUME I (British, c.1658–1741)
A George I helmet-shaped Ewer
London, 1726
15 in. (38 cm.) high.
(117 ozs.)
Sold with the basin illustrated opposite

DAVID WILLAUME I (British, c.1658–1741)
A George I shaped–circular Sideboard Dish
London, 1726
$25\frac{1}{2}$ in. (64.8 cm.) diameter
(317 ozs.)
Sold by the Trustees of Olive, Countess Fitzwilliam's
Chattels Settlement
London, 27 November 1991, £682,000 ($1,207,140)

A Charles II two-handled
circular Porringer and Cover
maker's mark CM
London, 1672
7¼ in. (18.5 cm.) high
(29 ozs.)
London, 8 July 1992, £40,700 ($78,306)

DAVID WILLAUME II (British, 1693–1761)
A George II silver Ewer
London, 1744
13 in. (33 cm.) high
(63 ozs.)
New York, 30 October 1991, $203,500
(£116,954)

George Booth, 2nd Earl of Warrington, a patron
of the leading Huguenot goldsmiths,
commissioned this ewer for one of the bedrooms
at Dunham Massey, his ancestral home. The Earl
formed a magnificent collection of silver, of
which his manuscript inventory, *The Particulars of
My Plate and Its Weight*, offers an illuminating
insight into his passion for collecting.

PAUL DE LAMERIE
(British, 1688–1751)
One of a Pair of George II
two-handled circular Baskets
London, 1734
12½ in. (32 cm.) wide;
5¼ in. (13.5 cm.) high
(81 ozs.)
London, 27 November 1991,
£572,000 ($1,012,440)

ROBERT COOPER
(British, c.1650–c.1720)
A Set of Twenty-Four
George I Dinner Plates
London, 1719
5⅝ in. (24.5 cm.) diameter
(422 ozs.)
New York, 28 April 1992,
$220,000 (£123,595)

Each plate is engraved with the
arms of Winnington impaling
those of Reade.

PAUL CRESPIN (British, 1694–1770)
A Set of Four George II Candlesticks
London, 1750–1
10½ in. (26.75 cm.) high
(137 ozs.)
London, 13 May 1992, £79,200 ($143,193)

Each candlestick is engraved with the crest of Tollemache within the Order of the Thistle for Lyonel, 4th Earl of Dysart, K.T. (1708–1770). Previously, their design has consistently been attributed to Juste-Aurèle Meissonnier. However, the design of similar gilt-bronze candlesticks in the Wallace Collection has been attributed by Sir Francis Watson to the Slotdz brothers.

OTTO KNOOP (Dutch, 1708–1742)
A silver Shabbat and Festival Hanging Lamp
Amsterdam, circa 1740
35$\frac{3}{4}$ in. (87 cm.) high
(55 ozs.)
Amsterdam, 27 May 1992, Fl.264,500 (£80,006)

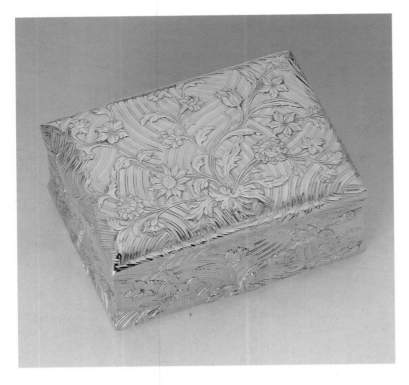

PHILIPPE-ANTOINE MAGIMEL (French, 169?–1772)
A Louis XV gold Snuff-Box
Paris, 1746–7
$3\frac{1}{8}$ in. (8 cm.) wide
Geneva, 19 November 1991, S.Fr.121,000 (£47,827)

JEAN DUCROLLAY (French, 1709–1761)
A Royal Louis XV gold Snuff-Box, with six miniatures under
glass mounted *à cage*, the interior with a miniature of Stanislas
Leszczinski and lined in the base with Japanese lacquer
Paris, 1750
$3\frac{1}{8}$ in. (7.9 cm.) wide
Geneva, 19 November 1991, S.Fr.115,500 (£45,653)

JEAN FORMEY (French, active 1754–1791)
A Louis XV vari-coloured gold Snuff-Box, decorated with
scenes in the manner of David Teniers the Younger
Paris, 1754–5
$2\frac{7}{8}$ in. (7.2 cm.) wide
Geneva, 19 May 1992, S.Fr.99,000 (£37,079)

JAMES COX (English, active 1749–1791)
A George III gold and enamel Table-Necessaire, with a
watch movement and concealed erotic scene
$3\frac{1}{8}$ in. (8 cm.) long
London, circa 1770
New York, 28 April 1992, $115,500 (£64,887)

James Cox, specialised in watches and clocks with
musical automata. One of his most famous creations is
the Peacock Clock made for Prince Potemkin for his
Tauride Palace, now in the Winter Palace, St.
Petersburg. One of the 'curious clocks' made for the
Emperor of China in 1776 is in the Jack and Belle
Linsky Collection, Metropolitan Museum of Art, New
York, while cabinet-form necessaires by Cox are in the
Gilbert Collection, Los Angeles and the al-Tajir
Collection, London. Both these collections also include
snuff boxes fitted with automata with agate panels
mounted *à cage* and with chased compartments similar
to the present example.

A gilt-metal mounted mother-of pearl Necessaire,
with singing bird Automaton and twin musical
movements by Frères Rochat, containing
French gold implements
10 in. (25·5 cm.) long
Geneva, circa 1825
London, 27 November 1991, £99,000 ($175,230)

JOHANN WILHELM KEIBEL
(Russian, 1788–1862)
A gold and emerald Snuff-Box
St. Petersburg, circa 1850
$3\frac{1}{2}$ in. (9 cm.) long
Geneva, 19 November 1991, S.Fr.198,000
(£78,261)

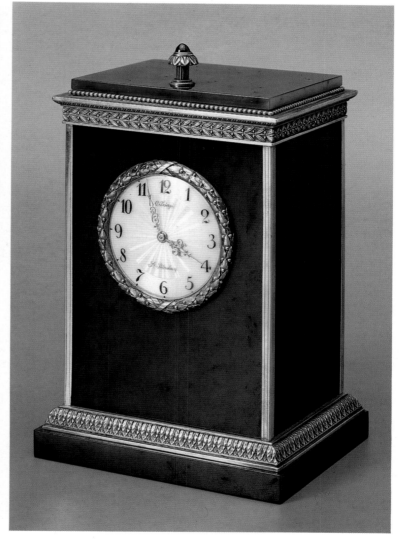

Top:
FABERGÉ
workmaster Michael Perchin (1860–1903)
An oval nephrite Charka with a large openwork gold handle in the Renaissance style, enamelled and set with a large foiled sapphire and four diamonds
St. Petersburg, 1899–1903, $5\frac{1}{8}$ in. (13 cm.) long
Geneva, 19 November 1991, S.Fr.63,800 (£25,218)

FABERGÉ
workmaster Julius Rappoport (1864–1916)
A gold rococo style Beaker, the baluster-shaped body set with coins of Catherine the Great and Elizabeth Petrovna
St. Petersburg, circa 1885, $3\frac{3}{8}$ in. (8.5 cm.) high
Geneva, 19 May 1992, S.Fr.52,800 (£19,775)

Above:
FABERGÉ
workmaster Michael Perchin (1860–1903)
An enamelled silver-gilt and pale-green bowenite Desk-Clock
St. Petersburg, 1899–1903, $6\frac{1}{2}$ in. (16.5 cm.) high
Geneva, 19 November 1991, S.Fr.88,000 (£34,783)

FABERGÉ
workmaster Henrik Wigström (1862–1923)
A rectangular minute-repeating silver-gilt mounted nephrite Desk-Clock
St. Petersburg, 1908–17, 5 in. (12.7 cm.) high
Geneva, 19 November 1991, S.Fr.126,500 (£50,000)

PORTRAIT MINIATURES

Opposite:
FRENCH SCHOOL, (c. 1662)
Anne of Austria, as Saint Anne, with Queen Marie-Thérèse of
France holding her Son, the Grand Dauphin, as the Virgin Mary
and the Infant Christ
oval, $8\frac{1}{8}$ in. (20.6 cm.) wide
Geneva, 19 May 1992, S.Fr. 101,200 (£37,903)

Very few French royal miniatures of this time are recorded; this
work is a fine example by an unidentified but highly talented
court painter.

LOUIS-AMI ARLAUD-JURINE (Swiss, 1751–1829)
A young Girl with a Doll
signed
oval, 3 in. (7.6 cm.) high
Geneva, 19 November 1991, S.Fr. 49,500 (£19,566)

JEAN-PHILIPPE GOULU (Swiss, 1786–1853)
A young Boy, seated, whipping his toy-horse
signed and dated 1812
3 in. (7.6 cm.) diameter
Geneva, 19 November 1991, S.Fr. 49,500 (£19,566)

Right:
JEAN-ETIENNE LIOTARD (Swiss, 1702–1789)
A Gentleman
enamel on copper
oval, $2\frac{1}{4}$ in. (5.7 cm.) high
Geneva, 19 November 1991, S.Fr. 55,000 (£21,740)

SAMUEL ANDREWS (British, 1767?–1807)
Lieutenant-Colonel Charles Russell Deare
oval, $2\frac{1}{2}$ in. (65 mm.) high
London, 4 March 1992, £12,000 ($20,812)

Deare (1749/50–1790) was commissioned into the Bengal
Artillery in 1769; he was killed by a cannon ball during the third
Mysore War.

JOSEPH DANIEL (British, d. 1806)
A double-sided Miniature of Sarah Bayly (illustrated) and her
Father, Zachary Bayly
oval, $2\frac{1}{2}$ in. (6.4cm) high, in a gold frame with blue enamel border
set with rose diamonds and split pearl reverse
London, 27 November 1991, £13,200 ($23,364)

JEWELLERY BY CARTIER

by Raymond Sancroft-Baker

The House of Cartier was founded in 1847 when Louis-François Cartier opened a shop at 29 rue Montorgueil, Paris. Within fifty years the firm had a worldwide reputation for quality, which it still retains. In order to meet the growing international demand branches were opened in London in 1902 and New York in 1909: those were run by Louis-François's grandsons, Jacques and Pierre, whose brother Louis was in charge of the Paris establishment.

In recent years the demand for signed pieces by Cartier has increased and the decision to hold a sale entitled *Jewellery by Cartier* last May in Geneva was fully justified. It was not only a great success but also tremendous fun to put together, including, as it did, many disparate objects which no other firm could have produced. The first few lots exemplified this: a set of gold hunting buttons, a cigarette holder and a pair of ear clips modelled as Yorkshire Terriers.

The distinguishing feature of many objects and items of jewellery made by Cartier was that these were stylized enough to be different, yet unfailing in appeal. If this slightly unorthodox approach had been tried by less accomplished manufacturers, the result might have been disappointing. Many books and numerous articles have been written about Cartier and, if I had only two words to characterise their work, I would settle for quality and design. Two lots illustrating this point were an Art Deco desk clock, the enamel of which imitated bloodstone extremely realistically, and the Art Deco mantel clock on which Burmese amber was used for the carved chimerae at either side of the enamel bezel which enclosed a carved jade dial. The whole effect was original, the lines clean and yet aesthetically pleasing.

Although the design for this clock was of oriental inspiration, it was not originally intended for the Far Eastern market, but because it employs oriental materials it was sold to a buyer from the Far East. This example is by no means unique and several other objects with jade and oriental motifs found new owners outside the traditional home for Cartier: Europe and America.

Among the 270 lots, there were numerous hand bags, some with jewelled clasps, including a *belle époque* example that incorporated a small watch, as well as scent flasks, cuff-links, cigarette cases and every type of jewellery in both precious and semi-precious stones, and an aquamarine tiara representing Cartier's imaginative approach. Octagonal rather than round pocketwatches were made and a wristwatch might be set on a segmented onyx bracelet instead of a leather strap. A small mystery clock of the model 'A' type, which sold for S.Fr.143,000 (£53,759), was based on an optical illusion as the hands seem to float in mid-air without any apparent connection with the movement: the hands are in fact fixed onto separate crystal discs with serrated metal rims which in turn are driven by gears that are hidden within the frame. Special mention must be made of the safe that was made to look like a Louis XV commode, with a marble top and ormolu mounts, the enamel sides and front imitating marquetry. This was sold by a collector in one of the Southern States of America and shipped to Geneva for the sale, at 600 kilograms, a major task. This extraordinary object fetched S.Fr.44,000 (£17,600), double its estimate.

The sale concluded with a 25.22 carat diamond set in a clip brooch. The innate purity and quality of the stone suggests that this came from the Golconda mines in India: it is similar to other such diamonds used in the French Crown Jewels. The sale which totalled S.Fr.10,032,770 (£3,771,718), will no doubt come to represent a landmark.

CARTIER
A marble, agate and enamel Elephant Table Clock, Barometer and Thermometer
circa 1905
Geneva, 21 May 1992, S.Fr.330,000 (£125,400)

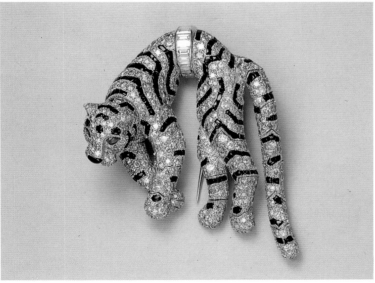

Left, from top:
CARTIER
An Art Deco oriental inspired Mantel Clock
circa 1925
Geneva, 21 May 1992, S.Fr.330,000 (£125,400)

CARTIER
A yellow diamond, emerald and onyx tiger clip Brooch
1980,
Geneva, 21 May 1992, S.Fr.143,000 (£54,340)

Right, from top:
CARTIER
A rock crystal, diamond and black onyx model 'A' mystery Clock
circa 1930
Geneva, 21 May 1992, S.Fr.143,000 (£53,759)

CARTIER
An Art Deco jade, coral, enamel and diamond Cigarette Case
circa 1927
Geneva, 21 May 1992, S.Fr.132,000 (£50,160)

Top:
CARTIER
A peridot and diamond Necklace
1936
Geneva, 21 May 1992, S.Fr.198,000 (£75,240)

Inset:
CARTIER
An Art Deco jade, black onyx and diamond Brooch
1923
Geneva, 21 May 1992, S.Fr.93,500 (£35,530)

Above:
CARTIER
An Art Deco emerald, diamond and
black enamel Bracelet
circa 1930
Geneva, 21 May 1992, S.Fr.88,000 (£33,440)

Above:
CARTIER
A sapphire and diamond Necklace
circa 1935
Geneva, 21 May 1992, S.Fr.550,000 (£209,000)

Inset:
CARTIER
A cabochon Kashmir sapphire Ring
40.87 carats
Geneva, 21 May 1992, S.Fr.660,000 (£250,800)

Right, from top:
CARTIER
A pair of Art Deco diamond and pearl Earrings
circa 1925
Geneva, 21 May 1992, S.Fr.137,500 (£52,250)

CARTIER
A fancy yellow diamond Ring
24.67 carats
Geneva, 21 May 1992, S.Fr.363,000 (£137,940)

CARTIER
An Art Deco diamond clip Brooch
circa 1930
25.22 carats
Geneva, 21 May 1992, S.Fr.935,000 (£355,300)

From left:
A brilliant-cut Diamond
32.58 carats, D colour and flawless
Geneva, 21 November 1991, S.Fr.3,168,000
(£1,267,200)

A pear-shaped diamond Ring
15.06 carats, D colour and VVS2
New York, 22 October 1991,
$440,000 (£255,200)

A rectangular-cut diamond Ring
16.05 carats, D colour and VVS2
New York, 10 December 1991, $396,000
(£217,800)

A brilliant-cut diamond Ring
7.01 carats, G colour and VS1
London, 12 February 1992,
£50,600 ($90,068)

A rectangular-cut fancy yellow diamond
Ring
15.29 carats
New York, 14 April 1992,
$154,000 (£87,780)

A rectangular-cut fancy intense yellow
diamond Ring
24.53 carats
St. Moritz, 20 February 1992,
S.Fr.660,000 (£257,400)

A pear-shaped fancy grey diamond Ring
11.02 carats
New York, 14 April 1992,
$165,000 (£94,050)

A marquise-cut diamond Ring
10.75 carats, D colour and VS2
New York, 10 December 1991,
$242,000 (£133,100)

WINSTON
A diamond Necklace
Geneva, 21 November 1991,
S.Fr.2,860,000 (£1,144,000)

Right:
WEBB
A pair of brilliant-cut diamond ear
Pendants
New York, 10 December 1991,
$79,200 (£43,560)

Far right:
WEBB
A diamond panther Bangle
New York, 10 December 1991,
$82,500 (£45,375)

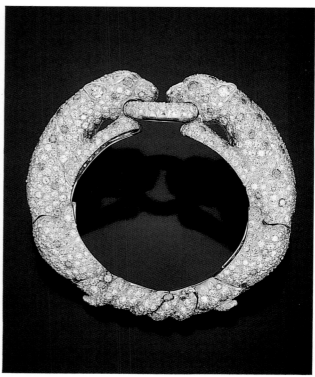

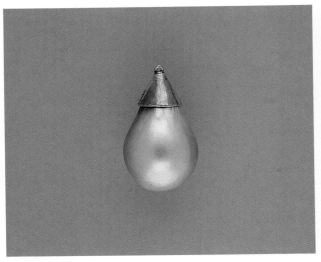

Above:
A pink diamond Necklace
Geneva, 21 May 1992, S.Fr.2,860,000 (£1,086,800)

Right, from top:
A grey pearl Pendant
292 grains
Geneva, 21 May 1992, S.Fr.682,000 (£259,160)

WEBB
A pair of cultured pearl and diamond ear Clips
New York, 10 June 1992, $39,600 (£22,572)

Opposite, below, from left:
A diamond Brooch
central stone 14.77 carats, D colour and VS1
Sold from the Collection of Caroline Ryan Foulke
New York, 14 April 1992, $385,000 (£219,450)

STERLE
A diamond Bracelet
Geneva, 21 November 1991, S.Fr.121,000 (£48,400)

A diamond cluster Brooch
circa 1840
London, 17 June 1992, £33,000 ($51,810)

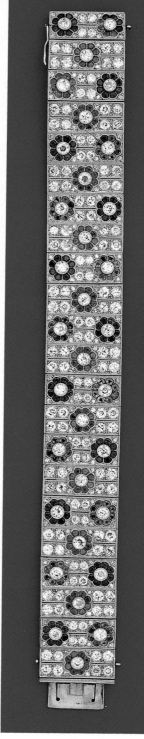

Top left:
VAN CLEEF & ARPELS
A diamond Necklace
Geneva, 21 May 1992, S.Fr.330,000 (£125,400)

Inset:
A rectangular-cut diamond Ring
18.69 carats
Geneva, 21 May 1992, S.Fr.616,000 (£234,080)

Top right:
An Art Deco diamond and gem-set Bracelet
London, 11 December 1991, £18,150 ($28,132)

Left:
WINSTON
A diamond Necklace
Sold from the Collection of Caroline
Ryan Foulke
New York, 14 April 1992,
$506,000 (£288,420)

Below left:
An antique diamond Brooch
circa 1860
New York, 14 April 1992,
$82,500 (£47,025)

Below right:
CARTIER
A carved coral, diamond and emerald
chimera Bangle
New York, 22 October 1991,
$63,800 (£37,000)

Top, from left:
WINSTON
A rectangular-cut emerald Ring
10.13 carats
New York, 22 October 1991,
$308,000 (£178,640)

CHAUMET
An Art Deco emerald and diamond
Brooch
circa 1935
central emerald 16.38 carats
Geneva, 21 May 1992,
S.Fr.2,288,000 (£869,440)

WINSTON
An emerald and diamond Pendant
central emerald 36.57 carats
Geneva, 21 November 1991,
S.Fr.1,705,000 (£682,000)

Above:
RUBEL
An Art Deco diamond and gem-set
Bracelet
circa 1925
Geneva, 21 May 1992,
S.Fr.264,000 (£100,320)

Right:
VAN CLEEF & ARPELS
An emerald and diamond leaf clip Brooch
Geneva, 21 May 1992,
S.Fr.104,500 (£39,710)

From left:
WINSTON
A sapphire and diamond Brooch
central sapphire 55.56 carats
Geneva, 21 May 1992, S.Fr.385,000
(£146,300)

A rectangular-cut Kashmir sapphire Ring
31.12 carats
Geneva, 21 May 1992,
S.Fr.1,628,000 (£618,640)

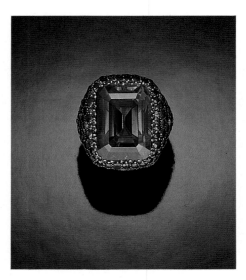

From left:
JAR
A rectangular-cut sapphire Ring
44.23 carats
New York, 14 April 1992,
$165,000 (£94,050)

CARTIER
A pair of sapphire and diamond ear
Pendants
Geneva, 21 November 1991,
S.Fr.253,000 (£101,200)

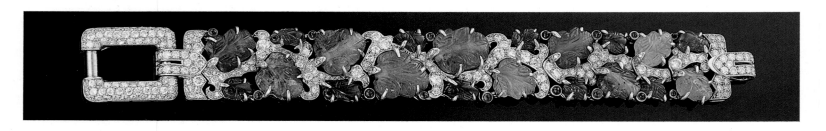

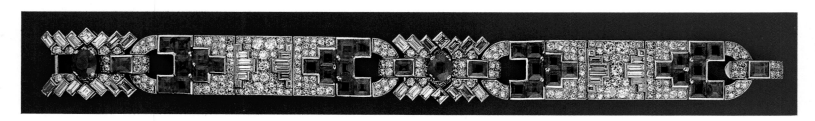

VAN CLEEF & ARPELS
A ruby and diamond Necklace
Geneva, 21 November 1991,
S.Fr.286,000 (£114,400)

Inset:
A ruby Ring
10.37 carats
St. Moritz, 20 February 1992,
S.Fr.396,000 (£154,440)

Below, right:
A Victorian ruby and diamond three-
stone Ring
circa 1880
London, 17th June 1992,
£46,200 ($83,160)

A Burmese ruby and diamond Ring
central ruby 9.82 carats
New York, 10 December 1991,
$440,000 (£242,000)

Below, far right:
VAN CLEEF & ARPELS
An invisibly-set ruby and diamond
flower Brooch
New York, 22 October 1991,
$220,000 (£127,600)

Opposite:
VAN CLEEF & ARPELS
A sapphire and diamond Bracelet
Geneva, 21 November 1991,
S.Fr.352,000 (£140,800)

CARTIER
An Art Deco carved gem and
diamond Bracelet
circa 1930
New York, 10 December 1991,
$137,500 (£75,625)

CARTIER
An Art Deco ruby and diamond
Bracelet
circa 1930
Glasgow, 10 September 1991,
£44,000 ($69,520)

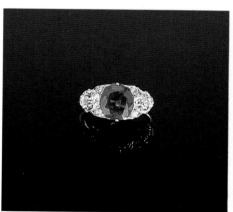

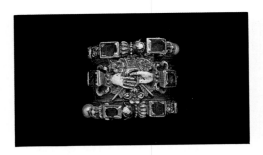

From left:
A Renaissance jewelled gold and enamel
marriage Ring
Dutch, dated 1610
London, 2 October 1991,
£74,800 ($118,184)

The Middleham Ring (enlarged)
gold, late 14th/early 15th Century
London, 2 October 1991,
£41,800 ($66,044)
Now in the Yorkshire Museum, York

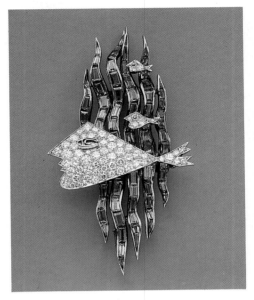

From left:
BARON HEGER DE LOWENFELD
Hebe
A diamond and sapphire clip Brooch,
designed by Georges Braque
Geneva, 21 November 1991,
S.Fr.121,000 (£48,400)

BARON HEGER DE LOWENFELD
Gaia
A diamond and peridot clip Brooch,
designed by Georges Braque
Geneva, 21 November 1991,
S.Fr.35,200 (£14,080)

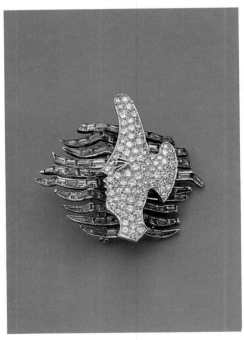

From left:
BARON HEGER DE LOWENFELD
Phoenix
A diamond and enamel clip Brooch,
designed by Georges Braque
Geneva, 21 November 1991,
S.Fr.55,000 (£22,000)

BARON HEGER DE LOWENFELD
Les Fils D'Eos
A diamond, lapis lazuli and gold clip
Brooch, designed by Georges Braque
Geneva, 21 November 1991,
S.Fr.41,800 (£16,720)

Left:
A pair of antique diamond, gold and
enamel Bangles, with miniatures of King
Friedrich Wilhelm IV of Prussia
(1795–1861) and his wife, Elisabeth
(1801–1873)
circa 1840
Geneva, 21 November 1991,
S.Fr.88,000 (£35,200)

This cross from the *Nuestra Señora de las Maravillas* which sank in 1656, is one of the most important pieces of jewellery of its type to have been recovered from the seabed and has survived in near perfect condition, despite a sojourn of over three hundred years in salt water. The unusual combination of decorative features such as the lobed outline and distinctively patterned reverse is uncharacteristic of mid-seventeeth-century Spanish work and points to a Colonial origin. The lobed surround is found in coins of Philip III (1598–1621) from mints such as Seville and re-appears again during the reign of Philip V (1780–24) on coins from mints in the New World. The same lobed surround is also found in Spanish seventeeth-century religious pendants in which the centre can be either figurative or set with gems. The reverse of the present cross is reminiscent of the etched decoration found on German Renaissance armour and metalwork with its complex medley of foliage, arabesques, circles and quatrefoils incorporating, in this instance, a fleur-de-lys cross inspired by one of the Spanish military orders. This fusion of decoration with its emphasis on scrollwork more typical of late sixteenth and early seventeenth-century Europe is unusual. The cross manifests a richness of materials and a boldness of form which sets it apart from the more fastidious designs favoured by goldsmiths in Barcelona and Seville, and is an important example of the sumptuous jewellery from the New World so admired in Europe.

A number of emerald crosses of Spanish and Spanish Colonial origin survive, including important examples from treasure ships such as the *Nuestra Señora de Atocha* (sank 1622) and the *San Pedro* (sank 1595), but none is directly comparable with this example. The same rather spiky goldwork is, however, found on an impressive emerald and gold 'rostrillo' with matching set of 19 dress ornaments donated to the Treasury of the Virgen de Gracia de Carmona in 1680 by Francisco de Rivera y Aral which are also of Spanish American origin. The richness of the jewels in this Treasury as well as the many others in Spain may give a clue as to the intended destiny of the *Maravillas* cross. It may have belonged to one of the Spanish grandees aboard the vessel or been intended

A Spanish Colonial emerald and gold Pectoral Cross
circa 1650
London, 28 May 1992, £231,000 ($411,180)

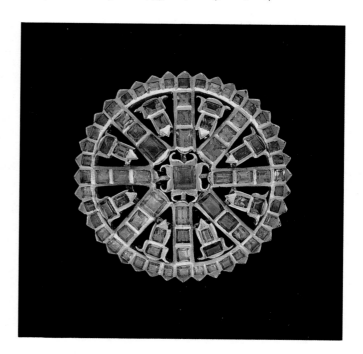

A Spanish Colonial emerald and gold Brooch
circa 1650
London, 28 May 1992, £55,000 ($98,395)

as a gift in Spain. A possible explanation is, that it was commissioned in the New World by a member of one of the Spanish orders of knighthood as a votive gift, in much the same way as a gold filigree chain was donated in 1659 to the Carmona Treasury by Captain Gregoria Morera, who fortuitously survived the perils of a voyage undertaken only three years after the fateful journey of the *Maravillas*.

CERAMICS

A Pair of very large Dutch Delft blue and white nine-tiered
pyramidal Tulipières
circa 1690
50½ in. (126 cm.) high
Amsterdam, 3 December 1991, Fl. 977,500 (£303,618)

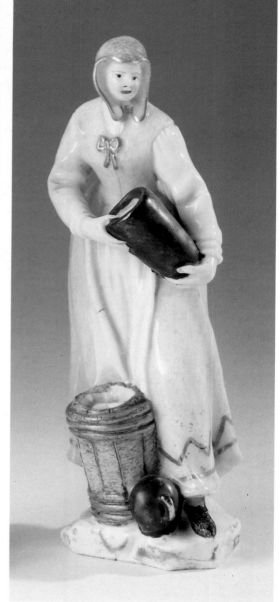

A Deruta blue and gold lustred Dish
circa 1525
17$\frac{1}{4}$ in. (43 cm.) diameter
London, 25 November 1991, £30,800 ($55,132)

Right:
A Capodimonte Figure of a Milkmaid
circa 1750
7 in. (17.5 cm.) high
Rome, 19 November 1991. L. 42,550,000 (£19,518)

One of a Pair of Savona Drug Jars from the factory of Jacques Boselly
circa 1760
8 in. (20 cm.) high
Monaco, 7 December 1992, Fr. 177,600 (£18,272)

Left:
A Meissen Royal presentation gold-mounted Snuff-Box,
painted by J.G. Höroldt, with a portrait of Augustus the Strong
circa 1730
2¾ in. (7 cm.) wide; 2 in. (5 cm.) high
London, 30 September 1991, £220,000 ($379,280)

A Meissen lobed square Tea-Caddy and Cover painted in the
manner of J.G. Höroldt
1725–30
4½ in. (11.5 cm.) high
London, 30 September 1991, £20,900 ($36,031)

Right:
A Meissen gold-mounted yellow-ground oval Snuff-Box,
painted in the manner of B.G. Haüer
circa 1740
3 in. (7.5 cm.) wide
London, 30 September 1991, £41,800 ($72,063)

A Meissen gold-mounted turquoise-ground circular Snuff-Box,
painted in the manner of I.J. Clauce after Watteau with figures
from the Italian Comedy
circa 1745
2¼ in. (5.5 cm.) wide
London, 30 September 1991, £41,800 ($72,063)

A Meissen large circular Dish from the Swan Service, modelled by J.J. Kandler and J.F. Eberlein for Count Brühl
1737–41
15⅛ in. (38 cm.) diameter
London, 30 September 1991, £41,800 ($72,063)

Right:
A Meissen kakiemon large shallow fluted Dish with a Johanneum mark
circa 1730
11⅔ in. (29 cm.) wide
Sold from the collection of Gertrude J. and Robert T. Anderson
London, 1 June 1992, £38,500 ($70,339)

A Meissen Box and Cover modelled as a Tortoise, probably by Georg Fritzsche
circa 1725
7¾ in. (19.5 cm.) long
London, 30 September 1991, £22,000 ($37,928)

The Meissen (Marcolini) 'Reepmaker' ornithological
Dinner Service
mostly 1774–80
Amsterdam, 12 May 1992, Fl. 460,000 (£139,309)

A Bow Figure of Kitty Clive in the role of 'The Fine Lady'
from Garrick's farce *Lethe*
circa 1750
10¼ in. (25.5 cm.) high
London, 25 November 1991, £8,250 ($14,767)

Right:
A Staffordshire creamware Dovecote of Whieldon type
circa 1755
8¾ in. (22 cm.) high
New York, 24 January 1992, $18,700 (£10,564)

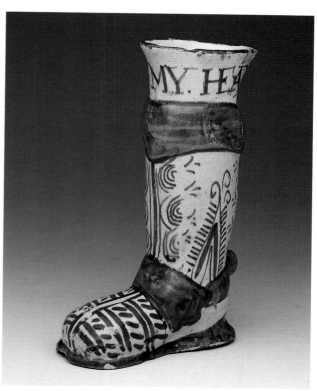

An English Delft (Southwark) blue and white Drinking-Vessel
modelled as a spurred Boot
circa 1650
7 in. (17.5 cm.) high
London, 25 November 1991, £12,100 ($21,659)

A North Bohemian (Kronstadt) 'Hausmaler' Flask, painted by Ignaz Preissler in Schwarzlot and Eisenrot enamels
1720–30
6¾ in. (17 cm.) high
London, 23 June 1992, £42,900 ($71,708)

A J. & L. Lobmeyr large circular Dish engraved by Karl Pietsch with *The Marriage of Neptune and Amphitrite*
1878–81
17 in. (42.5 cm.) diameter
London, 26 November 1991, £41,800 ($74,613)

DAUM (French)
A fine applied, etched and enamelled glass Vase
enamelled signature 'Daum Nancy'
11¾ in. (29.8 cm.) high
New York, 28 March 1992, $47,300 (£26,573)

GABRIEL ARGY-ROUSSEAU (French, 1885–1953)
A *pâte-de-verre* glass Vase
moulded signature 'G Argy-Rousseau'
9¾ in. (24.8 cm.) high
New York, 14 December 1991, $44,000 (£24,444)

TIFFANY STUDIOS (American)
A fine 'Trumpet Creeper' leaded glass and bronze Table Lamp
stamped signature 'Tiffany Studios New York, 28277 3'
27 in. (68.5 cm.) high; 18 in. (45.8 cm.) diameter of shade
New York, 14 December 1991, $400,000 (£244,444)

GALLE (French)
A double–overlay acid–etched Hydrangea Table Lamp
both base and shade with cameo signature 'Gallé'
$24\frac{3}{4}$ in. (63 cm.) high; 19 in. (48 cm.) diameter of shade
Geneva, 17 November 1991, S.Fr.297,000 (£117,392)

GREENE & GREENE (American)
An important Honduras mahogany, ebony and glass
Chandelier, executed in the workshops of Peter Hall and
Emil Lange for the dining room of the Robert R. Blacker
House, Pasadena, California
circa 1907
the ceiling plate $81\frac{1}{2} \times 71$ in. (207 × 180.3 cm.); the light
box $44\frac{3}{4} \times 33 \times 8\frac{3}{4}$ in. (113.7 × 83.3 × 22.2 cm.)
New York, 14 December 1991, $220,000 (£122,222)

Opposite top:
WILLIAM MORRIS (English, 1834–1896)
A rare 'Swan House' Hammersmith hand-knotted
Morris & Co. Carpet
circa 1908
$159\frac{1}{2} \times 150$ in. (396 × 380 cm.)
London, 5 February 1992, £33,000 ($59,136)

The Swan House carpets were originally designed by
William Morris, *circa* 1881, and commissioned by
Wickham Flowers, M.P. for the Old Swan House,
Chelsea Embankment. Their traditional designs illustrate
Morris's vast knowledge and understanding of the history
of carpet design and owe much of their inspiration to
sixteenth and seventeenth-century Turkish velvets and
Persian 'medallion' designs.

This unique carpet very closely resembles the original
watercolour for the Swan House. The variations would
indicate that it was a private commission.

CHARLES RENNIE MACKINTOSH, F.R.I.B.A.
(Scottish, 1868–1928)
Shop and Office Block in an Arcaded Street
signed 'Charles Rennie Mackintosh FRIBA, Architect'
pencil, pen and black ink and watercolour on paper
$11\frac{1}{4} \times 31\frac{1}{4}$ in. (28.5 × 79.5 cm.)
Glasgow, 25 September 1991, £45,100 ($77,887)

This and a companion drawing can be dated *circa* 1915, the year Mackintosh arrived in London. These recently discovered and undocumented drawings augment our understanding of Mackintosh's architectural work during this period, showing him working for the first time on a new scale – that of urban streetscape, designing probably for an overseas location and working in a style which contains references to his Glasgow work while anticipating the decorative designs of the London period.

Opposite:
JACQUES-EMILE RUHLMANN
(French, 1879–1933)
'Lit-Soleil', a macassar ebony Bed
branded 'Ruhlmann'
76½in. (194.4 cm.) high; 71 in. (180.3 cm.) wide;
89½in. (227.4 cm.) long
New York, 25 January 1992,
$132,000 (£74,576)

JACQUES-EMILE RUHLMANN
(French, 1879–1933)
'Ducharnebrouz', a rosewood and gilt bronze
Day Bed
20½in. (52 cm.) high; 35½in. (90 cm.) wide;
79 in. (200 cm.) long
Monaco, 8 December 1991,
Fr.339,600 (£41,111)

Right:
PAUL THEODORE FRANKL
(American, 1886–1958)
A Pair of lacquered wood and metal
'Skyscraper' Bookcases
each with metal tag 'Sky/Scraper/Furniture/
Frankl Galleries/4 East 48th Street/New York'
circa 1930
75 in. (190.5 cm.) high; 27 in. (68.5 cm.) wide;
11 in. (28 cm.) deep
New York, 6 June 1992,
$55,000 (£30,054)

JACQUES-EMILE RUHLMANN
(French, 1879–1933)
A Pair of alabaster Lamps for the 'Ile de France'
24¾ in. (63 cm.) high
Monaco, 8 December 1991,
Fr.517,000 (£53,167)

ANTIQUITIES

An Egyptian divine Head of the God Amun, wearing a characteristic crown surmounted by fragmentary double plumes
Reign of Taharqa, 690–664 B.C.
diorite
$11\frac{3}{8}$ in. (29.1 cm.) high
Sold from the collection of Mr. Alan M. May
London, 2 December 1991, £572,000 ($1,006,720)

This magnificent Egyptian head of the god Amun came from the excavations of Miss Margaret Benson in the Temple of Mut in Asher at Karnak, in 1896. After persistent pleading with the Antiquities' Service, Miss Benson and Miss Gourlay were given the concession to dig at the Mut Temple in South Karnak in the belief that it would yield no material. Over two hundred important statues of Dynasty XXV and XXVI (circa 7th-6th Century B.C.) were recovered by the two English ladies, for which they were rewarded with a few pieces. In 1985 part of the statue of the god's consort, Mut, which almost certainly belongs to this piece, was found by the expedition from the Brooklyn Museum, New York.

A Hellenistic Statue of the God Harpocrates
(Horus the Child)
circa 1st Century B.C. – early 1st Century A.D.
bronze
25¾ in. (65.5 cm.) high
London, 8 July 1992, £165,000 ($317,460)

The extraordinary size and superb quality of this bronze
suggest that it was made in a major urban centre, perhaps in
Asia Minor. Its subject, Harpocrates, was the son of the
Egyptian deities Isis and Osiris, but his cult was adopted
readily by Graeco-Roman worshippers, and spread
throughout the Roman Empire. This bronze shows the god
almost synthesized with the Greek Eros (he stands on tiptoe,
perhaps just alighting from flight); however, in antiquity he
would also have retained some of his Egyptian attributes, such
as the crown of Upper and Lower Egypt.

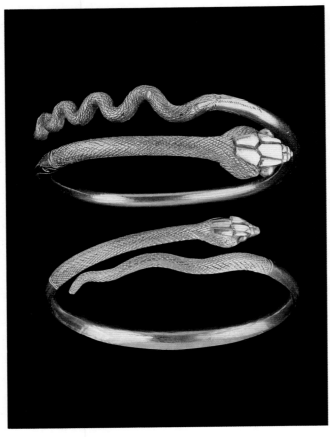

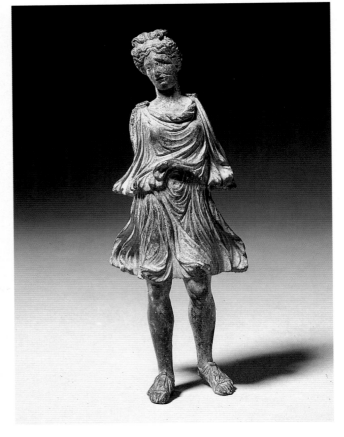

Top:
An Egyptian turquoise glazed composition
Pectoral in the form of a winged Isis
circa 1000 B.C., $9\frac{3}{4}$ in. (24.7 cm.) across wings
London, 8 July 1992, £11,000 ($21,164)

Above, left:
A Romano-Egyptian solid gold snake Bracelet
1st Century A.D., $3\frac{1}{2}$ in. (8.8 cm.) across, 150 g. weight
London, 8 July 1992, £22,000 ($42,328)

A Romano-Egyptian solid gold snake Bracelet
1st Century A.D., 3 in. (7.6 cm.) across maximum
London, 8 July 1992, £7,700 ($1,924)

Above:
A Hellenistic Statuette of Artemis
circa 4th Century B.C.
bronze
$5\frac{1}{4}$ in. (13.4 cm.) high
London, 2 December 1991, £35,200 ($61,952)

Above:
A Greek funerary Stele
second half of the 4th Century B.C.
Pentelic marble
31 in. (79 cm.) high
London, 2 December 1991, £33,000 ($58,080)

Top right:
A Roman cuirassed Bust of the Emperor Antoninus Pius
138–161 A.D.
marble
$37\frac{3}{4}$ in. (95.9 cm.) high
London, 8 July 1992, £44,000 ($84,656)

Right:
The Marbury Hall Roman Altar
1st Century A.D., upper part 18th Century
marble
$35\frac{1}{4}$ in. (89.5 cm.) high; $24\frac{7}{8}$ in. (63.3 cm.) diameter
London, 8 July 1992, £27,500 ($52,910)

ISLAMIC ART

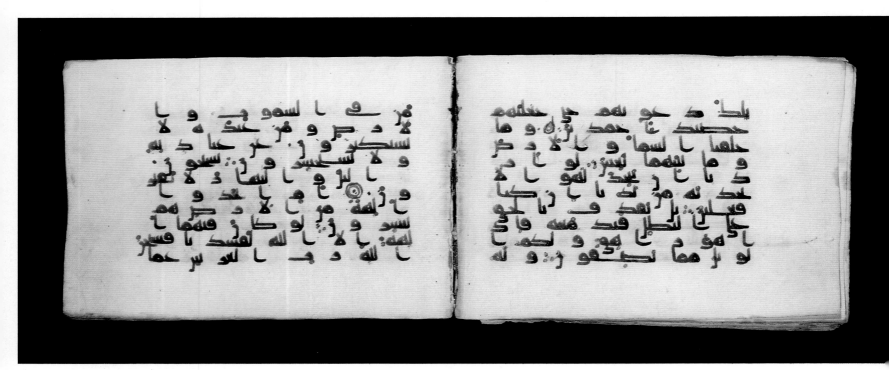

Top:
A Qur'an Section
comprising ch.v, *sura* al-Ma'idah to ch.ix, *sura* al-Tauba
North Africa, 13th Century
manuscript on vellum, 113ff.
folio 7 × 6 in. (17.8 × 15.3 cm.)
London, 28 April 1992, £60,500 ($105,875)

A large Qur'an Section
comprising ch. xx, *sura* Ta Ha, v.5 (part) to ch. xxxv,
sura al-Furquan v.15 (part)
Near East, 9th Century
manuscript on vellum, 88ff.
5½ in. × 7¾ in. (14 × 19.7 cm.)
London, 8 October 1991, £68,200 ($119,350)

An Iznik pottery Jug
Turkey, circa 1570
10 in. (25.2 cm.) high
London, 28 April 1992, £24,200 ($42,350)

Top:
A fine post-Sassanian bronze Ewer
Iran, 8th Century
11¾ in. (29.8 cm.) high
London, 28 April 1992, £25,300 ($44,275)

A post-Sassanian wheel-cut rounded light blue glass
Bowl
Nishapur, 8th–10th Century
3⅛ in. (7.9 cm. high); 4⅜ in. (11.2 cm.) diameter
London, 28 April 1992, £46,200 ($80,850)

Portrait of Fath 'Ali Shah Qajar
Persia, Qajar, circa 1820
oil on canvas
$72\frac{1}{4} \times 41\frac{1}{4}$ in. (183.5 × 105 cm.)
London, 28 April 1992, £39,600 ($69,300)

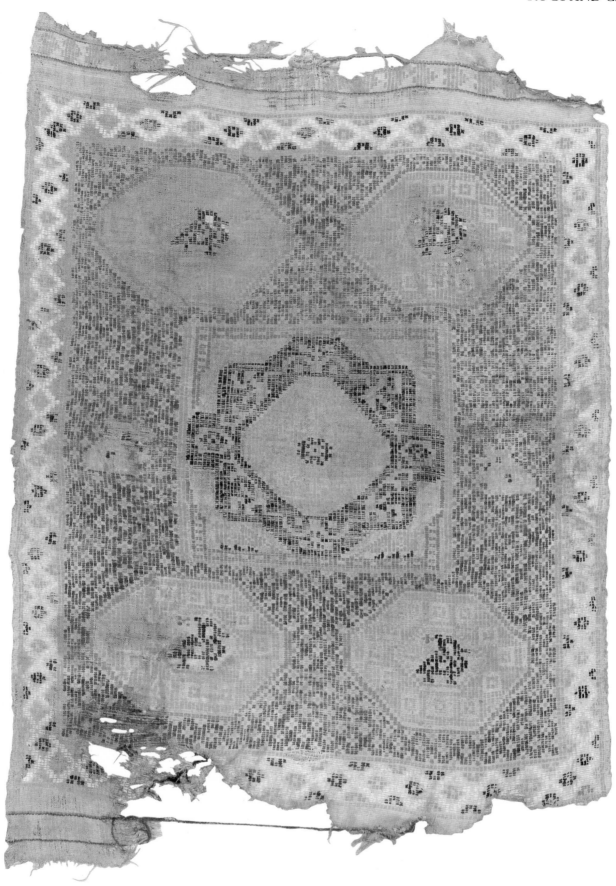

An Egyptian extra weft brocaded Rug
8th–10th Century A.D.
$45 \times 29\frac{3}{4}$ in. $(114 \times 75.5$ cm.)
London, 30 April 1992, £33,000 ($57,750)

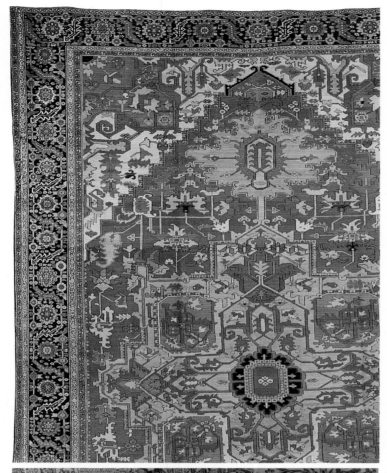

Above:
A Zareh Penyamin Koum Kapu silk and metal
thread Prayer Rug of 'Sultan's head' design
Turkey, circa 1900
55 × 37 in. (140 × 94 cm.)
London, 10 October 1992, £57,200 ($97,812)

Left, from top:
A Heriz Carpet (detail)
Iran, 19th Century
209 × 140 in. (543 × 355 cm.)
New York, 8 February 1992, $41,800 (£22,594)

A Sarouk Carpet (detail)
1878
356 × 188 in. (890 × 470 cm.)
Bologna, 8 June 1992, L.106,065,000 (£48,123)

Above, from left:
A Statuette of Buddha
Sakyamuni
made in China for the Tibetan
market, 15th Century,
marked Yongle and of the period
gilt copper
$10\frac{5}{8}$ in. (27 cm.) high
Amsterdam, 23 October 1991,
Fl.32,200 (£9,832)

A Figure of Syamatara
Nepal, late 14th Century
silver, on a gilt copper base
$5\frac{1}{2}$ in. (14 cm.) high
Amsterdam, 23 October 1991,
Fl.39,100 ($11,938)

Right:
A silver mounted carved ivory
Casket
Ceylon, second half of the
17th Century
$12\frac{1}{8} \times 6 \times 7\frac{3}{4}$ in.
(30.8 × 15.2 × 19.7 cm.)
London, 28 April 1992,
£13,200 ($23,100)

A rare well-modelled sancai-glazed pottery Figure of a
Fereghan Horse
Tang Dynasty
$21\frac{1}{4}$ in. (54 cm.) long
New York, 4 June 1992, $231,000 (£127,836)

Opposite:
An Imperial bronze Head of a Tiger, from the zodiac
fountain in Yuanming Yuan
Qianlong
12 in. (30.5 cm.) high
Hong Kong, 1 October 1991, H.K. $3,300,000
(£245,043)

A rare Pair of silver-inlaid bronze corner Mounts
Warring States
$4\frac{1}{8} \times 3\frac{1}{8}$ in. (10.5 × 7.9 cm.)
New York, 4 June 1992, $550,000 (£304,371)

An early Ming blue and white
'Dice' Bowl
Xuande six-character mark and of
the period
11 in. (28 cm.) diameter
Hong Kong, 1 October 1991,
H.K. $3,850,000 (£286,735)

A Ming-style blue and white Moon
Flask
Qianlong seal mark and of the
period
19¼ in. (49.2 cm.) high
Hong Kong, 31 March 1992,
H.K. $1,430,000 (£107,188)

A rare blue and white 'Music Party' Plate
circa 1700–10
33.8 cm. diameter
London, 11 May 1992,
£18,700 ($33,286)

A rare yellow and green-glazed incised Dragon Jar
Wanli six-character mark and of the period
7 in. (17.7 cm.) high
New York, 4 June 1992,
N.Y.$143,000 (£79,136)

THE VUNG TAU CARGO

by Colin Sheaf

No auction at Christie's this year more clearly revealed the Group's continued efforts, at a time of perceived worldwide economic instability, to maintain and extend its global influence and market leadership. In a number of ways, the sale in Amsterdam of the Vung Tau Cargo set new standards, both in the aggressive marketing of our auctioneering skills, and in effective sales presentation. Comprising some 28,000 pieces of Chinese porcelain, the cargo presented us with unprecedented initial organisational problems, but resulted finally in an auction which achieved 100% sold, a grand total of Fl.13,288,480 (£4,165,667), some three times the high estimate, and a very considerable amount of enthusiastic sale-related Press coverage. All of this came as a source of satisfaction to the joint London and Amsterdam team which had handled the sale negotiations and organisation; and, above all, to the nucleus of government officials, centred on the Vietnam Salvage Corporation, which had been instructed by the Government of Vietnam to supervise the recovery and sale of the Cargo.

It was this political background which made the sale of the Cargo an event unprecedented in the art world. Charity auctions have been held elsewhere on behalf of Communist governments. This was, however, the first time that a major auction house had negotiated a straightforward commercial contract, to hold a very public auction abroad of objects consigned on behalf of the government of a Communist country. In this case, the government of the Socialist Republic of Vietnam set up an inter-ministerial Committee, under the direct supervision of the Prime Minister, to arrange the very capitalist disposal at auction of a very Communist asset; the salvaged contents of a Chinese trading junk which sank off the southern coast in about 1690. Much of the cargo of export quality Chinese porcelain had survived a self-evident fire which burnt the ship to the waterline; a dozen charcoal-heated rice steamers, found randomly scattered around the wreck, may suggest how the accident came to happen. Located as a chance find by fishermen in 1989, the cargo was systematically lifted by specialist international teams attached to the Vietnam Salvage Corporation (VISAL), and supervised by Hallstrom Oceanics, the co-operative venture partner in the project. Responsibility for handling negotiations for the export and sale of the cargo went to Mr. Le Minh Cong, Director General of VISAL and his deputy director Mr. Huang Van Loc, who also provided invaluable translation assistance. Over fifteen months, and three trips by Christie's staff to Saigon, the contract was negotiated clause by clause and authorised by the various ministries involved; Security, Finance, Culture and Transportation, as well as the People's Committee of the Region of Vung Tau/Con Dao. Given the efforts involved to get the whole project under way, it put additional pressure on Christie's to achieve at least a satisfactory result for those government officials who had proposed a commercial art auction venture unprecedented in the Communist bloc.

The forthcoming sale was announced in Press Conferences conducted on 12 February in Amsterdam and London, and on 13 February in Saigon, Hong Kong, Singapore and Taipei. Immediately there was considerable Press and public interest; it was both an 'art' coup and a 'hard news' political story. A specially-commissioned fifteen-minute video received wide coverage. The objective was to show the way such porcelain would have been used in Europe at its time of manufacture. It included underwater footage of the salvage operation, interviews with porcelain experts, and, most novel, discussions between the distinguished British interior decorator Nina Campbell and the furniture designer David Linley about the way that such porcelain could be effectively used as interior decoration today. Inevitably, comparisons would be drawn between the Nanking Cargo, sold in Amsterdam with spectacular public interest in 1986, and the slightly earlier Chinese porcelain from this new shipwreck. But the Nanking cargo was export porcelain to eat off, and drink out of; table services, tea-bowls, chocolate cups, tens of thousands of utilitarian wares to dress a dining table or enhance the sophistication of a tea party. The Vung Tau Cargo was export porcelain from sixty years earlier, when it was still an object for conspicuous display in Europe. It was a late vestige of that medieval fascination for Oriental trifles as part of a 'Cabinet of Curiosities'; which turned at this period, in the hands of the interior designers like the French Huguenot emigré Daniel Marot, into the idea of using porcelain within overpowering architectural displays at the highest levels of fashionable society.

Bidders from Europe and Asia saw the point of this manner of decoration, and the sale of some 10,000 catalogues indicated that such a volume of export porcelain was unlikely to flood the market, a real fear at a time of world recession. Pre-auction exhibitions in London, Glasgow, Paris and Amsterdam maintained and increased public interest in this dispersal, and absentee commission bids continued to arrive very regularly before 7 April. The Amsterdam viewing rooms looked splendid: serried ranks of blue and white porcelain on shelves thirty metres long vied with complete wall installations resembling period drawing rooms; prompting a British art-world journalist to comment that it was the most attractive pre-sale viewing display he had ever seen.

When the six-member official Vietnamese delegation took their seats in the saleroom Press gallery to applause from a registered-bidder audience of five hundred people, it was clear that one major objective, generating an enthusiastic public response, had been achieved. Buyers from all the European countries competed with trade, private and museum bidders from Japan, Hong Kong, Singapore and Taiwan. A group of six major trade buyers from London, looking for stock to sell in Harrods and at exhibitions, ended up with a substantial proportion of the more interesting and decorative pieces.

A relay team of five auctioneers, in two salerooms, took some sixteen hours to sell the 1,011 lots. As the hammer fell on the last one, with the total comfortably over a quite unexpected four million pounds, there was no doubt that this sunken shipwreck had fully 'risen to the occasion'.

A Selection from the Vung Tau Cargo

A Pair of large blue and white Baluster
Vases and Covers
circa 1690
19¼ in. (49 cm.) high
Amsterdam, 7 and 8 April 1992,
Fl.39,100 (£12,257)

Twenty-four blue and white
scalloped-rimmed Saucers
circa 1690
6⅛ in. (15.5 cm.) diameter
Amsterdam, 7 and 8 April 1992,
Fl.27,600 (£8,804)

A *famille rose* part Dinner Service
Qianlong
Amsterdam, 7 and 8 April 1992,
Fl.258,750 (£78,314)

A Pair of large brilliantly-mottled jadeite Peacocks
15 in. (38.1 cm.) high
Hong Kong, 1 October 1991,
H.K.$3,740,000 (£277,715)

A magnificent large white jade Marriage Bowl
Qianlong
12½ in. (31.7 cm.) diameter
Hong Kong, 31 March 1992,
H.K.$4,620,000 (£344,776)

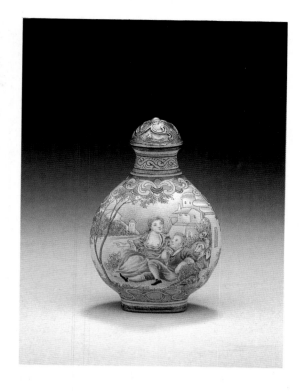

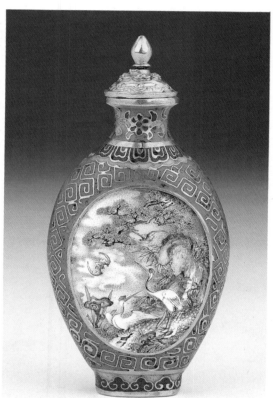

One of a remarkable Pair of massive cinnabar lacquer rectangular
Screens and Stands
18th–19th Century
82 in. × 38 in. (208 cm. × 95 cm.)
Hong Kong, 31 March 1992, H.K.$1,705,000 (£127,049)

A rare Beijing enamel *famille rose* European-subject Bottle
Qianlong blue-enamel four-character mark and of the period
New York, 4 June 1992, $93,500 (£51,743)

An Imperial *cloisonné* and Beijing enamel Snuff Bottle
Qianlong four-character mark and of the period
Hong Kong, 31 March 1992, H.K.$1,045,000 (£77,983)
Record auction price for an enamelled snuff bottle

Opposite:
XIANYU SHU (1256–1301)
Cursive Script Calligraphy (*cao shu*) (detail)
handscroll, ink on paper
$13\frac{5}{8} \times 195\frac{1}{2}$ in. (34.5 × 496.5 cm.)
New York, 2 June 1992, $330,000 (£182,320)

TANG YIN (1470–1523)
Drinking Wine in Spring Wind: from Landscape and Running
Script Calligraphy (*xing shu*)
Handscroll in two sections, ink and colour on paper
$11\frac{3}{4} \times 41\frac{1}{2}$ in. (30 × 105.5 cm.)
New York, 25 November 1991, $792,000 (£440,000)

WEN ZHENGMING (1470–1559)
Double Cypress
handscroll, ink on paper, dated 1535
$10\frac{1}{4} \times 74\frac{3}{4}$ in. (26 × 190 cm.)
New York, 2 June 1992, $242,000 (£133,701)

BADA SHANREN (Zhu Da, 1626–1705)
Bamboo, Rock and Bird; Lotus: from Flowers and Birds
an album of twelve leaves, ink on paper
each leaf $12 \times 10\frac{3}{4}$ in. (30.5 × 27.5 cm.)
New York, 25 November 1991, $605,000 (£336,111)

ZHANG DAQIAN (1899–1983)
Mount Ling Yan
scroll, ink and colour on silk, mounted and framed
$37\frac{1}{4} \times 104\frac{1}{8}$ in. (94.5 × 264.5 cm.)
Hong Kong, 30 September 1991, H.K.$4,290,000 (£320,627)

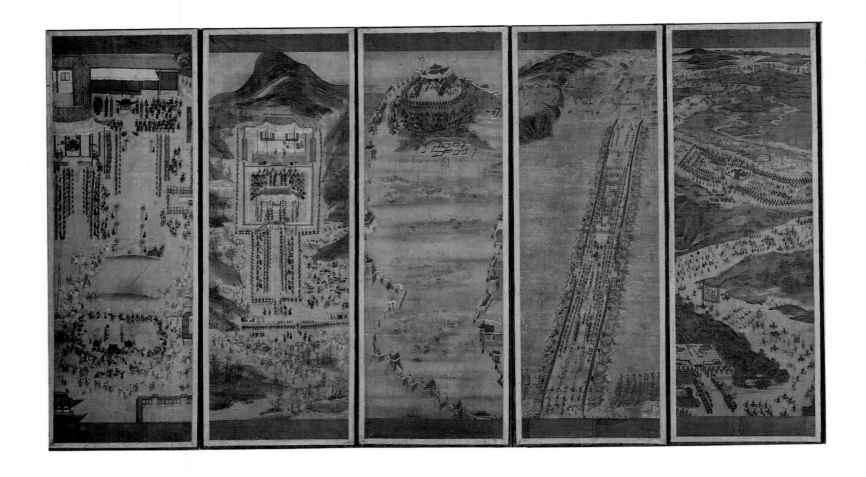

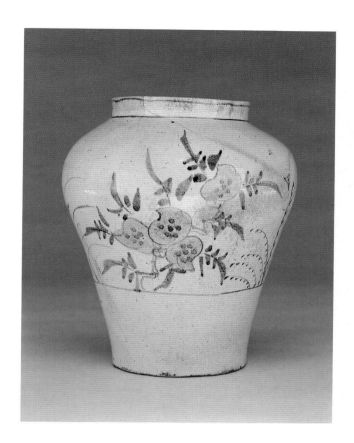

KOREAN SCHOOL, late 18th or early 19th Century
Scenes of Court Ritual (detail)
eight-panel screen, ink and colour on silk
$57\frac{1}{4} \times 20\frac{7}{8}$ in. (145.5 × 53 cm.)
New York, 24 October 1991, $550,000 (£323,529)

A blue and white Vase
Choson period, first half 18th Century
$10\frac{3}{4}$ in. (27.4 cm.) high
New York, 24 October 1991, $385,000 (£226,470)

KOREAN SCHOOL, 19th Century
Shipjangsaeng: The Ten Signs of Long Life (detail)
eight-panel screen, ink and colour on silk
$56\frac{3}{4} \times 158$ in. (144 × 425 cm.)
New York, 24 October 1991, $660,000 (£388,235)

An inlaid lacquer Stationery Box
Choson period, 16th Century
$11\frac{1}{4} \times 17\frac{1}{4} \times 5\frac{1}{4}$ in. (28.6 × 43.8 × 13.3 cm.)
New York, 22 April 1992, $550,000 (£314,285)

JAPANESE ART

One of a Pair of important two-leaf gold lacquer Screens
Meiji period (1863–1912)
each panel $88\frac{5}{8} \times 41$ in. (225 × 104.5 cm.)
London, 18 March 1992, £220,000 ($377,080)

Opposite:
An Export Ewer and Basin
17th Century
gold *hiramakie*, *hirame*, *nashiji*, and *kirigane* on a
black lacquer ground
the ewer $10\frac{1}{4}$ in. (25.5 cm.) high
the basin $21\frac{1}{4}$ in. (53 cm.) diameter
London, 11 November 1991, £104,500 ($183,397)

A Pair of Kakiemon Cockerels
late 17th or early 18th Century
11 in. (28 cm.) high
Sold by the Executors of the 6th Lord Ashburton, K.G., K.C.V.O.
London, 18 March 1992, £58,300 ($99,926)

Top:
JAPANESE SCHOOL, circa Genroku period (1688–1704)
Ise Monogatari: Tales of Ise (illustrated); *Sagoromo Monogatari:* Tale
of Sagoromo; *Hachikazuki:* The Bowl Girl; and *Urashima Taro*
ten volumes
$10\frac{5}{8} \times 7\frac{7}{8}$ in. (27 × 20 cm.)
New York, 23 October 1991, $198,000 (£116,470)

HIROSHIGE (1797–1858)
One from a complete Set of the *Fuji sanjurokkei:* The Thirty-Six
Views of Mount Fuji
signed, woodblock prints, $14\frac{3}{4} \times 10$ in. (37.7 × 25.5 cm.)
New York, 23 October 1991, $60,500 (£35,588)

Above:
TACHIBANA MINKO (active 1764–1772) and
Circle
Kitsune no yomeiri: The Fox's Wedding
woodblock prints
four from a set of six
each approx. 8 × 11 in. (20.5 × 28 cm.)
London, 11 November 1991, £99,000 ($173,745)

SAITO YOSHISHIGE (b. 1904)
Work no. 10
signed and dated 1961
oil on carved board
$71\frac{3}{8} \times 47\frac{5}{8}$ in. (181.4 × 121.1 cm.)
New York, 22 April 1992, $165,000 (£94,555)

THE COMPTON COLLECTION

by Sebastian Izzard

It is a rare occasion when a collection which is recognised to be pre-eminent of its type comes to the marketplace. Dr. Walter Compton bought his first Japanese sword blade in a New York Chinatown laundry for $6.00 at the age of fourteen. From this modest beginning he embarked on a lifelong commitment to the field that resulted in a collection of over one thousand Japanese swords and sword fittings. Along the way he found a stolen National Treasure blade which he gave back to Japan, and he exhibited many of his best pieces at the Japan House gallery in New York, in Japan and in France. Dr. Compton was well acquainted with the leading Japanese sword scholars of the day, Dr. Homma Junji and Dr. Sato Kanzan, who advised him as to the quality of his blades. Acting on their advice he rigorously pruned the collection to ensure that only the finest examples remained. He disposed of the remainder, thus reducing his collection of 750 blades to 380, which were stored in a special vault beneath his home in Elkhart, Indiana.

The news that the Compton Collection was to be offered for sale by Christie's New York caused a furore. Well before it had been catalogued, requests for lists of blades to be offered, estimates, catalogue orders and general enquiries poured into our offices, indicating the widespread international interest in Japanese swords in general and in this collection in particular. This unprecedented response swelled following the series of exhibitions of the collection in Tokyo, London, and Paris.

The first part of the Compton Collection was offered on 31 March in New York. The rooms were packed with buyers from the Far East, from Europe and from all over the United States. Bidding was strong throughout the sale: the previous world record was for a Japanese sword, established at Christie's New York in 1985, was equalled or broken twelve times during the sale. Like the 1985 sword, blades by the Ichimonji group of smiths proved the most popular, and a new world record was set for a Fukuoka Ichimonji *tachi* at $418,000. Shinto and Shinshinto blades also proved keenly sought after, a blade by Inoue Shinkai making $341,000 and one by Masayuki of Musashi $242,000. The total of $7,998,365 achieved for Part I of the Compton Collection, a record for any single owner collection of Japanese art, appears even more remarkable when one considers the difficult world-wide economic situation. Against a backdrop of turmoil in the Tokyo stock market, which saw a substantial drop from the time of our exhibition in Tokyo to the day of sale in New York, we entered the saleroom in a state of slight trepidation. These fears proved unfounded, as is shown by the figures, with Japanese bidders competing strongly among themselves and purchasing well over sixty per cent of the sale.

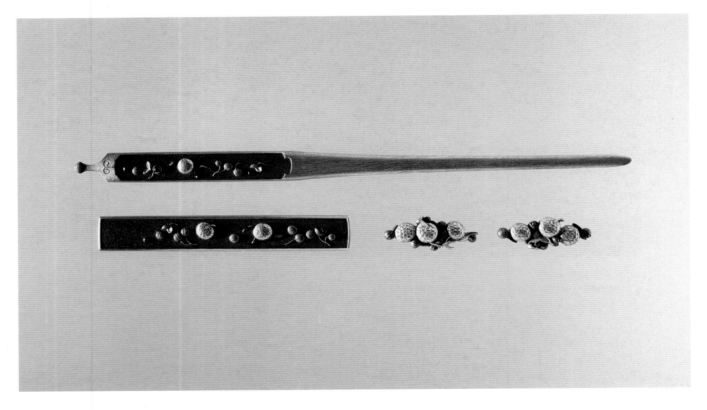

A Goto School *Mitokoromono*
Early Edo Period (circa 1650)
kogai: length $8\frac{1}{2}$ in. (21.4 cm.), width $\frac{1}{2}$ in. (1.2 cm.), thickness $\frac{3}{16}$ in. (5.5 mm.)
kozuka: length $3\frac{7}{8}$ in. (9.6 cm.), width $\frac{9}{16}$ in. (1.4 cm.), thickness $\frac{1}{4}$ in. (6.75 mm.)
menuki: length $1\frac{1}{2}$ in. (3.5 cm.), thickness $\frac{3}{16}$ in. (5.75 mm.)
New York, 31 March 1992, $26,400 (£15,260)

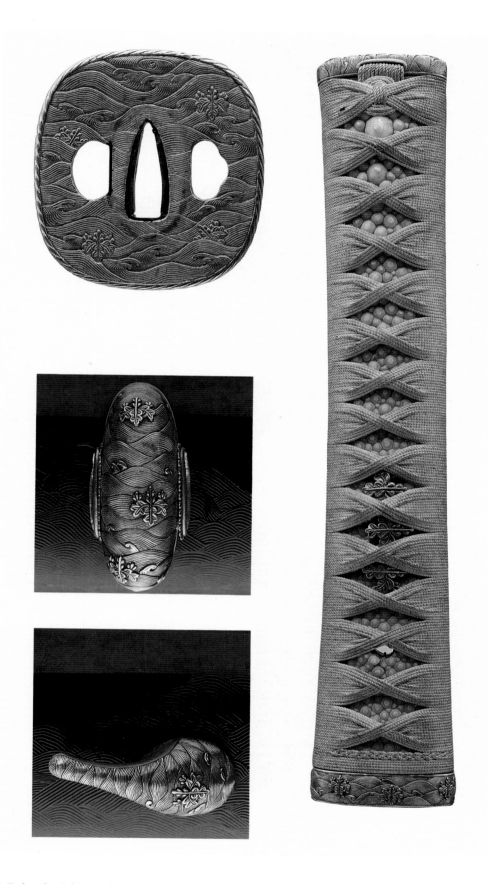

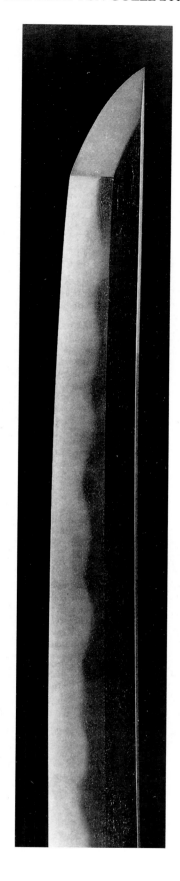

A Fukuoka Ichimonji *Tachi*
Kamakura period (2nd half of the 13th Century)
signed 'Ichi'
27¼ in. (69.3 cm.) long
31 March 1992, $418,000 (£241,618)
Record auction price for a sword

Top:

A Hirata School *Kozuka*

Early Edo period (circa 1625), attributed to Hirata Donin

$3\frac{5}{8}$ in. (9.4 cm.) long

New York, 31 March 1992, $104,500 (£60,580)

Record auction price for a *kozuka* (small auxiliary knife) and any single sword fitting

An Ishiguro School *Tsuba* (front and back)

Edo period (circa 1850), signed 'Ishiguro Masaaki' with *kao*

$2\frac{7}{8}$ in. (7.3 cm.) high × $2\frac{5}{8}$ in. (6.8 cm.) wide

New York, 31 March 1992, $88,000 (£50,867)

Record auction price for a single *tsuba*

A Goto School *Daisho Tsuba* (front and back)

Late Edo period (circa 1866), signed 'Toki Ni Toshi Nanajugo Raku Hakuo Saku' and 'Raku Hoku Kyo Hakuo Saku'

dai $3\frac{1}{4}$ in. (8.2 cm.) long × 3 in. (7.7 cm.) wide

sho $2\frac{7}{8}$ in. (7.5 cm.) long × $2\frac{3}{4}$ in. (6.9 cm.) wide

New York, 31 March 1992, $60,500 (£35,072)

An Osaka Inoue *Katana*
Edo Period, dated the 8th month of 1677, signed 'Inoue Shinkai'
$27\frac{3}{8}$ in. (69.5 cm.) long
New York, 31 March 1992, $341,000 (£197,681)

TRIBAL ART

THE McCARTY-COOPER COLLECTION OF TRIBAL ART

by Hermione Waterfield

William (Billy) McCarty-Cooper brought much joy to many people during his short life, as his multitude of friends will testify, and the sale of his collection of Tribal Art and Antiquities in New York was a joyous occasion. The crowd in the room hummed in happy anticipation as they were seated, and Christopher Burge took the sale at a lively pace, giving as much attention to the lots under $500 as those over $50,000.

Art from Gabon has long been a favourite with collectors and held a special place in Billy's affections. The Fang of that country carve wooden heads and figures to be placed on baskets containing the skull and some bones of revered ancestors, which are kept in household shrines and consulted as occasions arise. An enchanting head reminiscent of the work of Brancusi and Modigliani, which had been sold by the distinguished Parisian dealer Charles Ratton to the pioneer of African art appreciation, James Johnson Sweeney, made three times what it had realised in November 1986. A female figure, also sold by Charles Ratton, astonished those present by the price it realised – the figures from the northern Fang are usually more static in pose than those from the south, but this female had an exceptionally animated expression and could be accounted one of the best from that area. That fire seldom burns in the same place twice might account for the fact that a male figure from the southern Fang realised $110,000 less than when it was the subject for a passionate battle in May 1989 when it realised $660,000.

In Eastern Gabon the Kota cover their highly stylized wooden figures with sheets of copper and brass in a form so admired by Braque that he made a copy in cardboard: it was thought to have perished during the war, but happily emerged from a drawer in a Parisian basement. The group in the sale realised between $11,000 and $165,000. A rare mask for the Ngontang Society of the Fang, depicting a European and of a type so admired by Derain and Vlaminck that they had their example cast in bronze, made $49,500.

Billy enjoyed inviting scholars as well as enthusiasts to dine at Oriole Drive, to share with him his joy in tribal art, and many were kind enough to share their knowledge when we were compiling the catalogue entries. Frederick Lamp sent us proofs of his publication on the Baga, giving the names of the spirits personified in the colourful wooden dance crests and their place in the lives of the people of Guinea. The festivals are still celebrated, but some of the characters no longer participate, such as the powerful female astride a horse, known as *Yombofissa* and generally regarded as a water spirit, which realised $30,800. Her long braided tresses of fibre hung about her shoulders and she showed extensive traces of red paint, a colour used against witchcraft and manifestations of evil, being the colour of fire and therefore repellent to witches. Two bird crests, said to represent pelicans and called *A-Bemp*, flew up to $14,300 and $12,100; the first was painted blue and white, with three smaller birds on its back, the second was of a cubist design, banded in red and blue with a white breast.

For the Genval Kuba king figure, probably representing *Kot a Mbweeky II*, we were able to quote from a letter written to William Fagg by Dr. Albert Maesen, the leading authority on the art of Zaire at the Musée Royal de l'Afrique Centrale, Tervuren (outside Brussels), of whose death we learnt with sadness shortly before the sale.

Billy McCarty-Cooper was intrigued, as was Max Ernst, by the dolls of the Ashanti of Ghana, with their disc-like heads and narrow cylindrical bodies designed to slot into the back of a woman's cloth wrapper. The exact function of the dolls is now lost, but it is generally agreed that they were carved to ensure many healthy children to the possessor. Understandably a great number were carved and used by the Ashanti during the last century, and have since found their way into collections: the prices ranging from $1,760 to $3,080 for the five in the sale were well above expectation. Similarly the prices of between $1,980 and $4,180 for the heddle pulleys, carved to support the warp threads for the looms in West Africa, were all above the top estimates. They were an engaging group carved with bird finials, horned heads and a sinuous creature some believed to represent an elephant, others an aardvark (an African burrowing quadruped). The other surprise from the West African section of the sale was $2,420 for a small brass elephant cast to weigh gold. This device for conveying unspoken messages during the exchange of gold in Ghana and Côte d'Ivoire is thought to have been introduced during the seventeenth century.

The art of Africa formed the major part of the McCarty-Cooper collection but a few Pacific artefacts were selected for their abstract forms. The superb Fijian headrest came from the Melanesian Mission, whose members converted that island and the formidable King Cakobau to Christianity. The long and gentle curve of the cross bar had an enhancing ripple effect which was achieved by binding the live branch and rubbing it with a pebble before it was cut and carved. The background of bark cloth on which it was photographed had been purchased for only a few dollars and amazed the assembled throng by the price it realised. Much barkcloth is still used today in Fiji and Tonga, when chiefs are wrapped in hundreds of yards of the material on ceremonial occasions, but the short lengths in the sale showed signs of wear and were probably from the beginning of this century. A bowl from Wuvulu (Matty Island), conceived in a series of curves resulting in the distinctive form produced only on that island, made $30,800: it bore the label from the last century of the Hamburg dealer Gustav Umlauff.

The signatures and dedications on the fly leaves of the books that made up the first four lots of the sale revealed the interest that Douglas Cooper had in tribal art: he was hoping to arrange, with Paul Guillaume, an exhibition entitled 'Confrontations', which would have explored similar themes to those pursued in the 1984 exhibition at the Museum of Modern Art in New York.

Far left:
A Fang female Reliquary
Figure
Ntumu of Northern Gabon,
late 19th Century
wood with brass panel
$21\frac{5}{8}$ in. (55 cm.) high
New York, 19 May 1992,
$440,000 (£240,437)

Left:
A Fang Head
Betsi of Gabon,
late 19th Century
wood
$11\frac{1}{8}$ in. (28.2 cm.) high
New York, 19 May 1992,
$352,000 (£192,349)

A Fiji Headrest
19th Century
wood, coconut fibre
$25\frac{1}{2}$ in. (65 cm.) long
New York, 19 May 1992,
$77,000 (£42,076)

Two Lengths of Fiji bark
Cloth
$135\frac{1}{2} \times 25\frac{1}{4}$ in. (344 × 64 cm.)
and $74\frac{3}{4} \times 44\frac{1}{2}$ in.
(190 × 113 cm.)
New York, 19 May 1992,
$2,090 (£1,142)

An Ubangi slit Drum
Northern Zaire, first quarter, 20th Century
wood
98¾ in. (251 cm.) long
London, 23 June 1992, £82,500 ($153,285)
Bought by the National Museum of African Art,
Smithsonian Institute, Washington, D.C.

A Group of Seminole Beadwork
Southeastern United States, mid-19th Century
the pouch and sash of glass beads on cloth
the moccasins of glass beads on skin
London, 23 June 1992, £34,100 ($63,357)

A Songye Prestige Stool
Zaire, first quarter, 20th Century
wood with brass panel
$25\frac{1}{4}$ in. (64 cm.) high
London, 3 December 1991, £121,000 ($208,000)
Bought by the Art Institute of Chicago

This piece was acquired in Lusambo, central Zaire, in 1924 by Mr and Mrs Schepens. The stool is one of a small group believed to be by the same master carver. Of the eleven stools which can be attributed to his hand only one other has a single male figure support, seven having female supports, and two double figure supports.

PRINTED BOOKS AND MANUSCRIPTS
THE LIVERPOOL COPY OF THE 36-LINE BIBLE

by Felix de Marez Oyens

For centuries the invention of printing has occupied the minds and fancies of historians and antiquarians, bibliographers and book collectors. This interest has not been limited to a coterie of specialists; scholars of every feather and almost any member of the general reading public seem to have formed an idea of the circumstances shrouding the origin of the black art. The event is frequently described as momentous and *clichés* abound. In the last hundred years or so important but widely scattered work has been done on the subject, mostly published in German or English in scholarly journals of limited circulation. Although a large amount of both raw and refined materials is therefore available, a modern comprehensive study remains to be written. In any discussion of the invention and early development of typography towers the figure of Johann Gutenberg of Mainz. He may well form the best argument against the schools of thought that preach the inevitability of historical events and their independence from the individual men and women who prominently figure in them. In spite of his various associations Gutenberg appears to stand on his own; intellectual, political and social history would unquestionably have run a different course without him.

Full-length biographies of the inventor do intermittently appear, but none deserves to become a classic or even standard. Oddly, our knowledge of Gutenberg and his early rivals is very limited and imprecise, while their productions can be rather more fruitfully studied. The importance of the invention of printing is often mentioned in the same breath as that of those two other great European discoveries (or rediscoveries) of the late Middle Ages and early Renaissance, gunpowder and America. In the common consciousness Columbus's discovery far outdistances the other two, but all three conspired to change the world.

On 27 November 1991 any thunder that could be heard during a sale in Christie's Great Room had nothing to do with gunpowder, but a few connoisseurs will have had both Gutenberg and Columbus on their mind when the auctioneer knocked down the last lot. The sale of the 36-line Bible (B36) took place in St. James's, but before describing it one should perhaps recall earlier rounds of Gutenbergian sales at Christie's on Park Avenue. On 7 April 1978 the Offenburg Church of the Holy Cross – Syston Park – William Makellar – Eugene Augustus Hoffman – New York General Theological Seminary copy of the 42-line Bible (B42) was sold for $2,200,000; it is now located at the Württembergische Landesbibliothek in Stuttgart. On 22 October 1987 the Gosford – Amherst of Hackney – Dyson Perrins – Philip Frere – Estelle Doheny copy of volume 1 only of the same edition of the Vulgate sold for $5,390,000 to the Maruzen Co. of Tokyo. Both sales established new auction-record prices for a printed book, and the latter stands to this day. It is of course entirely appropriate that the first substantial printed book should also be the most expensive. Ever since the eighteenth century when B42 was recognized as the 'Gutenberg Bible', collectors of early printed books have considered it the greatest prize, and long is the roll of European and American bibliophiles who have battled for

it in the salerooms, or sent agents to exploit the many bouts of political upheaval on the Continent and the concomitant secularizations of monasteries. Until our own time there has been a steady enough trickle of supply to keep the appetite of the most ambitious collectors and librarians whetted. (A total of 48 copies survives, and in 1978 alone – *annus mirabilis* of modern Gutenberg lore – three copies were on the New York market!)

To bibliophiles B36 is the only incunable to have exercised the same kind of legendary appeal as B42. It already formed the subject of a bibliographical monograph in 1760: Johann Georg Schellhorn the elder, *De Antiquissima Latinorum Bibliorum Editione ceu primo artis typographicae foetu*. For the next 130 years the two Bible editions vied for priority until Göttingen University librarian, Karl Dziatzko, proved beyond any doubt that B36 was reprinted from B42; contemporary manuscript use of its paper stocks was found within the diocese of Bamberg rather than Mainz and dated from the late rather than the early or mid-1450s. Christie's catalogue argued at length that B36 was printed by Albrecht Pfister in Bamberg and not by Gutenberg. Its type-fount is a late manifestation of the so-called Donatus-Kalender type (DK type), which had been developed through various castings by Gutenberg in Mainz no later than the B42 fount. Pfister's compositors showed close familiarity with the complicated Gutenbergian type-system by consistently selecting the correct 'abutting' and 'non-abutting' sorts, and it is highly probable that one or more journeymen accompanied the removal of DK materials from Mainz to Bamberg.

The edition size of B36 may have been less than half that of B42 as its intended market was geographically more limited (Franconian and Bavarian religious houses as opposed to those from the Upper Rhine to the Thames). Thus B36 is today much rarer both in institutional libraries and in private hands than B42; only 15 copies in varying states of completeness are extant. Not since 1789, when the Maffeo Pinelli copy of volume 2 was sold in London for 14 guineas to Sir George Shuckburgh, had any copy or even a substantial fragment appeared at auction. In 1814 Shuckburgh's son-in-law, Charles Jenkinson, later 3rd Earl of Liverpool, exchanged his copy for most of the Würzburg *Schottenkloster* set in the unmatched collection of incunabula formed by the 2nd Earl Spencer. It is this book, the Würzburg 'Scottish' Benedictine Monastery of St. James the Great – Spencer – Liverpool copy of the 36-line Bible, that was offered as the last lot in Christie's Autumn sale of *Highly Important Early Printed Books and Illuminated Manuscripts*.

The incunable fetched £1,100,000 and was knocked down to the American booksellers, H. P. Kraus. It is unknown what books Columbus took along on his voyages to the New World – his Bible would have been of small format – but tens of thousands of incunables have crossed the Atlantic since, including over a dozen copies of the Gutenberg Bible. (A printing press was established in Mexico less than fifty years after the Spanish first set foot on the continent.) However, the Liverpool B36 is the first copy of this

pographical monument to enter an American collec-
on. It is now preserved at the Scheide Library in
rinceton, and a more appropriate destination on either
le of the Atlantic does not exist. It is shelved near the
rfurt *Predigerkirche* – Brinley copy of B42 (the second
py of the Gutenberg Bible to have made the crossing),
e unique Latin Calixtus Bull of 1456, the 31-line
dulgence, the unique bifolium of the 33-line Donatus
inted by Gutenberg and Fust *circa* 1453–54, the 1457
d 1459 Mainz Psalters, the third issue of the Mainz
atholicon, a complete set of all incunable editions of the
ble in German, a remarkable run of 11 incunable
itons of the Bible in Italian, the Subiaco Lactantius, the
oligno Dante, an uncut copy of the Aldine Aristotle, at
ast 4 Caxtons (including the first illustrated English
inted book), two blockbooks, as well as two exceed-
gly important Anglo-Saxon manuscripts including the
lebrated Blickling Homilies; the library also contains
nong many other treasures an eighteenth-century
ock-printed Buddhist charm, colonial and Revolu-
onary printed Americana including the Declaration of
dependence, and autograph music by Bach and
eethoven.

The taste and technique of three generations of
heides have formed what is now in several respects the
nest private book collection in the world. The history of
s formation has been described in Julian P. Boyd, *The
heide Library* (Privately printed 1947) and in a special
sue of *The Princeton University Library Chronicle*
XXVII, Winter 1976, no. 2). The purchase of the
6-line Bible by the present owner of the library, William
urd Scheide, is an exciting new chapter in this history.

BIBLIA LATINA. [Bamberg: Printer of the 36-line Bible (Albrecht
Pfister), circa 1459–60 (not after 1461)]. Royal 2° (39.5 x 28 cm.)
Folio 75/9 (*recto*)
London, 27 November 1991, £1,100,000 ($1,927,200)

Book of Hours, use of Utrecht, Haarlem and
Zwolle, circa 1470–80
illuminated manuscript on vellum, 165 leaves,
41 three- and four-line initials, 8 larger initials,
and 7 fine full-page miniatures by the Masters
of the Zwolle Bible, bound in contemporary
blind-stamped calf over wooden boards
$7\frac{5}{8} \times 5\frac{5}{8}$ in. (19.5 × 14.3 cm.)
Sold by the Heirs of Edward F. Searles and
Benjamin Allen Rowland of Massachusetts
London, 24 June 1992, £143,000 ($265,694)

A fine example of regional division in the
production of an illuminated Book of Hours in
the northern and eastern Netherlands; the
manuscript was written in Haarlem, its
miniatures commissioned from Zwolle.

Jacobus de Cessolis (active late 13th–
early 14th Century), *De Ludo Scachorum*,
Strassburg, Heinrich Knoblochtzer,
1 September 1483
chancery folio and royal quarto, with
woodcut illustrations
Sold from the Dr. Robert Blass Library
South Kensington, 8 May 1992,
£19,800 ($35,660)

Heldenbuch, Strassburg, Johann Prüss, circa 1480
chancery folio, 163 woodcuts repeated to 230
impressions, in a contemporary Westphalian
binding
London, 27 November 1991,
£352,000 ($623,040)

The extremely rare first edition of this highly
important body of thirteenth-century German epic
poetry, its recension based on the mid-fifteenth-
century manuscript *Strassburger Heldenbuch* from the
workshop of Diebolt Lauber. The woodcuts are
among the finest work of the early Strassburg
school. Only eight other copies are recorded.

A NAUTICAL LIBRARY: THE DUPONT COLLECTION

by Nina Musinsky

On 8 October 1991 the Pierre S. duPont III collection of Navigation, Cartography and Literature of the Sea was sold at Christie's New York. A senior executive of the DuPont Co. and a great-great-grandson of its founder, duPont, who died in 1988, was a retiring man who shunned publicity in spite of his position on the boards of several major charities and as father of a governor and Presidential candidate. The sale of his library thus came as a surprise to many in the book world, who were unaware of the existence of this unusually coherent and imaginative collection.

Not since the early seventies had a major library with a maritime focus come on the market. The Boies Penrose collection and part of Harrison D. Horblit's collection, sold in London in 1971 and 1974, were both broad in scope, encompassing general travel and exploration, trade, and early science, while the Scott Library from the Royal Institution of Naval Architects, sold at Christie's in 1974, was more narrowly focused on the technical aspects of navigation and naval architecture. DuPont, a devoted sailor, had taken a different course, forming his collection around the specific yet wide-ranging theme of the ocean voyage, which enabled him to appropriately include in it not only rare classics of the voyages of discovery (principally to the Americas), but also nineteenth-century novels of the sea, pilot books and maritime atlases, rare seventeenth and eighteenth-century pamphlets on pirates, and early navigational treatises. Most of these were purchased in the fifties, and copies of many of the rarer items had not appeared at auction since.

Comprising 330 books in 255 lots, the collection sold for a total of $2,310,154 to a variety of international bidders, with a strong showing by the European and particularly the French trade, attracted by an interesting group of rare early French works of exploration. These included fine copies of both the first and second editions of Champlain's *Voyages* (1613 and 1632), which sold respectively for $99,000 and for $52,800. The 1590 French translation of Waghenaer's *Spieghel der Zeevaerdt*, the first French edition of the first printed pilot book to incorporate sea charts, had not appeared at auction for at least 60 years; the duPont copy fetched $40,700. An abridged translation of Peter Martyr's first three *Decades*, entitled *Extraict ou Recueil des Isles nouvellement trouvees..*(1532), and the first collection of voyages printed in French, was another rarity that fetched a strong price at $48,400. A copy of the more common first English edition (1555), prettily bound in eighteenth-century red morocco, did nearly as well, more than doubling a conservative estimate of $12,000–18,000, at $46,200.

Another very interesting French translation of an English voyage was *Le Voyage de l'Illustre Seigneur et Chevalier François Drach* (ie., Drake), printed in 1627 and containing what is probably the earliest map showing Drake's circumnavigation of the globe ($71,500). This was one of a small group of Drake items that included the star lot of the sale, a magnificent set of Baptista Boazio's five hand-coloured engraved maps and view-plans illustrating Drake's West Indian voyage and four towns that were victims of his raids. The set was originally published to accompany

Walter Bigges and Master Croftes' *Summarie and true discourse of Sir Francis Drake's West Indian Voyage* (London, 1589; the Leiden 1588 Latin edition, the preceding lot, fetched $8,800), and has been called 'the most interesting and important published graphic work pertaining to Drake and his career' (H.P.Kraus, *Sir Francis Drake, a Pictorial Biography*, Amsterdam, 1970). Although the history of these maps remains to be fully elucidated, their beauty, rarity, and importance (the view of St. Augustine is the earliest known engraving of any locality now part of the United States) were widely appreciated, and the set, estimated at $70,000–90,000, sold for $231,000.

The most complete set of the de Brys' *Great and Small Voyages* to appear at auction in New York or London since 1945, and which duPont had purchased from Henry Stevens (the great compiler of de Bry sets), fetched the second highest price of the sale, at $154,000.

The collector's success in locating landmarks of the cartographical documentation of the New World was evident in his selection of pilot books and sea charts. A copy of the first edition of *The English Pilot, The Fourth Book* (1689), containing the first important series of charts of the North American coast to be published in England, was the first copy of this edition to appear at auction in half a century; it fetched $39,600. An equally scarce pilot's guide by the cartographer William Gerard de Brahm, *The Atlantic Pilot* (1772), containing the first published charts showing the currents of the Gulf Stream, and of which only two or three copies are known, sold for $8,800. A very fine set of Braddock Mead's six-sheet *Chart of North and South America* (1753), which with its separately issued descriptive text constituted the most authoritative account at the time of the early discoveries on the Northwest Coast, doubled the high estimate at $13,200. The duPont collection also included a printed statement submitted to the British Government by Joseph F.W. Desbarres, author of *The Atlantic Neptune* (1774–9), claiming arrears for expenses he incurred during his survey of the North American coast; a unique copy with extensive annotations by the author, it sold for $14,300. Notwithstanding these and other outstanding examples, such as a fine copy of the 1513 edition of Ptolemy's *Geographie* ($77,000), books of cartographical interest did not dominate the duPont collection, but were rather a natural expression of the unifying historical theme. The multiplicity of links of each book to the rest of the collection accounted for the strong prices fetched not only by the many rare items but also by such fairly common books as the first and second editions of Exquemelin's *Bucaniers* (both 1684–5), which sold for respectively $2,860 and $1,760, or for the success of a series of contemporary accounts of the perpetrations of notorious pirates. Taken individually, many of the books in the duPont collection were of relatively obscure interest; but in the context of other volumes, their intrinsic value was recognised. This mutual enrichment is the true mark of a *collection* in the fullest sense of the word, endowing its parts with the lasting aura of a distinguished provenance.

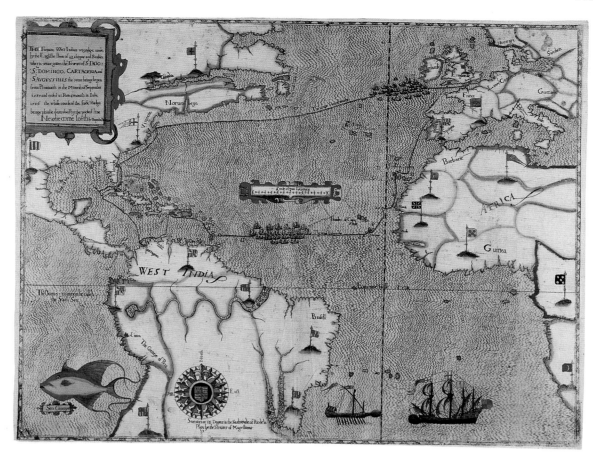

Baptista Boazio (Italian, active1588–1606), Five hand-coloured engraved Maps to illustrate *Sir Francis Drake's A summarie and true discorse of Voyage to the West Indies*, published in Leiden in 1588 and in London in 1589, comprising a map of Drake's voyage, and plans of Santiago on Cape Verde Island, Santo Domingo in Hispaniola, Cartagena de Indias and St. Augustine in Florida, each approximately $16\frac{5}{8} \times 21\frac{5}{8}$ in. (42.2×55.7 cm.)
New York, 8 October 1991, $231,000 (£134,302)

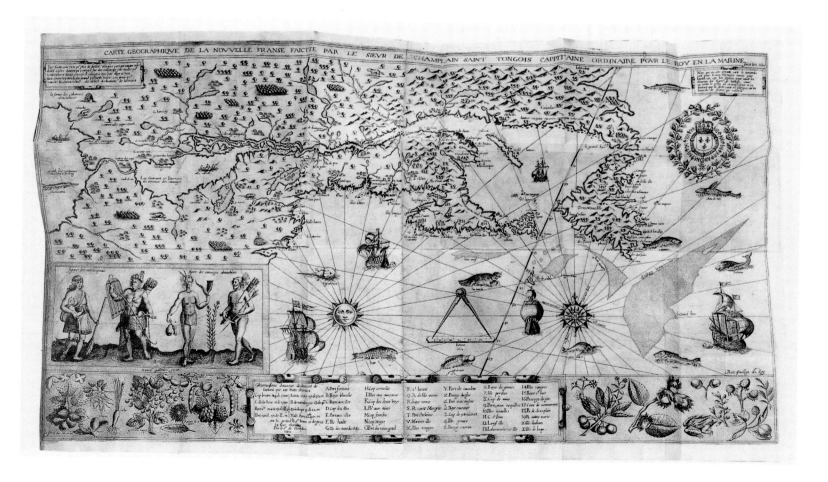

Samuel de Champlain (French, d. 1635), *Les Voyages du Sieur de Champlain Xaintongeois, Capitaine ordinaire pour le Roy, en la marine.*
Divisez en deux livres. Ou, Journal tres-fidele des observations faites és descouvertures de la Nouvelle France, Paris, 1613
first edition, with the rare folding map 'carte geographique de la nouvelle Franse', quarto, contemporary limp vellum
New York, 8 October 1991, $99,000 (£57,558)

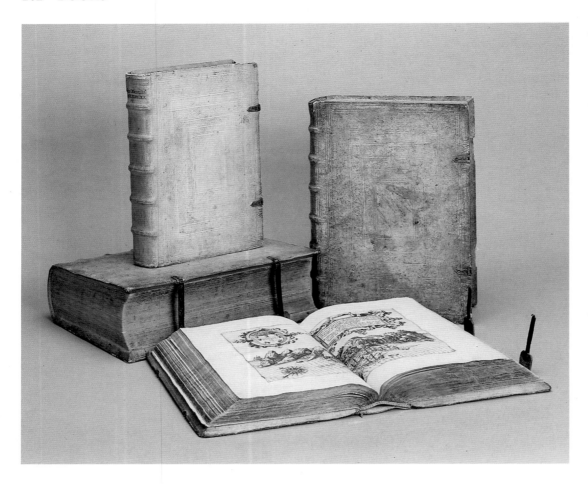

Johann Theodor and Johann Israel de Bry, [The Great and Small Voyages], text in Latin, Frankfurt and Oppenheim, 1590–1624
Parts I–XII only (of 15) of the Great Voyages, bound in two volumes, parts I–X only (of 14) of the Small Voyages, bound in two volumes, folio, contemporary blind-stamped pigskin over wooden boards
London, 31 October 1991,
£143,000 ($228,800)

Johannes Blaeu, *Atlas Maior sive cosmographia blaviana*, first edition in Latin, Amsterdam, J. Blaeu, 1662
11 volumes, folio, 594 engraved maps and plans finely coloured by hand, contemporary vellum
Rome, 10 December 1991,
L.218,500,000 (£101,533)
Record auction price for a printed book sold in Italy

Species Lilij crüenh. Goldgilgen.
52

Pseudoacorus. Gelb wasser gilgen.

gold Gilgen

wasser: Gilgen:

Joachim Camerarius, the younger (German, 1534–1598), Manuscript Florilegium, Nuremberg, circa 1589
473 drawings of ornamental plants, arranged seasonally for the most part, watercolour and bodycolour, on 194 leaves, each approximately $14\frac{3}{8} \times 9\frac{3}{8}$ in. (36.5 × 24.5 cm.), bound in 18th Century mottled calf
London, 20 May 1992, £638,000 ($1,161,160)

One of the earliest and most magnificent pictorial records of flowers in a sixteenth-century garden, this is of importance for its connection with the greatest German garden of the period, that of Prince-Bishop Johann Conrad von Gemmingen at Eichstätt, which was designed and supervised by Camerarius.

NUMIDA VULTURINA; (Hardw.)

Opposite:
John James Audubon (1785–1851), *The Birds of America; from Original Drawings*, London, published by the author, 1827–38 four volumes, double elephant folio, engraved titles with 435 hand-coloured etchings with aquatint engraving by William Home Lizars of Edinburgh, Robert Havell Sr. and Robert Havell Jr. of London, after Audubon's original life-size watercolours, the University of Edinburgh's original subscriber's copy
New York, 24 April 1992, $4,070,000 (£2,279,200)
Record auction price for any illustrated book and for any printed Americanum

Audubon wrote in his journal on 7 December 1826: 'Received a short note from Professor Jameson desiring that I should put the University of Edinburgh [down]as a subscriber for my work. I was highly pleased with this, [it] being a powerful leader'. The University is shown as number 9 on Audubon's final list of European subscribers published in 1839. With an edition size approaching 200 copies (Audubon's final list of all subscribers totals 161), *The Birds of America* appears on the market quite frequently. Indeed, since 1973, sixteen copies have been sold, although eleven of these were sold on a sheet-by-sheet basis and are now dispersed. There are two distinguishing features of the University of Edinburgh's copy. One is its binding: the plates are arranged by families and not by the numerical and chronological sequence in which they were published. This arrangement has allowed the traditional first plates from each volume (Turkey cock, Raven, Canada Goose and canvas-backed Duck) to remain in especially fine condition. It is one of only five sets in existence today to have been bound in this order and Christie's commissioned the rebacking by Aquarius, over the original boards and sewing, in order to emphasise the importance of the book as a whole, rather than as a collection of plates. The other feature is the overall condition of the book: it is an exceptionally fine copy with the plates in superb, vividly coloured impressions

and showing remarkably little evidence of handling. The purchaser, a private collector (who also bought the University's set of Gould's works), has the satisfaction of joining an elite group of eleven private individual owners of copies of *The Birds of America*. Only two of these eleven copies, both in England, remain in the families of the original subscribers.

Above:
John Gould (1804–1881), [A Set of fourteen Works on Ornithology], London, published by the Author, 1831–88 44 bound volumes and 9 original fascicles, large folio, 3242 hand-coloured lithographed plates by John and Elizabeth Gould, Edward Lear, W. Hart, H.C. Richter and Joseph Wolf, the University of Edinburgh's subscriber's set
New York, 24 April 1992, $880,000 (£492,800)

YÁKOTLÚS – QUATSINO

Edward S. Curtis, *The North American Indian being a series of*
Volumes picturing and describing the Indians of the United States and
Alaska ... edited by Frederick Webb Hodge, New York, 1907–30
40 volumes, quarto and large folio, the 20 portfolios containing
723 photogravures in sepia, a mixed set, with most of the
photogravures in the rarest state printed on Japanese tissue,
limited edition, number 147 of 500 proposed sets, of which
probably only 272 sets were produced
New York, 5 December 1991, $198,000 (£110,614)

Jean Cocteau (1889–1963), an unpublished autograph
Manuscript containing numerous notes and reflexions on
different themes, with eight original drawings, 43 pages quarto,
circa 1929–30, in half-cloth binding with sketches by the author
and entitled 'Opium'
Geneva, 18 November 1991, S.Fr.165,000 (£65,218)

Riviere & Son, binders
Alexis François Artaud de Montor, *The Lives and Times of the
Popes*, New York, The Catholic Publication Society of America,
1910–11, bound circa 1925
Seventeen volumes comprising fifteen volumes of text and two
boxes, extra-illustrated with 304 letters and documents from
pontiffs, kings, regents and other historical figures plus 1077
portraits of popes, bound in red levant morocco, lavishly gilt with
variously coloured onlays, each cover with a representation of the
Virgin and papal arms and the monogram of Cardinal Mundelein,
and set with four garnets and four chalcedonies
New York, 5 December 1991, $99,000 (£55,649)

THE SPIRO COLLECTION OF AMERICAN HISTORICAL LETTERS AND DOCUMENTS

by Chris Coover

The collecting of American historical manuscripts, which has become such an active area in recent years, is more venerable than might be expected. Jared Sparks (1789–1866), the first editor of the writings of George Washington, is usually credited with being the first serious collector of such documents. In the course of his research the historian corresponded with members of Washington's family, his political associates and surviving officers of the Continental Army who had served under him. Many original letters and papers were loaned to Sparks. Some he returned, but others, like Washington's 64-page holograph draft of his discarded first inaugural address (1789), he kept (in this case, at least, Sparks apparently had the approval of Washington's descendants). Today, only twelve leaves and a handful of fragments of this important manuscript are extant; virtually all are known to have been given away by Sparks as mementos of the first President. A typical leaf (pages 57–8) bearing Sparks' characteristic manuscript label made $82,500 in the sale of the collection of Mr. & Mrs. Harry Spiro on 14 May 1992. Since Sparks' day, the letters of American Presidents have been actively collected by many. Good or bad, capable or incompetent, the holders of this office serve as archetypes of the national character for Americans.

The Spiro Collection was relatively small, comprising only 143 lots and containing not quite 200 pieces, and had been brought together solely by purchase at auction in a comparatively brief period, starting in the 1978 dispersal at Sotheby Parke Bernet of the extensive manuscript collection of the late Philip D. Sang of Chicago. The Spiros were unusually fastidious in matters of condition (which Sang was not), and they wisely concentrated on letters of significant political, diplomatic or military content. Even relatively minor historical figures, therefore, were represented by extremely important letters. A letter of John Hay, President Lincoln's private secretary, for example, anticipated the public announcement of the Emancipation Proclamation by two months. This remarkable letter sold for a record $24,200; more modest letters of Hay are often available for as little as $500. The Spiros' selectivity was amply rewarded when the sale in which their collection was offered achieved the best results of any such auction in the last decade, totalling nearly $3 million. Startling price records were set for letters of a host of historical figures including George Washington ($137,500 for a letter dated July 1776), Benjamin Franklin ($44,000), John Quincy Adams ($10,450 for a letter on a British-American naval controversy, the *Chesapeake-Leopard* incident), Jefferson Davis ($34,200 for his last pay voucher as President of the Confederate States of America), Harriet Beecher Stowe ($17,600 for a letter presenting a copy of *Uncle Tom's Cabin* to Prince Albert and Queen Victoria), and John Adams ($209,000 for an extraordinary letter describing his first interview as Minister to Great Britain with King George III).

The documents in the Spiro Collection ranged from the Colonial period (notably a superlatively rare autograph letter of Roger Williams, founder of Rhode Island, regarding captives held by the Indian tribes, $28,600), to the modern era (a 1951 letter of

Congressman J. F. Kennedy), but its especial strengths were in letters and documents of the period of the American Revolution, 1775–83, and the Civil War of 1861–5. In addition to several important Washington manuscripts the collection featured a fine letter of General Benedict Arnold, a military genius who ably served the American cause early in the conflict but became disillusioned and turned traitor. In his letter of July 1780 Arnold alluded provocatively to his being offered command of the garrison and forts at West Point on the Hudson, which stronghold he was on the verge of betraying to British General Sir Henry Clinton: a scant two months later the chance capture of Major John André by pickets exposed the plot ($12,100). Sir Henry Clinton's original parchment commisson as Major General, signed by George III, was present ($4,400), as were letters of Admiral Richard Howe and his brother, Sir William Howe and an autograph letter of George III to the Admiral. In addition, the Spiros amassed no fewer than five manuscripts or letters of John Hancock, one of them jointly signed by Hancock and the Boston brewer and patriot Samuel Adams.

The chief political adversaries of the Civil War, Abraham Lincoln and Confederate President Jefferson Davis, were strongly represented, as were the military commanders of the North and South, Generals Ulysses S. Grant and Robert E. Lee. Five letters of Lincoln's were included, notably one dated 6 November 1862 to General Butler in New Orleans inquiring meaningfully for details regarding the use of free black labour on the plantations of Union-held Louisiana ($60,500). The most valuable manuscript in the sale, however, was Lincoln's autograph excerpt from his 1863 address to Congress, vowing to uphold the Emancipation Proclamation, which made $462,000 (see details in caption). Perhaps even more remarkable, though, was the extraordinary $409,000 paid for Lincoln's brief (21-word) autograph telegram to General Grant in Virginia, in which the President, having just perceived Grant's bold tactical plan to shift the entire Union army to a new front, informs him: 'Have just read your despatch of 1 p.m. yesterday. I begin to see it. You will succeed. God bless you.'

One of the most celebrated naval actions of the Civil War was the triumph of Rear Admiral David G. Farragut in successfully running the gauntlet with his squadron between two strong Confederate forts on the lower Mississippi, thereby seizing the port and city of New Orleans, effectively splitting the Confederacy along the line of the Mississippi. The Spiro Collection contained Farragut's own hand-drawn battle-plan and a list of ships in the squadron, which was the object of very spirited bidding and finally brought a record $44,000. Several good Grant letters of war date were offered; one, in which the Union commander peremptorily orders a dilatory General to 'take Mobile [Alabama]and hold it', sold for $33,000, a record for any Grant letter.

The short-lived Confederate States of America were represented by some fine manuscripts, especially President Jefferson Davis's graceful letter to Queen Victoria (whom he addressed as 'great and good friend') introducing James M. Mason, newly appointed Confederate Minister to Great Britain. When Mason and a compatriot, John Slidell, Minister to France, embarked for Europe on a British packet, the *Trent*, in November 1861, the ship was detained on the high seas by an over-zealous Union naval commander and Mason and Slidell were removed and incarcerated, precipitating one of the most rancorous and dangerous diplomatic crises between Great Britain and the United States since the War of 1812. In the end Lincoln's Secretary of State, William H. Seward, wisely ordered the two diplomats to be released, averting the threat of hostilities.

Robert E. Lee remains the enduring symbol of the lost Confederate cause, and the value of his letters has at least quadrupled in the last few years. The Spiro Collection boasted some fine examples. One, proclaiming a day of fasting and prayer for the army in penance for the disastrous defeats at Vicksburg and Gettysburg, containing the striking phrase, 'the defenders of a just cause should be pure,' and stating that 'we have relied too much on our arms for the achievement of our independence,' provoked frenzied bidding. Although estimated at $5,000 to $7,000, it was finally sold for an astonishing $52,800. Another letter of Lee's purchased at Christie's in 1980 for a modest $1,760, giving instructions for the mustering of the first Virginia regiments in the Spring of 1861, fetched $41,800, attesting to the exceptional rise of interest in this area in the intervening twelve years.

From left:

Abraham Lincoln (1809–1865), an autograph Quotation from his Address to Congress, 8 December 1863, vowing not to 'retract or modify the Emancipation Proclamation on 19 September, to take effect on 1 January 1864. It freed all slaves in the states and territories in rebellion against the Federal government; only with the passage of the 13th Amendment to the Constitution (ratified in December 1865) was slavery completely eradicated.
New York, 14 May 1992, $462,000 (£253,846)

George Washington (1732–1799), an autograph Letter signed to Benjamin Franklin, New York, July 1776, regarding the U.S. Continental Congress' official response to the belated peace initiatives of Sir William Howe and Admiral Sir Richard Howe. The Congress had adopted the Declaration of Independence the same month as this letter, which Washington left undated, which is believed to have been written on or shortly before 30 July, confirming that Franklin's official reply to Howe had been forwarded to the Admiral on board his flagship *Eagle*, anchored off Staten Island. Less than a month later hostilities between Great Britain and the former colonies erupted in the Battle of Long Island.
New York, 14 May 1992, $137,500 (£75,549)

Franz Schubert (1797–1828), a working autograph Manuscript signed and dated of the Quartet B Flat Major (no. 8), Deutsch no. 112, Opus 168, black ink with numerous corrections and erasure 36 pages, oblong quarto, $9\frac{1}{4} \times 12\frac{1}{2}$ in. (23.5 × 32 cm.), Vienna, 5–13 September 1814
London, 24 June 1992,
£297,000 ($551,826)

Published only posthumously in 1862, this quartet was given its public performance at the *Musikvereinsaal* on 23 February 1862 by the Josef Hellmesberger quartet

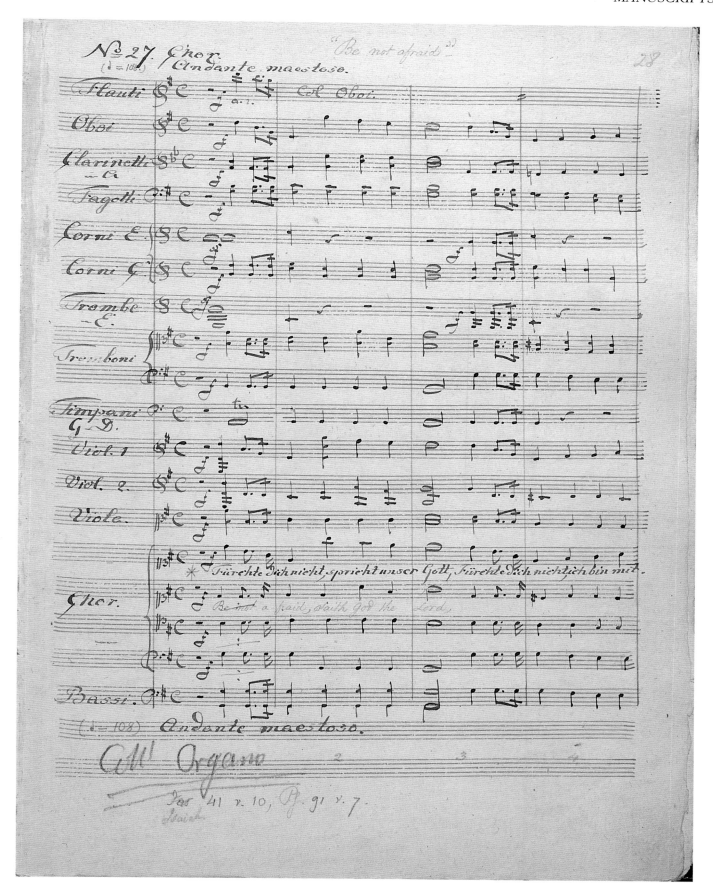

Opposite:
Heinrich Heine (1797–1856), 'Sie schifften wohl über das salzige
Meer', an autograph manuscript Draft with numerous deletions
and alterations to the poem, written in ink, 13 pages, quarto,
$10\frac{1}{4} \times 9$ in. (26.2 × 22.5 cm.)
Sold from the Gottschalk Collection
London, 16 December 1991, £22,000 ($39,820)

A hitherto unknown draft with numerous variants of a poem
based on the Brothers Grimm's *Die treue Braut* (The True Bride),
a ballad translated from mediaeval Danish heroic verse

Above:
Felix Mendelssohn Bartholdy (1809–1847), *Elijah*, a manuscript
full Score written by the copyist Eduard Henschke, with over
200 autograph annotations by the composer, with notes by the
translator William Bartholomew, and performing notes by the
organist Henry Gauntlett, over 500 pages, folio, $13 \times 9\frac{3}{4}$ in.
(32.6 × 24.6 cm.), Leipzig, London and Birmingham, 1846
London, 16 December 1991, £107,800 ($195,118)

The score used by the organist for the first public performance of
the oratorio at Birmingham on 26 August 1846

PHOTOGRAPHS

EDWARD S. CURTIS (American, 1868–1954)
Chief Joseph, Nez Percé
toned platinum print on heavy paper, 1903
$16\frac{5}{8} \times 13\frac{1}{4}$ in. (42 × 33 cm.)
New York, 15 April 1992, $26,400 (£15,000)

Only one or two examples of this unpublished image
are known to exist.

Opposite:
GUSTAVE LE GRAY (French, 1820–1882)
The Great Wave, Sète
albumen print from two negatives, 1856–9
$12\frac{3}{8} \times 15\frac{1}{2}$ in. (31 × 39 cm.)
London, 31 October 1991, £18,700 ($31,042)

PAUL STRAND (American, 1890–1976)
Venice
platinum print, 1911
$9\frac{1}{2} \times 12\frac{1}{2}$ in. (24 × 31.5 cm.)
New York, 15 April 1992, $55,000 (£31,250)

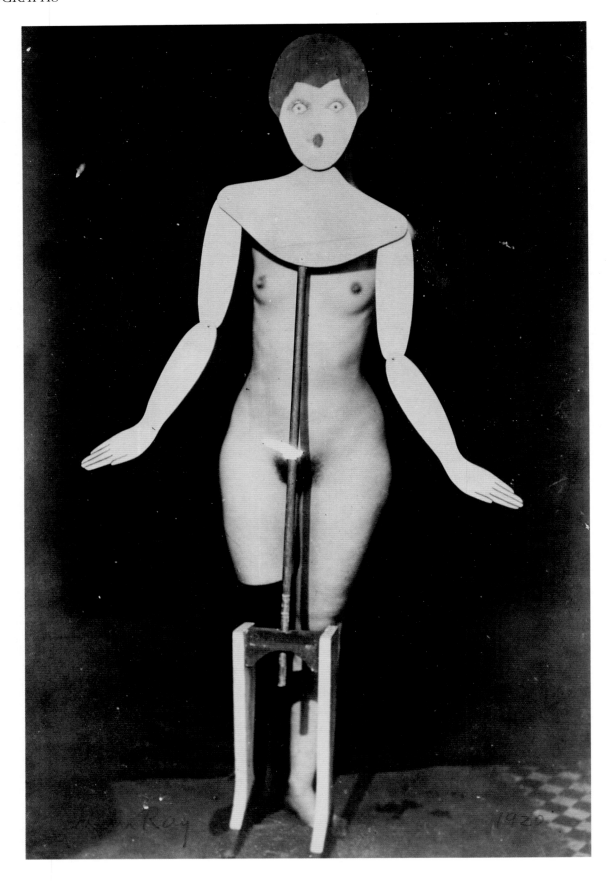

MAN RAY (American, 1890–1976)
Portmanteau (Coat Stand)
gelatin silver print, 1920
$9\frac{1}{4} \times 6$ in. (23.5 × 15 cm.)
New York, 10 October 1991, $66,000 (£38,596)

CONSTANTIN BRANCUSI
(Romanian, 1876–1957)
Leda
gelatin silver print, 1923
$6\frac{5}{8} \times 8\frac{7}{8}$ in. (16.7 × 22.5 cm.)
New York, 15 April 1992, $30,800 (£17,500)

HERBERT BAYER (American, 1900–1985)
In Search of Times Past
mixed media photocollage of gelatin silver prints, half-tone
elements, hand-applied gouache and black ink, 1959
$9\frac{1}{2} \times 13\frac{3}{8}$ in. (24 × 34 cm.)
New York, 15 April 1992, $121,000 (£68,750)
Record auction price for a work by the artist

The reverse of Flying Officer Manser's Victoria Cross

Above:
A rare late Elizabethan Lesser George of the Order of the Garter enamelled gold with 24 hog-back cut diamonds and a pendant pearl
$2\frac{3}{4} \times 1\frac{1}{2}$ in. (7 × 3.9 cm.)
London, 21 October 1991, £72,600 ($124,218)
Record auction price for a piece of British insignia

This was formerly in the collections of Alfred de Rothschild and Robert Lehman

Left:
The 'Thousand Bomber' Raid Victoria Cross, awarded posthumously to Flying Officer L. T. Manser, No. 50 Squadron, Royal Air Force, 21 October 1942
London, 24 April 1992, £57,200 ($100,614)

This Victoria Cross was awarded for 'determination and valour of the highest order' displayed by Flying Officer Manser during the mass raid on Cologne on the night of 30 May 1942. Despite his Manchester aircraft being hit even before reaching his objective, Flying Officer Manser managed to control the aircraft under heavy defensive ground fire and reach his target, dispose of his bomb load and start the journey home. During this the aircraft was hit several times 'and when a crash was inevitable, Flying Officer Manser ordered the crew to bale out.... While the crew were descending to safety they saw the aircraft still carrying their gallant captain plunge to earth and burst into flames.' (*London Gazette*, 23 October 1942)

The City of London Freedom Box and Large Naval Gold Medal for the Battle of St. Vincent, 1797, awarded to Vice-Admiral William Waldegrave, 1st Baron Radstock London, 20 November 1991, £115,500 and £28,600 ($197,620 and $47,908)

The gold and enamel Freedom Box, by James Morisset (hallmarked for London, 1797–8), is inscribed on the inside cover '...that the Thanks of this court be given to Vice Admiral the Hon. Willm. Waldegrave ... for gallant behaviour on the 18th of February last in defeating the Spanish fleet....' The only other time a Freedom Box and Naval Gold Medal have appeared together at auction was at Christie's in 1895 when the Medals and Awards to Rear Admiral Lord Nelson were sold. Nelson's box for St. Vincent sold for £1,050

Upper left, from top:
A Roman gold Aureus of Numerian (Emperor 283–4 A.D.)
(enlarged)
New York, 9 December 1991, $33,000 (£18,262)

A Roman gold Aureus of Magna Urbica (enlarged)
New York, 9 December 1991, $30,800 (£17,045)

This Aureus was struck to celebrate Magna Urbica's marriage in
283 A.D. to the Emperor Carinus.

Centre:
A Roman gold Aureus of Clodius Albinus (enlarged)
(Caesar 193–5 A.D., and Emperor 195–7 A.D.)
New York, 9 December 1991, $137,500 (£76,093)

Upper right, from top:
An extremely fine United States of America Half Cent of 1794
(enlarged)
London, 18 February 1992, £39,600 ($69,181)

This example of one of the United States' earliest coins, was one
of a group of coins collected at the end of the eighteenth century,
from the mint at Philadelphia, by an ancestor of the vendor.

A 'Georgia Gold Rush' 2½ Dollar gold coin struck by Mr
Templeton Reid, Milledgeville, Georgia, 1830 (enlarged)
New York, 13 September 1991, $19,250 (£11,617)

North America's first 'gold-rush' was to Southern Apalachia after
gold was found in Georgia and North Carolina as early as 1799.
Mr Reid made gold coins for a period of only about four months,
during which he produced some 1,500 pieces with face values of
$10, $5, and $2½. Most were melted down and about two dozen
are known today.

Above:
A gold Bar recovered from the *Nuestra Señora de las Maravillas*
approximately 9¼ × 1⅛ in. (23.5 × 2.8 cm.)
24¼ oz. (757.1 gr.)
London, 28 May 1992, £11,550 ($20,662)

A gold Bar recovered from the *Nuestra Señora de las Maravillas*
approximately 8 × 11.8 in. (20.3 × 2.9 cm.)
22 oz. (688.7 gr.)
London, 28 May 1992, £11,000 ($19,679)

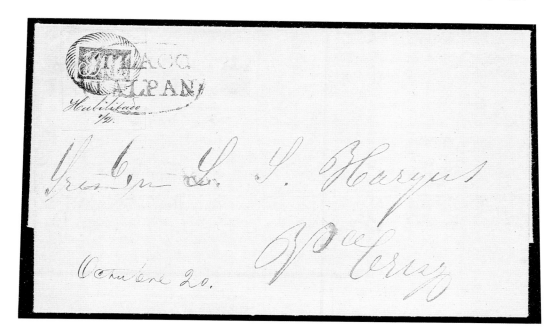

Mexico, 1856
The Tlacotalpan provisional $\frac{1}{2}$ real
black on cover
New York, 12 June 1992,
$110,000 (£59,459)

United States, 1893
The $5 Columbian plate number
and imprint block of six
New York, 25 September 1991,
$104,500 (£60,509)

United States, 1860
The only known Pony Express
Cover addressed to Abraham
Lincoln bearing the 'Running
Pony' handstamp
New York, 29 October 1991,
$154,000 (£91,124)

Top left:
Transvaal, 1870
A block of four of the 6d. ultramarine,
including a tête-bêche pair
London, 25 February 1992,
£13,200 ($22,994)

Top right:
Rhodesia, 1910–3
'Double Head' 1d. block of eight, giving
four pairs imperforate between
New York, 11 March 1992,
$52,800 (£28,711)

Middle:
South Australia, 1855
A unique used Block of 21 6d.
London, 3 June 1992,
£13,200 ($23,839)

Right:
Austrian Levant/Malta, 1857
An entire Letter from Australind,
Western Australia, to Malta showing the
extremely rare example of the oval
'Agenzia del Lloyd Austriaco/Malta'
handstamp
Zurich, 18 June 1992,
S.Fr.112,500 (£42,710)

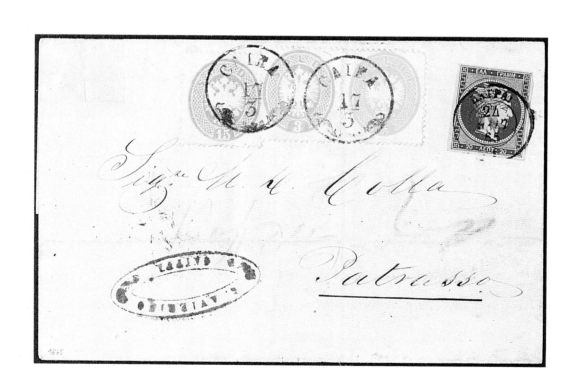

Above:
British Consular Post Offices in Siam,
1882–5
Overprinted 'B' and surcharged 'TWO
CENTS' on 32c., a corner block
comprising surcharge triplets
London, 19 September 1991,
£17,600 ($29,128)

Top right:
Great Britain, 1912–22
The 1d. tête-bêche pair
London, 7 May 1992,
£50,820 ($90,866)

Middle:
Chile, 1855
A Cover bearing two pairs of the 1854
5 centavos deep chocolate,
Gillet Printing
Zurich, 5 December 1991,
S.Fr.60,750 (£24,088)

Right:
Holy Land, 1865
An entire Letter from Caifa to Patras via
Smyrna, a rare usage of Austrian Levant
in combination with Greece, Large
Hermes Head
Zurich, 18 June 1992,
S.Fr.40,500 (£15,375)

MUSICAL INSTRUMENTS

ANTONIO STRADIVARI (Italian, 1644–1737)
A Violoncello, the Bonjour
Cremona, circa 1690
length of back 30 in. (76.3 cm.)
Sold by Robert Cohen, Esq.
London, 18 March 1992, £605,000 ($1,034,550)

GIOVANNI BATTISTA GUADAGNINI (Italian, circa
1711–1786)
A Violoncello, the Davidov
Turin, 1780
length of back $28\frac{1}{16}$ in. (71.2 cm.)
Sold from the Estate of the late Joseph di Tullio
London, 6 November 1991, £154,000 ($271,040)

ANTONIO STRADIVARI (Italian, 1644–1737)
A Violin, the Schreiber
Cremona, 1712
length of back $14\frac{1}{16}$ in. (35.8 cm.)
Sold by the David Lloyd Kreeger Foundation, Washington,
D.C.
London, 18 March 1992, £352,000 ($601,920)

PETER J. BRESSAN (British, 1663–1731)
A Pair of stained boxwood treble (alto) Recorders
London
lengths 20 in. (50.8 cm.) and $19\frac{15}{16}$ in. (50.7 cm.)
in their original box
London, 3 July 1992, £25,300 ($48,070)

Top, from left:
PIERRE FOUCHER
A rare and early French gold, enamel and diamond-set
Watch (back and front)
Paris, circa 1660
$2\frac{1}{4}$ in. (5.3 cm.) diameter
Geneva, 20 November 1991, S.Fr.792,000 (£314,286)

HUAUD LE PUISNE (1655–1723) (Case),
HOENDSHKER (Movement)
An enamelled gold verge Watch, finely painted with
Roman Charity after Simon Vouet
Dresden
$1\frac{1}{2}$ in. (4 cm.) diameter
New York, 28 October 1991, $38,500 (£22,647)

Above, from left:
GOUNOUILHOU
A gold and enamel double musical minute
repeating automaton Watch with Alarm
circa 1820
$2\frac{1}{2}$ in. (6.3 cm.) diameter
Geneva, 20 May 1992, S.Fr.121,000 (£45,660)

Manner of PHILIPPE DU BOIS
An 18 carat gold quarter repeating automaton cheeping bird
Watch with two monkey jacquemarts
circa 1790
$2\frac{5}{8}$ in. (6.55 cm.) diameter
Geneva, 20 May 1992, S.Fr. 165,000 (£62,264)

Top, from left:

PATEK PHILIPPE & CO.

An 18 carat pink gold perpetual calendar chronograph
Wristwatch with moonphases, No. 867241
Geneva, circa 1948, 1¾ in. (3.5 cm.) diameter
Geneva, 20 May 1992, S.Fr.143,000 (£53,962)

ROLEX

A steel antimagnetic split-second chronograph
Wristwatch, from a limited edition of 12
1940s, 1¾ in. (4.3 cm.) diameter
London, 2 October 1991, £27,500 ($47,850)

CARTIER

An 18 carat gold minute repeating perpetual calendar Pasha
Wristwatch
1½ in. (3.7 cm.) diameter,
London, 8 May 1992, £35,200 ($63,043)

Above, from left:

CHARLES FRODSHAM

A gold openface minute repeating split-second Chronograph
with one-minute Tourbillon, No. 09849
London, 1920, 2½ in. (6.4 cm.) diameter,
New York, 28 October 1991, $176,000 (£103,529)

AUDEMARS PIGUET

A platinum minute repeating Wristwatch with diamonds
and sapphires, No. 30828
circa 1925, 3⅜ in. (3.6 cm.) long
Geneva, 20 November 1991, S.Fr.165,000 (£65,477)

PATEK PHILIPPE & CO.

An 18 carat gold minute repeating, perpetual calendar,
moonphases and split-second chronograph Watch, No. 174149
Geneva, circa 1965, 2¼ in. (5.7 cm.) diameter,
Geneva, 20 November 1991, S.Fr.209,000 (£82,957)

SCHLOSS DYCK AND ITS ARMOURY

by Peter Hawkins

Schloss Dyck, near Düsseldorf in north-west Germany, dates mainly from the middle of the seventeenth century, although a castle existed on the site as early as 1094. In 1656 Ernst Salentin, Altgraf (*Comes Antiquus*) zu Salm-Reifferscheidt-Dyck, founder of the branch of the family that still owns it, began the major rebuilding programme that was to culminate in the beautiful baroque 'water-castle' that exists today. He was also the founder of the armoury, although a number of pieces date from before his time, and were presumably part of an earlier family collection.

Like most German castles Schloss Dyck had a *Gewehrkammer* containing personal arms of the family and the equipment of their retainers, as well as sporting weapons that were lent to guests, and curiosities and works of art more appropriate to a *Kunstkammer* than to the chase. Most of the inherited German family armouries which survived into the present century were dispersed between the wars, notably the outstanding collection of the Grand-Dukes of Saxe-Weimar at Ettersburg Castle in 1927. Even the Royal Armouries at Dresden and the collection of the Princes of Liechtenstein were reduced by successive disposals. Only one has been offered at auction since World War II: the smaller and less important *Gewehrkammer* of the Counts von Giech which was sold in London in 1974. At Schloss Dyck the armoury survived virtually intact probably from the seventeenth century, and certainly since the nineteenth century, with the exception of only one pair of pistols, sold in 1953. In all it comprised some 700 pieces, including nearly 200 wheel-lock firearms. The armoury was augmented by all Ernst Salentin's successors, but principally by his son Franz Ernst (1659–1727) and the latter's great-grandson Josef (1773–1861). The second of these was, among other things, a distinguished botanist and author, the founder with Thomas Blaikie of a celebrated park with gardens at Dyck, and a Prince of the French Empire from 1804, and of Prussia from 1816. His son, Alfred (1811–88), was responsible in 1877 for having the armoury arranged in the nineteenth-century manner with all but the best pieces displayed as wall-trophies along with game-heads and antlers. In 1906 his successor commissioned a catalogue from Max von Ehrenthal, the distinguished curator of the Saxon Royal Armoury at Dresden.

The arrangement of the armoury was retained until the outbreak of World War II, when its contents were stored in a mine for safe keeping. In 1961 a complete restoration of the whole building, damaged during the war, was begun on the instructions of the late Princess Cecilie zu Salm-Reifferscheidt-Dyck. The armoury, in which she showed a particular interest, was then arranged in a contemporary fashion and opened to the public on a regular basis in 1967.

Divided for sale in London into two parts, the collection has been dispersed to enthusiasts in the United States, the United Kingdom and the Continent of Europe.

Most of the outstanding pieces were to be found among the firearms, where the strength of the collection lay, and mainly in the sporting guns and rifles. In line with the local princely taste for the pursuit of fur rather than feather, the rifles far outnumbered the guns, and it was appropriate that the highest price of all be reserved for the wheel-lock rifle of *circa* 1680 stocked by Johann Michael Maucher of Schwäbisch-Gmünd, and that it should be acquired by the museum in the town of its origin. The figure of £137,500 establishes a new auction record for any European firearm at auction. Though now one of the most famous of all the German gunstockers, Maucher was also celebrated in his time for carving figures, vases and decorative objects of all kinds in ivory and wood, as confirmed by the inclusion in his signature on the rifle of 'Sculptor (*Bildhauer*) and Gunstocker', in that order. Of the thirty or so surviving examples of Maucher's work as a gunstocker, the vast majority are now in public collections.

Of the flintlock longarms, the most attractive and interesting was probably the double fowling-piece of *circa* 1820, made at Dyck in the Parisian manner for Prince Josef, by his personal gunsmith Pierre Greverath. Prince Josef had been married to a French wife since 1803, and had between 1800 and 1820 spent each winter in Paris. However it is highly unusual for a German princely family to have retained their own court gunmaker at so late a date, rather than ordering first-rate guns from Paris or London. Helped by its direct links with the family history, Prince Josef's gun made £27,500, and was the most expensive among the interesting group of firearms by local makers not found elsewhere.

In the pistol section the honours went to a pair of flintlock pistols of *circa* 1650, by Felix Werder, goldsmith gunmaker of Zurich, with characteristic gilt-brass barrels, locks and mounts, but unique in his *oeuvre* by virtue of being double-barrelled. Restrained only by their condition, the pistols reached £63,800.

The total for the first part of the Dyck armoury was £1,052,040 ($1,847,382), already surpassing the previous record for a European *Gewehrkammer* at auction.

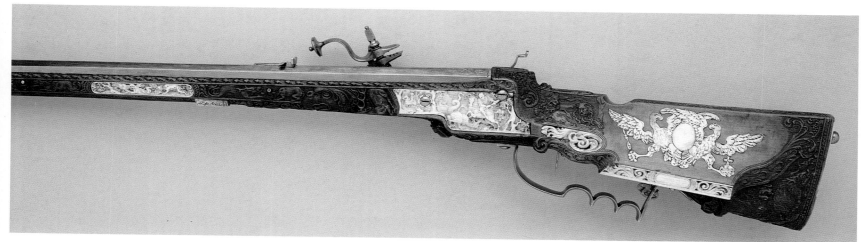

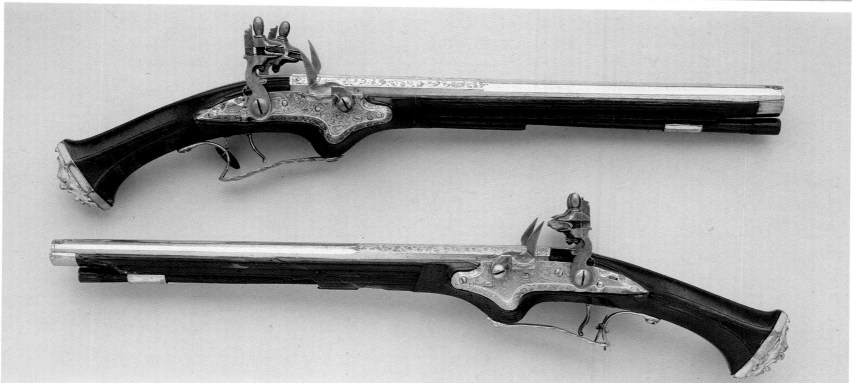

Top:
JOHANN MICHAEL MAUCHER (German, 1645–1701)
An important wheel-lock Sporting Rifle
Schwäbisch-Gmünd, circa 1680
$30\frac{1}{4}$ in. (77.5 cm.) barrel
London, 15 April 1992, £137,500 ($240,572)
Record auction price for a European firearm
Middle:
FELIX WERDER (Swiss, 1591–1673)
An important Pair of Swiss d.b. single-trigger flintlock Pistols
Zurich, circa 1650
20 in. (51 cm.)
London, 15 April 1992, £63,800 ($112,032)

Above:
PIERRE GREVERATH (German, 1750–1828)
A fine German d.b. flintlock Fowling-piece
Dyck, circa 1820
$34\frac{3}{4}$ in. (88.8 cm.) barrels
London, 15 April 1992, £27,500 ($48,290)

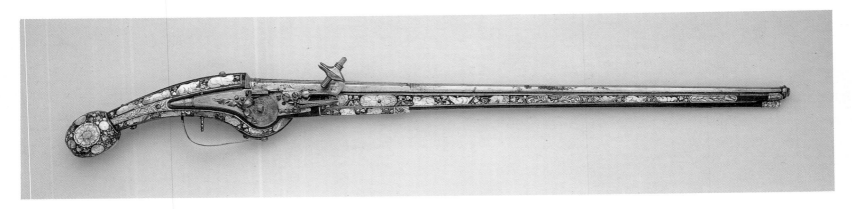

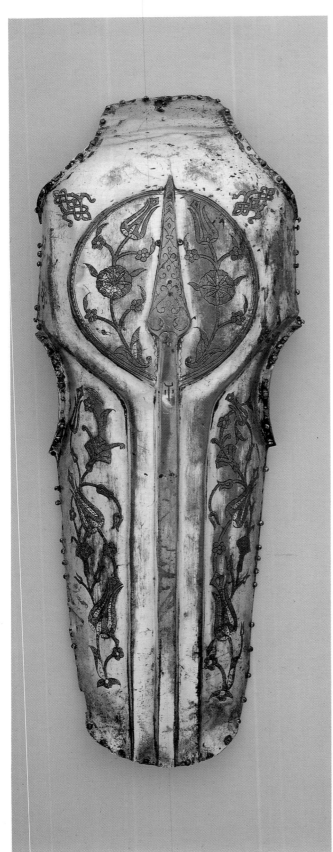

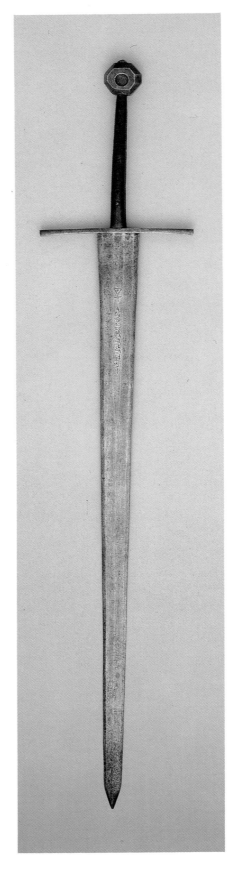

A French long wheel-lock holster
Pistol
circa 1600–10
32¾ in. (83.2 cm.)
London, 20 November 1991,
£30,800 ($55,070)

An Ottoman gilt-copper Chanfron
second half of the 16th Century
23 in. (58.8 cm.)
London, 20 November 1991,
£71,500 ($118,690)

An Italian Medieval Sword
early 14th Century
33¾ in. (83.8 cm.) blade
London, 20 November 1991,
£30,800 ($51,128)

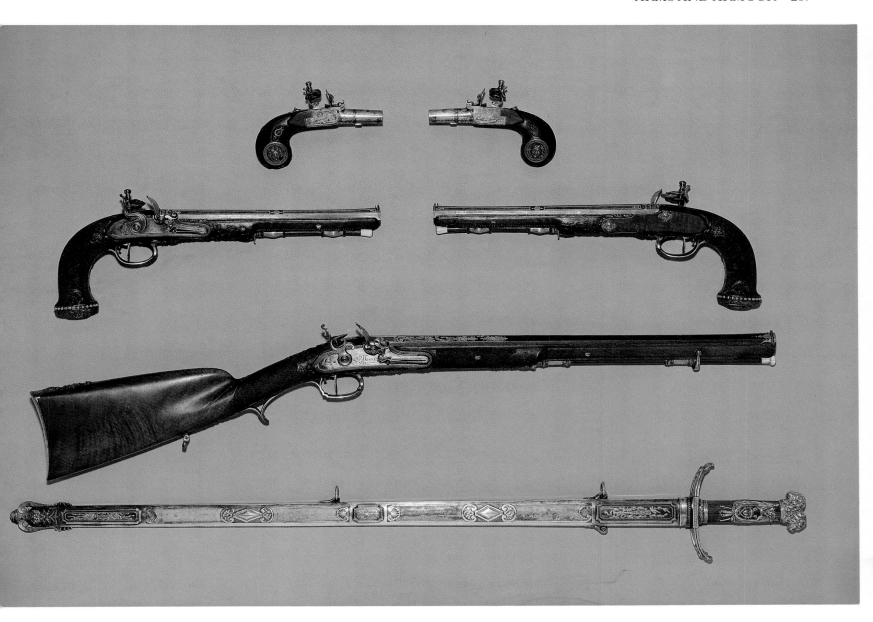

NICOLAS-NOËL BOUTET (French, c.1761–1833)

A Garniture of Flintlock Firearms and a Sword, presented to Napoleon in 1797, comprising a pair of pocket pistols, a pair of rifled carriage pistols, a rifled carbine, their accessories including a signed silver-mounted horn flask, and a dress sword, Versailles

pocket pistols 6¼ in. (16 cm.)
carriage pistols 16 in. (40.5 cm.)
rifled carbine, barrel 19½ in. (49 cm.)
sword blade 30 in. (76.5 cm.)
London, 20 November 1991, £114,500 ($191,730)

When this garniture was exhibited by T. Gwenapp at the Oplotheca Exhibition in 1816, its history was recorded as follows:

> Presented to Napoleon by the Directory of the French Republic in 1797 as a testimony of their approbation in consequence of his beating the Austrians and Sardinians, and forcing the King of Sardinia into a hasty peace. The Sword is the one Bonaparte carried in his hand when he drove the Council of Five Hundred out of St. Cloud, and became in consequence First Consul.

> When Bonaparte was made Emperor, he gave the case as a present to Marshall Junot, Duke of Abrantes, with whom it remained until his death. The Duchess of Abrantes having remained faithful to Louis XVIII, on the return of Napoleon from Elba, the latter deprived her of her pension. The Duchess being an extravagant woman, was, during Napoleon's short reign, obliged to part with a number of precious and scarce things, and amongst the rest, this case of arms, given by Napoleon to her husband. It was purchased by an officer then in the command of the French Emperor, and after the battle of Waterloo was brought to this country.

The garniture was acquired by Robert, 3rd Lord Clonbrock in 1833.

HOLLAND & HOLLAND
A matched Pair of 12-bore (2¾ in.) 'Modele de Luxe Self-Opener' sidelock ejector Guns, No. 40000/40537 (40000A)
London, circa 1976
London, 6 November 1991,
£28,600 ($50,364)

J. PURDEY
A Pair of ·410 (3 in.) self-opening sidelock ejector Guns, No. 28323/4
London, circa 1980
Sold from the collection of the late Sir Joseph Nickerson
London, 6 November 1991,
£37,400 ($65,861)

BOSS
A Pair of lightweight 12-bore round-body single-trigger self-opening sidelock ejector Guns, No. 8599/600
London, circa 1938
Sold by Lady Mairi Bury, J.P.
London, 6 November 1991,
£33,000 ($58,113)

HOLLAND & HOLLAND
A Pair of 12-bore (2¾ in.) 'Game Conservancy Royal Self-Opener' sidelock ejector Guns, No. 40500/1
London, circa 1979
London, 15 July 1992,
£29,700 ($56,608)

HOLLAND & HOLLAND
A lightweight 12-bore (2 in.)
single-trigger 'Royal Centenary
Self-Opener' sidelock ejector
Gun, No. 33226
London, circa 1937
London, 15 July 1992,
£8,250 ($15,724)

HOLLAND & HOLLAND
A 12-bore 'Royal Self-Opener'
sidelock ejector Gun,
No. 30776
London, circa 1928
London, 15 July 1992,
£9,020 ($17,192)

J. DICKSON
A 12-bore assisted-opening
round-action ejector Gun,
No. 6187
London, circa 1909
Sold by Simon Boyd, Esq.
London, 16 November 1991,
£8,800 ($15,496)

PURDEY
A Kelly-engraved 12-bore
2¾ in.) self-opening sidelock
ejector Gun, No. 28855
London, circa 1985
London, 6 November 1991,
£14,850 ($26,150)

THE MURAD III GLOBES

by Tom Lamb

On 30 October 1991 a new world record of £1,023,000 ($1,757,560) was set for a pair of gilt metal globes, made for Sultan Murad III, grandson of Suleiman the Magnificent, and attributed to the workshop of Gerard Mercator, the most important cartographer of the sixteenth century. The success of the sale was due to the research carried out by some ten specialists in varying disciplines who contributed to our catalogue.

The story began some nine months previously when the globes arrived at our Scientific Instruments department. Standing 40cm high, on Dutch style stands, with a diameter of 29cm, they were discoloured and stained by tobacco smoke, but remarkably intact, only lacking several screws and two hour circle pointers. Although unsigned, the first clue to their origin lay in the Latin cartouche on the terrestrial globe 'AMURATHES TERTIUS Magni in coelo Dei soly:manus solus omnium regnum mundi rex imperator sultha:nus Turcarum: 1579', and the large flamboyant *tughra* (the sultan's personal cypher) on the celestial, indicating that the globes were dedicated to Sultan Murad III, and bore his cypher.

Jeremy Collins as head of the Scientific Instruments department asked my opinion as a map specialist and together a plan of research was devised. The importance of this remarkable pair of globes was unmistakable; the quality of the engraving was exceptional, the construction magnificent. No Globes of such quality and calibre had been seen on the market in recent times, and these would require detailed research in a variety of disciplines, historical and geographical. The obvious questions posed were, if as the dedication suggested the globes were made for Murad III, who made them and who commissioned them? Unfortunately their history could only be traced back to the late nineteenth century.

Research was initiated on two fronts, working from the evidence of the objects themselves, and on the historical background. The first aspect to be investigated was the engraving, construction and metallurgy of the globes. Professor Gerard Turner of Imperial College, London examined the forms of the horizon circles, and the style and variant forms of the engraving, concluding that both globes were made in a short period as a pair by more than one craftsman. However, the horizon rings were modelled on those on Gerard Mercator's pair of globes of 1541 and 1551. As Gerard Mercator was the greatest cartographer of the sixteenth century, copies of his globes would not be unusual. Further evidence of a connection with Mercator arose from a study of the celestial and geographical images by Dr. Elly Dekker of Leiden University. Dr. Dekker carried out a detailed analysis of the positions of over 1000 stars and their constellation figures. She showed that the constellation figures were modelled on Mercator's printed globe of 1551. However, it was also noted that the star positions were taken not from Mercator but from Schoner's catalogue published in 1551 and 1561. Dr. Dekker's analysis of the geography on the terrestrial globe also provided further important information. It showed that the form of the terrestrial globe was modelled on Mercator's globe of 1541, but the depiction of the coastlines and place names were taken from his world map of 1569. This controversial wall-map was drawn up on Mercator's new projection, and had not been widely circulated by 1579.

Of greater interest was the analysis of the 15 legends used to describe unknown areas around the world. Of these 15 legends, 14 followed the 1569 wall-map: the legend for the area known as 'Beach' for Northern Australia, varied and could only be located on one other map of the period, that published in 1587 by Mercator's second son Rumold. Rumold worked for his father from the 1560s, and with his brother Arnold virtually ran the family business in Duisburg from 1570. This connection suggested that Rumold might have had access to the notes of the construction of this globe. Furthermore the radical north polar depiction seen on the globes and on the 1569 wall-map is only found on one other contemporary image, an engraving of 1574 of Mercator with a similar globe by his friend Frans Hogenberg.

While the evidence of the globes indicated their connection with Mercator's workshop, the question as to who might have commissioned them remained. Research on this angle was carried out by Dr. Julian Raby of the Oxford Institute of Oriental Studies and Priscilla Thomas, consultant with the book department. The late 1570s was a particularly interesting period of diplomatic activity by the Spanish, French and English at the Sublime Porte at Istanbul, and gifts were an essential part of that diplomacy. Available records of gifts in the relevant years did not include any globes. In fact it is likely that if these globes had been a diplomatic gift, the wording of the cartouche would have implied this. A second form of gift arrived from states in the Ottoman sphere of influence, the Ragusans, Wallachians, Transylvanians and Poles who all provided annual tribute, but in no case is there an obvious link with Duisburg. One obvious candidate for such a gift was the Habsburg Court, which from 1547 until 1606 made an annual payment to the Sultan. This amounted to 30,000 ducats annually, the greater part in the form of gold and silver vessels, as well as clocks and automata. Fortunately the archives of the Habsburgs have largely survived in Vienna. Dr. Gottfried Mraz kindly checked the records of *the Turkenverehrung* ('presents') to the Sublime Porte for 1578–82, but again without success. Another source of gifts was Venice. A search through the relevant archives again drew a blank.

This left one final possibility, that the globes had been ordered by the Sultan himself or by someone in his Court for presentation to him. The *tughra* on the celestial globe was remarkably accurate, and no other object of the fifteenth and sixteenth centuries, apart from documents, is known with so large and elaborate a version of the Sultan's personal cypher. An examination of both the dedicatory inscription and the quality of the *tughra* suggests an explanation for their manufacture. The Ottoman *tughra* was the Sultan's personal cypher, used to confirm the legality of documents and mark works of art; however, the arabesque decoration of the *tughra* on this celestial globe is European in inspiration. The quality of the rendering of the Ottoman *tughra* is in direct contrast to the poor form of the Latin inscription, which also lacks the normal ingratiating titles and would not have been prepared by an official secretariat either in Europe or Istanbul.

Why was such a pair of European globes ordered for Murad III and who might have acted on his behalf? On the first question the date on the globes proved important. Murad III succeeded to the Sultanate in 1574, and was encouraged by his Hodja to establish an observatory in the European quarter of Istanbul at Tophane. The building was completed in 1577 and was equipped with the finest instruments, including quadrants, an astrolabe, and large European globes described by Salomon Schweygger in 1578 as being a pair about 5 feet high. The history of this Observatory was, however, short-lived. The Mufti, spurred on by jealousy of the Hodja, issued a *fetwa*, or decree, for the destruction of the

Attributed to the Workshop of GERARD MERCATOR (German, 1512–1594)

The Terrestrial Globe, from a Pair of gilt-metal Globes, bearing the *tughra* and Latin inscriptions of Sultan Murad III probably Duisburg, 1579

$11\frac{5}{8}$ in. (29.6 cm.) diameter; $15\frac{3}{4}$ in. (40 cm.) overall height; 15 in. (38 cm.) overall width

London, 30 October 1991, £1,023,000 ($1,757,560)

Record auction price for a pair of globes

Attributed to the
Workshop of
GERARD MERCATO[R]
(German, 1512–1594)
The Celestial Globe

observatory, and this was demolished by the Jannissaries in the winter of 1579. It is said that all the instruments were destroyed.

A possible intermediary between the Ottoman court and Duisberg was Gabriel Defrens, a multi-lingual dragoman, probably Burgundian, who was employed by the Odabashi, the sultan's personal attendant at the Topkapi Palace. In 1580, the Austrian ambassador, von Sinzendorff wrote to Emperor Rudolf II warning him that Defrens had just left Istanbul for Europe, travelling to Ragusa, Venice, and thence to Augsburg and Nuremberg. His real purpose was espionage, and von Sinzendorff judged him 'an agent most dangerous for Christendom'. As for his ostensible mission, 'he just recently had it made known and recognised that he would buy clocks and suchlike instruments there [Augsburg and Nuremberg] and finally travel towards England'. The report is dated 17 September 1580, but von Sinzendorff makes it clear that Defrens had made the journey before and was well acquainted with the roads. It seems that he

had travelled in 1579 in the retinue of the retiring French envoy, Sebastien de Juye. It is possible that Defrens visited Mercator at Duisburg. Whoever placed the order must have supplied a copy of the *tughra*, and Defrens might well have carried documents with him. We know Defrens wrote French well and Italian: his Latin was only passable (von Sinzendorff seems to imply that his Turkish was no better). This could explain why the Latin inscription lacks the appropriate phrasing of diplomatic protocol. Had the globes reached Istanbul, they would probably have been melted down, like the instruments in the Tophane Observatory.

Thus, by careful research and some good fortune, a case for the attribution of the globes to the workshop of Mercator was made, the interest of Sultan Murad III in such instruments established, and a possible connection between Istanbul and Duisburg suggested. I am sure the present owner will treasure these magnificent globes and perhaps one day a document or letter will be found to shed further light on their history.

Above:
DUDLEY ADAMS (British, 1762–1830)
A Pair of Library Globes
London, 1789
18 in. (46 cm.) diameter; $44\frac{1}{2}$ in. (112 cm.) overall height
London, 20 May 1992, £35,200 ($64,064)

Top right:
J. LANCASTER & SON
A patent ladies Watch Camera
Birmingham, circa 1889
South Kensington, 12 March 1992,
£29,700 ($50,697)
Record auction price for a camera

Right:
A 16 mm. metal-body Lucky Strike cigarette packet
Camera; with a metal-body light meter disguised as an
Ohio Safety match box
circa 1949–1950
South Kensington, 12 March 1992,
£18,700 ($31,920)
One of a collection of over 300 'Spy', subminiature and detective
cameras, which realised £296,043 ($505,331), a record total for an
auction of cameras

THEN AND NOW:
25 YEARS OF COSTUME, TEXTILE AND FAN SALES

by Susan Mayor

On 14 July 1992 Christie's South Kensington celebrated 25 years of costume and textile sales at Christie's with an impressive sale of seventeenth, eighteenth and nineteenth-century costume and needlework. Inevitably it brought back memories of previous outstanding sales in the field; the Wied sale of 1967, the Chanel sale of 1978, the Iklé sale of 1989 and the 1987 sale of seventeeth-century needlework which fetched £1,000,000, still the record in this sphere. But the anniversary sale had triumphs in its own right. An early eighteenth-century Italian petenlair and petticoat embroidered in brightly coloured wools was sold for £16,500: a much simpler chintz open robe fetched the same sum. Other lots included two eighteenth-century printed cotton dresses (£13,200 and £6,820), a black woollen seventeenth-century jacket (£4,180), a seventeenth-century linen glove (£2,860), a little boy's skeleton suit (£1,760), a trained beaded evening dress of about 1912 (£2,640) and a beautiful but stained eighteenth-century embroidered English coverlet (£8,800).

Such items are becoming increasingly rare. 25 years ago fine eighteenth-century costume appeared regularly in sales: now it is unusual to find examples in fresh condition. As a result prices continue to rise. Fans in particular have become increasingly popular, sought avidly by collectors throughout the world.

One group of 47 lots in our anniversary sale stirred memories of the great Warner pattern book sale of 1971. This was a collection of pattern books and designs of Bianchini-Ferrier dating from 1918–1940. Whereas the Warner Archive chiefly comprised eighteenth and nineteenth-century albums of woven silk, the Bianchini-Ferrier volumes contained swatches with designs from the '20s and '30s by Raoul Dufy, Robert Bonfils and Charles Martin for Paul Poiret, Jeanne Lanvin and others. In 1971 bidders for the Warner volumes were all English: in 1992 bidders for the Bianchini albums came from all over the world. Clearly interest in antique textiles has become not only stronger but strikingly international.

One area was not represented in this Anniversary sale. There were none of the royal or ceremonial memorabilia which over the years have aroused such interest: for example King Charles I's nightcap sold in 1983, Prince Rupert of the Rhine's hose and jump sold in 1980, or the Elizabethan Lord Chancellor's bourse, possibly that of Sir Christopher Hatton, which was sold in 1986. Even so, there were more than enough treasures to attract major museum bidders – ten or more from all over the world. After a thousand sales in 25 years the market for costume and textiles continues to thrive.

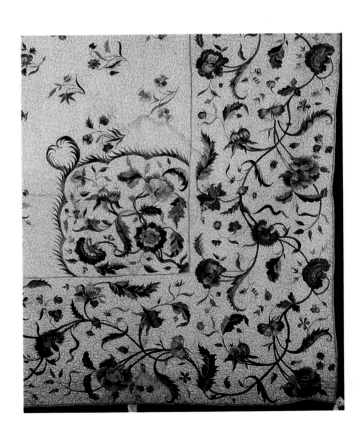

Opposite, from top:
An open Robe *à la polonnaise* of chintz, printed with exotic scrolling flowers in red, blue and purple
English, circa 1780
South Kensington, 14 July 1992,
£16,500 ($31,627)

A Coverlet, embroidered in brightly coloured silks, the whole ground false quilted in yellow silk with a vermicular pattern
English, circa 1730
85 × 74 in. (216 × 188 cm.)
South Kensington, 14 July 1992,
£8,800 ($16,816)

Above:
A rare Petenlair and Petticoat, of fine linen, embroidered in brightly coloured wools with birds, blackamoors and jesters among exotic fruits and flowers, the petticoat worked with four jesters each holding a flower against a landscape with castles
Italian, probably Venetian, circa 1720
South Kensington, 14 July 1992,
£16,500 ($31,531)

Top:
A ballooning Fan, painted with the ascent of Messieurs Charles et
Robert, and two smaller vignettes of balloons
satin
French, 1783
11 in. (28 cm.) diameter
South Kensington, 2 June 1992, £4,620 ($8,362)

Left:
A Chinese Imperial Consort's Robe of yellow silk embroidered
with dragons and five of the twelve symbols of authority
mid 19th Century
South Kensington, 28 April 1992, £11,550 ($20,443)

Right:
LINCOLN BENNETT & CO
Sir Winston Churchill's grey Homburg
initialled in gold 'W.S.C.'
South Kensington, 15 November 1991, £7,260 ($12,813)
Record auction price for an item of Churchill's clothing

Above:
ORRY-KELLY
A Marilyn Monroe sheer black beaded and
sequined Cocktail Dress for the film, *Some Like it
Hot*
1959
New York, 29 June 1992, $38,500 (£20,348)
Record auction price for a Monroe costume

This chiffon cocktail dress was used to particular
effect in the scene from *Some Like it Hot* in which
Monroe, perched atop a piano sings 'I'm through
with love' in the hotel lounge.

Top right:
Michael Jackson's white rhinestone Stage Glove,
encrusted with sparkling hand-sewn imitation
diamonds, the woven label with 'Western Costume
Co. Hollywood' and printed with the name
'Michael Jackson'
South Kensington, 19 December 1991,
£16,500 ($29,997)

Right:
John Lennon's leather Jacket
South Kensington, 7 May 1992,
£24,200 ($43,269)
Record auction price for an item of Beatles'
clothing

This was worn at the start of Lennon's career in
Hamburg and the Cavern Club in Liverpool, *circa*
1960, before the influence of their manager
Brian Epstein caused the 'Fab Four' to smarten up
their image

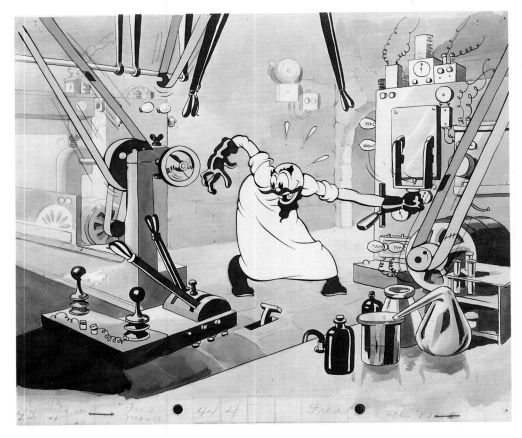

Top:
WALT DISNEY STUDIOS
The Witch's Castle Dungeon
Production Background for the film *Snow White and the Seven Dwarfs*, 1937
watercolour on paper
$11\frac{1}{2} \times 35$ in. (29.2 × 89 cm.)
New York, 27 June 1992, $71,500 (£38,235)

Above, from left:
WALT DISNEY STUDIOS
The Mad Doctor in his Laboratory
Production Background for the film *The Mad Doctor*, 1933
black and white gouache on full celluloid applied to a watercolour
$9\frac{1}{2} \times 11\frac{1}{2}$ in. (24.5 × 29.2 cm.)
South Kensington, 27 April 1992, £10,450 ($18,392)

ORSI (1889–1947)
Poster for *La Revue Nègre*
lithograph in colours, printed by Phogor, Paris, 1925
63 × 48 in. (160 × 122 cm.)
London, 3 June 1992, £7,150 ($12,912)

Above:
A painted tinplate Märklin 4-Volt electric Ocean Liner 'Augusta Victoria', believed to be one of only five in existence, with original detailing including lifeboats, deck winches, companionway ladders and working searchlights
German, circa 1910
46½ in. (118 cm.) long
South Kensington, 21 May 1992,
£41,800 ($76,201)
Record auction price for a European toy

Right:
A Rock and Graner 'O' Gauge armoured Train, modelled after the prototype used in the Boer War
German, circa 1900
South Kensington, 16 December 1992,
£14,850 ($26,108)

A composition-headed clockwork musical Automaton, with
Pierrot serenading the moon
1890
22 in. (56 cm.) high
South Kensington, 12 September 1991, £31,900 ($52,443)
Record auction price for an automaton

As the music plays the moon rolls his brown lashed eyes and
opens and closes his mouth, while Pierrot turns to him, strums his
guitar and nods his head.

Above:

NICOLE FRÈRES
A Grand Format Musical Box, No.32037, playing four overtures
(*Der Freischütz, Robert le Diable, William Tell* and *La Fille du Régiment*)
$28\frac{1}{2}$ in. (72 cm.) wide; cylinder $16\frac{3}{4} \times 3\frac{7}{8}$ in. (42×9.8 cm.)
diameter
South Kensington, 5 December 1991, £16,500 ($29,683)

Top right:

A painted wooden Butcher's Shop, with living quarters above
$30\frac{1}{2}$ in. (77.5 cm.) high; $26\frac{1}{2}$ in. (67.3 cm.) wide;
$15\frac{1}{2}$ in. (39.5 cm.) deep
South Kensington, 24 October 1991, £9,900 ($16,830)

Middle right:

A fossilised Egg of a Dinosaur, probably of the great Sauropod
Dinosaur Hypselosaurus, of the Maastrichtian period
70,000,000 B.C.
$7\frac{1}{8}$ in. (18.2 cm.) long; $5\frac{3}{4}$ in. (14.6 cm.) wide
South Kensington, 2 July 1992, £5,500 ($10,444)

Above:

ERNEST HOWARD SHEPARD (British, 1879–1976)
'So Pooh pushed and pushed and pushed his way through
the hole', illustration for A.A. Milne, *Winnie-The-Pooh*,
1926, p.23
pencil, pen and black ink
$3\frac{5}{8} \times 4\frac{1}{2}$ in. (9.2×11.5 cm.)
South Kensington, 10 July 1992, £9,020 ($17,011)

A French Prisoner-of-War Model of a
100-gun Man-of-War
boxwood
$9\frac{1}{4} \times 13$ in. (23.4 × 33 cm.)
South Kensington, 14 April 1992,
£12,000 ($21,072)

A collection of 85 Signal-Messages sent and received by
the White Star Liner, R.M.S. 'Titanic', 12–15 April
1912
South Kensington, 14 April 1992, £66,000 ($115,896)
Record auction price for 'Titanic' ephemera

These important 'Titanic' messages included the crucial
S.O.S. message 'Sinking wants immediate assistance',
the last ever message sent by the 'Titanic' at 11.10 p.m.
on 14 April 1912. This set of 85 signals was part of a
unique collection of 448 Marconi radio signals which
realised a total of £95,700 ($168,049). These included
the 'Titanic' ice messages £5,280 ($9,271), the
'Carpathia' Captain's messages sent and received
£7,700 ($13,521) and private survivor messages sent
from the 'Carpathia' £2,200 ($3,863).

MOTOR CARS

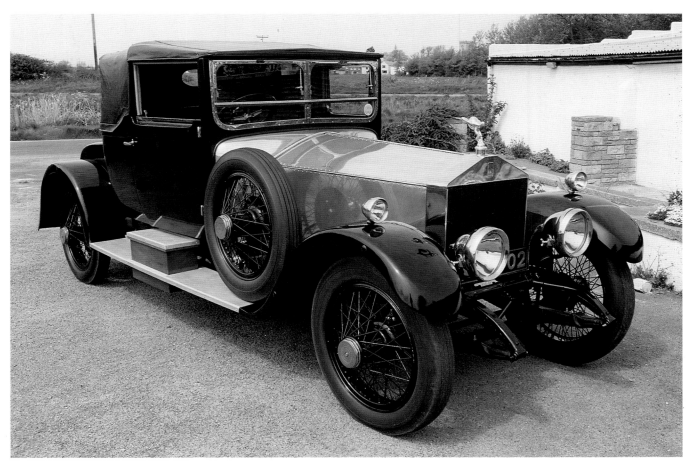

Top:
A 1926 Lincoln Sport Roadster Model L-151
Coachwork by Locke & Co.
Pebble Beach, California, 18 August 1991,
$77,000 (£46,108)

Above:
A 1920/21 Rolls-Royce 40/50 HP Silver Ghost Doctor's Coupé
Coachwork by Windovers of London
Palace House, Beaulieu, Hampshire, 20 June 1992,
£44,000 ($81,488)

<table>
<tr><td>

Top:
A 1964 Alfa Romeo Giulia TZ1
Coachwork by Zagato
Pebble Beach, California, 18 August 1991,
$264,000 (£158,084)

</td><td>

Above:
A 1935 Duesenberg Model SJ Convertible Coupé
Coachwork by Bohman & Schwarz
Pebble Beach, California, 18 August 1991,
$1,155,000 (£691,617)

</td></tr>
</table>

Top:
A 1967 Ford GT40 Mk.I Racing Coupé
Darling Harbour, Sydney, 16 March 1992,
Aus. $550,000 (£244,010)

Above:
A 1984 Lotus 95T Renault Formula One Grand Prix Race Car
Sold from the Monteverdi Collection
Auto-Museum, Binningen-Basel, Switzerland, 11 April 1992,
S.Fr. 170,500 (£65,076)

WINE

by Michael Broadbent

THE 25TH AND 225TH ANNIVERSARY SALES

The season celebrated two notable anniversaries. On 5 December 1766 James Christie's soon-to-be-famous gavel came down on lot 1 of his first sale, a four-day event. Lots 30–4 consisted of 15 dozen 'fine claret' and lots 35–9 of 24 dozen 'fine old maderia' (sic). They were offered at 'per dozen' in lots of 3 dozen bottles, still the same method and average lot size as today. 225 years later, to the day, we held a sale of Finest and Rarest Wines which included, appropriately, a range of excellent claret and one of the best collections of old madeira ever to appear on the market.

Earlier in the autumn, the second day of a two-day sale of Fine and Rare Wines was held on the 25th anniversary of the first sale of the first-ever specialist wine department. The comparison of prices between 11 October 1991 and 11 October 1966 makes interesting reading, a reflection not just of inflation but, more hearteningly, of the development of what is now a truly international market. The highest prices paid at the opening wine auction in 1966 were for Quinta do Noval of the famous 1931 vintage: two dozen bottles from the cellars of Pembroke College, Oxford which sold for 1,950 and 2,000 shillings per dozen, £97.50 and £100 in today's currency. Exactly 25 years later a single bottle of '31 Noval realised £682 ($1,227)

THE LATE ROBERT MAXWELL'S WINES

Such is the allure of notoriety that 'Fine Wines from the cellars of Headington Hill Hall' proved the biggest draw of the season. Clearly the big man knew and liked his wines, preferring fittingly large bottles. Magnums abounded: so did buyers, a full to overflowing saleroom packed with many new faces attracted by irresistible press coverage. Although there were only 223 lots, all sold, many above our estimate, for a grand total in excess of £92,400 ($166,320). The highest individual price was £550 for an *impériale* (8 bottle capacity) of Château Figeac 1970.

CHÂTEAU LATOUR

If pristine private cellars are highly regarded in the saleroom, even more so is wine straight from the château. A magnificent range of vintages, from 1918 to 1988, was shipped from Bordeaux for a sale on 21 November organised to celebrate the launch of *Latour; a History of the Château and its remarkable Proprietors*, by Nicholas Faith (Christie's Wine Publications). Leading the many high prices was £3,960 ($7,128) paid for an *impériale* of the 1961.

THE WINE & SPIRIT TRADES' BENEVOLENT SOCIETY

As Chairman of the Society 1991/2, it was doubly appropriate for me to organise an auction of Fine Wines and Spirits at Christie's in aid of the Society. Thanks to the support of major overseas producers, including 31 premium Californian wineries, leading German estates, Bordeaux château proprietors and growers in the Rhône and Burgundy, whose wines, specially shipped to London, formed over half the sale: over £44,000 ($79,200) was achieved, a record for any British charity wine auction.

Another novel and very successful event was a fashion show, Hartnell at Christie's, sponsored by Perrier, with champagne by Moët & Chandon and wines for the supper donated by Château Margaux. The most prestigious annual wine trade gathering, the Benevolent Banquet, was presided over by our Chairman, Lord Carrington, at the Hilton Hotel.

FINEST AND RAREST WINES

Of all the sales we hold, the most spectacular are those of Finest and Rarest Wines. The first of its kind was the famous Rosebery sale in May 1967. The most recent, on 18 June, was one of the best for several years. It included a very rare, possibly unique, jeroboam of 1864 Latour from the cellars of Hatfield House. This sold for £5,940 ($10,692). A substantial portion of the sale comprised the remaining stocks from the cellars of Caviar Kaspia in Paris; including no fewer than four bottles of 1844 Lafite in impeccable condition, two of the magnificent 1846, and bottles of the 1891, 1892 and 1893 and many other vintages of this great first-growth château. There was also an unprecedented quantity of the greatest vintages of Château d'Yquem, including a magnum and six bottles of the famous 1921, and five of the magnificent 1929.

OVERSEAS SALES

Our regular Spring and Autumn auctions in Geneva and Amsterdam vary in size; some are routine 'bread and butter' sales, some spectacular. Our recent Geneva sales have been notable for their size and effectiveness, with high individual prices and totals. Our third annual wine sale in Tokyo, was held over two days last October. Christie's Wine Inc. in Chicago had a very active season with important sales in Chicago and Los Angeles. These are now the biggest one-day wine auctions, American bidders sitting patiently through 1,200 to 1,400 lots during a non-stop session. One of the attractions is the pre-sale tasting at which bottles of first growths, Romanée-Conti burgundies and other top wines of great, some quite old, vintages are opened – a splendid way for the local wine buffs, and the many who fly in from elsewhere, to spend an agreeable Saturday tasting and buying.

SOUTH KENSINGTON, THE CITY AND GLASGOW

Though King Street is the hub of the United Kingdom fine wine market, Christie's South Kensington, with its own wine department organises very popular monthly sales. Held for the convenience of private buyers in the early evening, the sales are preceded by tastings. For those who work in the City, lunchtime tastings and wine auctions are held regularly at The Institute of Chartered Accountants. Christie's Glasgow now specialises mainly – and very appropriately – in auctions of Scotch whisky. An outstanding sale of its type was held last autumn, 333 lots of rare blends and old malts realising £74,167 ($133,501), the highest price being £5,500 ($9,900) for a 64 year old Macallan.

THE MOST NOTABLE PRICES ACHIEVED IN 1991/2

RED BORDEAUX

1844 Ch. Lafite £1,980 ($3,564) per bottle
1846 Ch. Lafite £1,870 ($3,366) per bottle
1864 Ch. Latour £5,940 ($10,692) per jeroboam
1874 Ch. Mouton-Rothschild £1,045 ($1,881) per bottle
1900 Ch. Lafite £682 ($1,228) per bottle
1921 Ch. Pétrus £9,020 ($16,236) per impériale
1924 Ch. Mouton-Rothschild £5,500 ($9,900) per jeroboam
1928 Ch. Beychevelle £1,815 ($3,267) per 6 magnums
1928 Ch. Pétrus £4,840 ($8,712) per double-magnum
1929 Ch. Pétrus £5,500 ($9,900) per double-magnum
1937 Ch. Pétrus £4,070 ($7,326) per jeroboam
1945 Ch. Mouton-Rothschild £1,045 ($1,881) per bottle
1945 Ch. Mouton-Rothschild £2,145 ($3,861) per magnum
1945 Ch. Mouton-Rothschild £2,310 ($4,158) per double-magnum
1945 Ch. Pétrus £4,400 ($7,920) per double-magnum
1947 Ch. Pétrus £2,090 ($3,762) per magnum
1953 Ch. Lafite £2,750 ($4,950) per 6 magnums
1959 Ch. Mouton-Rothschild £3,080 ($5,544) per dozen
1959 Ch. Lafite £2,530 ($4,554) per 6 magnums
1961 Ch. Lafite £3,190 ($5,742) per dozen
1961 Ch. Palmer £3,080 ($5,544) per dozen
1961 Ch. Margaux £2,860 ($5,148) per 6 magnums
1961 Ch. Ducru-Beaucaillou £1,430 ($2,574) per 6 magnums
1961 Ch. Latour £3,740 ($6,732) per 6 magnums
1961 Ch. Pétrus £16,500 ($29,700) per impériale
1961 La Mission Haut-Brion £2,750 ($4,950) per dozen
1963 Ch. Mouton-Rothschild £396 ($713) per bottle
1970 Ch. Pétrus £4,400 ($7,920) per dozen
1975 Ch. Pétrus £2,420 ($4,356) per 6 magnums
1982 Ch. Pétrus £3,190 ($5,742) per dozen

SAUTERNES

1869 Ch. d'Yquem £1,595 ($2,871) per bottle
1891 Ch. d'Yquem £572 ($1,030) per bottle
1893 Ch. d'Yquem £935 ($1,683) per bottle
1921 Ch. d'Yquem £748 ($1,346) per bottle
1929 Ch. d'Yquem £550 ($990) per bottle
1976 Ch. d'Yquem £1,540 ($2,772) per 6 magnums

RED BURGUNDY

1929 Romanée-Conti £715 ($1,287) per bottle
1945 Musigny, V.V. de Vogüé £264 ($475) per bottle
1947 Musigny, V.V. de Vogüé £3,300 ($5,940) per dozen
1949 Musigny, V.V. de Vogüé £440 ($792) per magnum
1969 Romanée-Conti £495 ($891) per bottle
1971 La Tâche £1,980 ($3,564) per dozen
1985 Echézeaux (H. Jayer) £1,320 ($2,376) per dozen

WHITE BURGUNDY

1971 Chevalier-Montrachet, Demoiselles (L. Latour)
£1,210 ($2,178) per dozen
1982 Montrachet (DRC) £1,870 ($3,366) per dozen
1983 Montrachet (DRC) £2,860 ($5,148) per dozen
1985 Montrachet (DRC) £3,190 ($5,742) per dozen

RHÔNE

1961 Hermitage, La Chapelle £3,300 ($5,940) per dozen
1966 Côte-Rôtie, La Mouline £495 ($891) per bottle

LOIRE

1928 Anjou Prunier £770 ($1,386) per dozen
1945 Moulin Touchais £616 ($1,109) per dozen

ALSACE

1976 Gewurztraminer, Cuvée Anne £715 ($1,287) per dozen

ITALY

1978 Sassicaia £572 ($1,030) per dozen

VINTAGE PORT

1881 Cockburn £352 ($634) per bottle
1912 Cockburn £204 ($366) per magnum
1927 Taylor £143 ($257) per bottle
1927 Fonseca £171 ($307) per bottle
1941 Quinta do Noval £176 ($317) per bottle
1945 Taylor £231 ($416) per bottle
1945 Taylor £2,750 ($4,950) per dozen
1947 Noval, Nacional £286 ($515) per bottle
1948 Fonseca £1,375 ($2,475) per dozen
1963 Fonseca £572 ($1,030) per dozen
1963 Noval, Nacional £4,070 ($7,326) per dozen
1966 Noval, Nacional £1,320 ($2,376) per dozen

MADEIRA

1792 Blandy's £990 ($1,782) per bottle
1875 Bastardo £198 ($356) per bottle

TOKAY

1920 Eszencia £374 ($673) per half litre
1947 Eszencia £341 ($614) per half litre

CHAMPAGNE

1949 Dom Pérignon £198 ($356) per bottle
1961 Dom Pérignon £352 ($634) per magnum
1964 Krug £968 ($1,742) per 6 magnums
1966 Dom Pérignon £682 ($1,228) per dozen
1979 Roederer Cristal £594 ($1,069) per dozen

COGNAC

1805 Rés.de l'Empéreur £506 ($911) per bottle
1811 Napoléon, G.F.C. £462 ($832) per bottle
1848 Grande Champ.des Héritiers £286 ($515) per bottle

SCOTCH WHISKY

The Macallan, distilled 1926, bottled 1980 £5,500 ($9,900) per bottle
Lagavulin, distilled 1881, bottled 1911 £3,520 ($6,336) per bottle
Dallas Dhu, distilled 1921, bottled 1985 £3,080 ($5,544) per bottle
Glen Grant, 59 year old £2,750 ($4,950) per bottle

Château Latour – Vintage 1864, Jeroboam
Sold by the Marquess of Salisbury
London, 18 June, 1992, £5,940 ($10,692)

International Offices

Salerooms

UNITED KINGDOM

London, King Street
Christie, Manson & Woods Ltd.
8 King Street, St. James's
London SW1Y 6QT
Tel: (071) 839 9060. Telex: 916429
Fax: (071) 839 1611
Chairman: The Hon. Charles Allsopp

South Kensington
Christie's South Kensington Ltd.
85 Old Brompton Road
London SW7 3LD
Tel: (071) 581 7611. Telex: 922061
Fax: (071) 584 0431
Chairman: W. A. Coleridge, F.R.I.C.S.

Scotland
Christie's Scotland Ltd.
164-166 Bath Street
Glasgow G2 4TG
Tel: (041) 332 8134. Telex: 779901
Fax: (041) 332 5759
Chairman: Sir Ilay Campbell, Bt.

Robson Lowe at Christie's
8 King Street, St. James's
London SW1Y 6QT
Tel: (071) 839 9060. Telex: 916429
Fax: (071) 389 2688

UNITED STATES

Christie, Manson & Woods International, Inc.
502 Park Avenue
New York, New York 10022
Tel: (212) 546 1000. Telex: 620721
Fax: (212) 980 8163
President: Christopher Burge
Executive Vice Presidents:
Stephen S. Lash, Doris P. Meister

Christie's East
219 East 67th Street
New York, New York 10021
Tel: (212) 606 0400.
Telex: 672 0346
Fax: (212) 737 6076
President: Kathleen Guzman

EUROPE

Italy
Christie's (Int.) S.A.
Palazzo Massimo Lancellotti
Piazza Navona 114
Rome 00186
Tel: (396) 687 2787
Fax: (396) 686 99 02
Chairman: Maurizio Lodi-Fe
Francesco Semmola

Monaco
Christie's Monaco S.A.M.
Park Palace, 98000 Monte Carlo
Tel: (33) 93 25 19 33. Telex: 489287
Fax: (33) 93 50 38 64
Marie Gavot-Mamboury

Switzerland
Christie's (Int.) S.A.
8 Place de la Taconnerie
1204 Geneva
Tel: (4122) 311 1766
Fax: (4122) 311 5559
Chairman of Christie's Europe:
François Curiel
Dan Klein

The Netherlands
Christie's Amsterdam B.V.
Cornelis Schuytstraat 57
1071 JG Amsterdam
Tel: (3120) 5 75 52 55
Fax: (3120) 6 64 08 99
Chairman: Charles André de la Porte

HONG KONG

Christie's Swire (Hong Kong) Ltd.
2804-6 Alexandra House
16-20 Chater Road, Hong Kong
Tel: (852) 521 5396. Telex: 72014
Fax: (852) 845 2646
Chairman: Baroness Lydia Dunn, D.B.E.
Alice Yuan Piccus

AUSTRALIA

Melbourne
Christie's Australia Pty. Ltd.
1 Darling Street
South Yarra
Victoria 3141
Tel: (613) 820 4311
Fax: (613) 820 4876
Chairman: James B. Leslie, A.Q., M.C.
Roger McIlroy

Representatives

UNITED KINGDOM AND IRELAND

Highlands
John Douglas-Menzies
Mounteagle, Hill of Fearn
Ross-shire IV20 1RP
Tel: (086283) 2866
Fax: (086283) 2720

Tayside, Fife and Grampian
Roy Miller, F.R.I.C.S.
3/5 Mill Street, Perth PH1 5JB
Tel: (0738) 43088

Edinburgh
Roy Miller, F.R.I.C.S.
5 Wemyss Place
Edinburgh EH3 6DH
Tel: (031) 225 4756/7
Fax: (031) 225 1723

Borders
Gerald Trotter
The Wellnage, Duns
Berwickshire TD11 3EJ
Tel: (0361) 82550

South West Scotland
James Hunter Blair
Blairquhan, Maybole
Ayrshire KA19 7LZ
Tel: (06557) 239

Northumbria
Aidan Cuthbert
Eastfield House
Main Street, Corbridge
Northumberland NE45 5LA
Tel: (0434) 633181

North-West
Victor Gubbins, F.R.I.C.S.
Eden Lacy, Lazonby, Penrith
Cumbria CA10 1BZ
Tel: (0768) 898800
Fax: (0768) 898020

Yorkshire
Sir Nicholas Brooksbank, Bt.
192 Huntington Road
York YO3 9BN
Tel: (0904) 630911
Fax: (0904) 644448

Cheshire
Richard Roundell, F.R.I.C.S.
Dorfold Hall, Nantwich
Cheshire CW5 8LD
Tel: (0270) 627024
Fax: (0270) 628723

West Midlands
Michael Thompson
Stanley Hall, Bridgnorth
Shropshire WV16 4SP
Tel: (0746) 761891
Fax: (0746) 761831

East Midlands
The Hon. Lady Hastings
Mrs. William Proby
The Stables, Milton Hall
Peterborough PE6 7AA
Tel: (0733) 380781
Bruce Clayton, F.S.V.A.
Park House, Park Lane, Harpole
Northampton NN7 4BT
Tel: (0604) 831551

Cotswolds
Viscount Ebrington
Rupert de Zoete *Consultant*
111 The Promenade, Cheltenham
Gloucestershire GL50 1PS
Tel: (0242) 518999
Fax: (0242) 576240

East Anglia
Charles Bingham-Newland
Sackville Place
44-48 Magdalen Street
Norwich NR3 1JU
Tel: (0603) 614546
Fax: (0603) 633740

Essex and Hertfordshire
James Service
Hawkins Harvest
Great Barfield, Essex CM7 4QW
Tel: (0371) 810189
Fax: (0371) 810028

South East
Christopher Proudfoot
Wellesley House
Manor Road
Hurstpierpoint
West Sussex BN6 9UH
Tel: (0273) 835575
Fax: (0273) 835576
Keith Middlemas, *Consultant*
and at
The Old Rectory, Fawkham
Longfield, Kent DA3 8LX
Tel: (0474) 702854

Hampshire and Berkshire
Richard Wills
Middleton Estate Office
Longparish, Andover
Hampshire SP11 6PL
Tel: (0264) 72211
Fax: (0264) 72271

South Dorset and Hampshire
Nigel Thimbleby
Wolfeton House, Dorchester
Dorset DT2 9QN
Tel: (0305) 268748

West Country and Wiltshire
Richard de Pelet
Huntsman's Lodge
Inwood, Templecombe
Somerset BA8 0PF
Tel: (0963) 70518
Fax: (0963) 7060

Cornwall
Christopher Petherick
Porthpean House, St. Austell
Cornwall PL26 6AX
Tel: (0726) 64672

Devon
The Hon. George Lopes, A.R.I.C.S.
Gnaton Estate Office
Yealmpton, Plymouth
Devon PL8 2HU
Tel: (0752) 880636

Channel Islands
Richard de la Hey
58 David Place, St. Helier, Jersey
Tel: (0534) 77582
Fax: (0534) 77540

Isle of Man
The Marchioness Conyngham
Myrtle Hill, Andreas Road
Ramsey, Isle of Man
Tel: (0624) 814502

Northern Ireland
Danny Kinahan
Castle Upton, Templepatrick
Co. Antrim BT39 0AH
Tel: (08494) 33480
Fax: (08494) 33410

Ireland
Desmond Fitz-Gerald,
Knight of Glin
Glin Castle, Glin, Co. Limerick
Fax: (010 35361) 6834 364
Private Residence
52 Waterloo Road, Dublin 4
Tel: (010 3531) 68 05 85
Fax: (010 3531) 68 02 71

UNITED STATES

Baltimore
Betsy Gordon Matthai
100 West Road, Suite 300
Baltimore, Maryland 21204
Tel: (301) 832 7555
Fax: (301) 825 9222

Boston
Elizabeth M. Chapin
Perry T. Rathbone, *Consultant*
Brigitte Bradford
P.O. Box 2723, Massachusetts 022
Tel: (617) 576 0400
Fax: (617) 876 7725

Chicago
Frances Blair, Lisa Cavanaugh
Laura de Frise, Susan Florence
200 West Superior Street
Chicago, Illinois 60610
Tel: (312) 787 2765
Fax: (312) 951 7449

Dallas
Carolyn Foxworth
7047 Elmridge Drive
Dallas, Texas 75240
Tel: (214) 239 0098
Fax: (214) 386 6102

Los Angeles
Terry Stanfill, Hannah Shore
Ursula Hermacinski
James de Givenchy (Jewellery)
342 North Rodeo Drive
Beverly Hills, California 90210
Tel: (310) 275 5534. Telex: 6711872
Fax: (310) 275 9748

Miami
Mary Hoeveler
110 Merrick Way, Suite 2A
Coral Gables, Florida 33134
Tel: (305) 445 1487
Fax: (305) 441 6561

New Orleans
John Fowler, P.O. Box 15529
New Orleans, La. 70175
Tel: (504) 899 2380
Fax: (504) 899 9531

Newport
Betsy D. Ray,
Ralph Carpenter *Consultant*
228 Spring Street
Newport, Rhode Island 02840
Tel: (401) 849 9222
Fax: (401) 849 6322

Palm Beach
Helen Cluett, Lucy Ullmann
251 Royal Palm Way
Palm Beach, Fla. 33480
Tel: (407) 833 6952
Fax: (407) 833 0007

Philadelphia
Paul Ingersoll, Molly Wood
P.O. Box 1112, Bryn Mawr
Pennsylvania 19010
Tel: (215) 525 5493
Fax: (215) 525 0967

San Francisco
Ellanor Notides, Elizabeth Allyn
3516 Sacramento Street
San Francisco, California 94118
Tel: (415) 346 6633
Fax: (415) 346 8084

Washington
John Gardner, Nuala Pell,
Marya Oja
Hamilton Court
1228 31st Street N.W.
Washington, D.C. 20007
Tel: (202) 333 7459
Fax: (202) 342 0537

WORLDWIDE
Argentina
Fernando Sánchez Zinny
César Feldman *Consultant*
Libertad 1269, 1012 Buenos Aires
Tel: (514) 814 0577
Fax: (541) 11 2785

Australia
Sydney
Janelle Dawes
298 New South Head Road
Double Bay, Sydney N.S.W. 2028
Tel: (612) 326 1422. Telex: 26343
Fax: (612) 327 8439
Adelaide
Ian Bruce
193 Hutt Street
Adelaide 5000
Tel: (618) 232 2860
Fax: (618) 232 6508

Austria
Christie's Kunstauktionen GmbH
Dr. Johanna Schönburg-Hartenstein
Kohlmarkt 4, 1010 Vienna
Tel: (431) 533 1635
Tax: (431) 533 7166

Belgium
Brussels
Bernard Steyaert
Janine Duesberg
Christie's Belgium S.A.
33 Boulevard de Waterloo
1000 Brussels
Tel: (322) 512 8830
Fax: (322) 513 3279
Antwerp
Annette Van Thillo-Gerard
Arenbergstraat 1, 2000 Antwerp
Tel: (323) 233 2371

Brazil
Rio De Janeiro
Maria-Thereza de Azevedo Sodré
Consultant
Ave. Rui Barbosa, 582
22250 Rio de Janeiro
Tel: (5521) 551 1467
Telex: 213 4285
Sao Paulo
Paulo Figueiredo
rua dr. Mello Alves, 717 c.l.
01417 Sao Paulo
Tel: (5511) 881 3478
Fax: (5511) 280 3357

Canada
Suzanne E. Davis
Christie, Manson & Woods
International, Inc.
170 Bloor Street, Suite 210
Toronto, Ontario M5S 1T9
Tel: (416) 960 2063
Fax: (416) 960 8815

Colombia
Harry M. Hanabergh
Aptdo. Aereo 250670
Calle 71, No. 13-10, Bogota,
Colombia
Tel: (571) 211 5049
Fax: (571) 255 1442

Denmark
Birgitta Hillingsø
Dronningens Tværgade 10
1302 Copenhagen K
Tel: (45) 33 32 70 75
Fax: (45) 33 13 00 75

Finland
Barbro Schauman
Ulrikagatan 3 A, 00140 Helsinki
Tel: (3580) 60 82 12
Fax: (3580) 66 06 87

France
Paris
Humphrey Butler
Christine Petit
Bertrand du Vignaud
Christie's France S.A.
6 rue Paul Baudry, 75008 Paris
Tel: (331) 42 56 17 66
Fax: (331) 42 56 26 01
Aix-en-Provence
Fabienne Albertini
2 rue Matheron
13100 Aix-en-Provence
Tel: (33) 42 96 43 94
Fax: (33) 42 23 98 59

Bordeaux
Marie-Cécile Moueix
Tel: (33) 56 81 65 47
Lyon
Christiane de Meaux
Tel: (33) 78 43 72 44

Germany
Düsseldorf
Christie's (Deutschland) GmbH
Jorg-Michael Bertz
Inselstrasse 15
D-4000 Dusseldorf 30
Tel: (49211) 498 2986
Fax: (49211) 492 0339
Hamburg
Christiane Gräfin zu Rantzau
Wentzelstrasse 21
D-2000 Hamburg 60
Tel: (4940) 279 4073
Fax: (4940) 270 4497
Munich
Fürstin zu Hohenlohe-Langenburg
Residenzstrasse 27
D-8000 Munich 2
Tel: (4989) 22 95 39
Fax: (4989) 29 63 02
Frankfurt
Dorothee Freifrau von Moreau
Savignystrasse 42
D-6000 Frankfurt am Main 1
Tel: (4969) 74 50 21
Fax: (4969) 75 20 79
Berlin
Marianne Kewenig
Fasanenstrasse 72
D-1000 Berlin 15
Tel: (4930) 882 7778
Fax: (4930) 883 8768

Israel
Mary Gilben
Christie's (Israel) Limited
Asia House
4 Weizmann Street
Tel Aviv 64239
Tel: (9723) 6950695/6950671
Fax: (9723) 6952751

Italy
Milan
Isabelle von Schoenfeldt *Consultant*
Christie's (Int.) S.A.
3 via Manin
20121 Milan
Tel: (392) 2900 1374
Fax: (392) 2900 1157
Turin
Sandro Perrone di San Martino
Corso Matteotti 33
10121 Turin
Tel: (3911) 548 819
Naples
Angela Carola Perrotti
Via Fiorelli 5
80121 Naples
Tel: (3981) 764 27 88
Savona
Rag. Flaminio Spinetti
Via Mazzini 97/99r
17100 Savona
Tel: (3919) 88 00 22 or 80 43 87

Japan
Sachiko Hibiya
Koji Yamada
Christie's Japan Limited
Ichibankan Bldg., B1
3-12, Ginza 5-chome
Chuo-ku
Tokyo 104
Tel: (813) 3571 0668
Tax: (813) 3571 5853

Luxembourg
Countess Marina von Kamarowsky
88, Avenue de la Faiencerie
L 1510 Luxembourg
Tel: (352) 47 24 86
Fax: (352) 47 52 44

Mexico
P.O. Box 105-158, Mexico 11570
Tel: (525) 531 1686/1806

Norway
Ulla Solitair Hjort
Christie's
Colbjornsensgt. 1
N-0256 Oslo 2
Tel: (472) 44 12 42
Fax: (472) 55 92 36

Portugal
Antonio M. G. Santos Mendonça
R. Conde de Almoster 44, 1°Esq.
1500 Lisbon
Tel: (3511) 78 63 83
Fax: (3511) 60 95 10

Singapore
Irene Lee
Mrs. Cecilia Ong *Consultant*
Tanglin P.O. Box 0212
Singapore 9124
Tel: (65) 738 2710
Fax: (65) 732 9723

Spain
Casilda Fz-Villaverde y Silva
Juan Varez
Christie's Ilberica S.L.
Valenzuela 7, Madrid 28014
Tel: (341) 532 66 26/7
Fax: (341) 523 12 40

Sweden
Stockholm
Christie's Sweden AB
Lillemor Malmström
Sturegatan 26, 11436 Stockholm
Tel: (468) 662 0131
Fax: (468) 660 0725
South of Sweden
Baroness Irma Silfverschiold
230 41 Klagerup
Tel: (4640) 44 03 60
Fax: (4640) 44 03 71
Gothenburg
Mrs. S. Wiklund
Försvarsgatan 12
42176 Västra Frölunda
Gothenburg
Tel: (4631) 69 40 68
Fax: (4631) 69 40 68

Switzerland
Zurich
Maria Reinshagen
Christie's (Int.) A.G.
Steinwiesplatz, 8032 Zurich
Tel: (411) 262 0505
Fax: (411) 251 0471

Taiwan
Anthony Lin
Christie's Swire Taiwan
6th Floor, 369 Fu-Hsing North Road
Taipei 10483, Taiwan, R.O.C.
Tel: (886) 2 718 1612
Fax: (886) 2 718 3702

Venezuela
Alain Jathière
5 Avenida Cachimbo II
Los Chorros, Caracas
Tel: (582) 2380503. Telex: 24950
Fax: (582) 357613

INDEX

INDEX OF PATRONS AND COLLECTORS